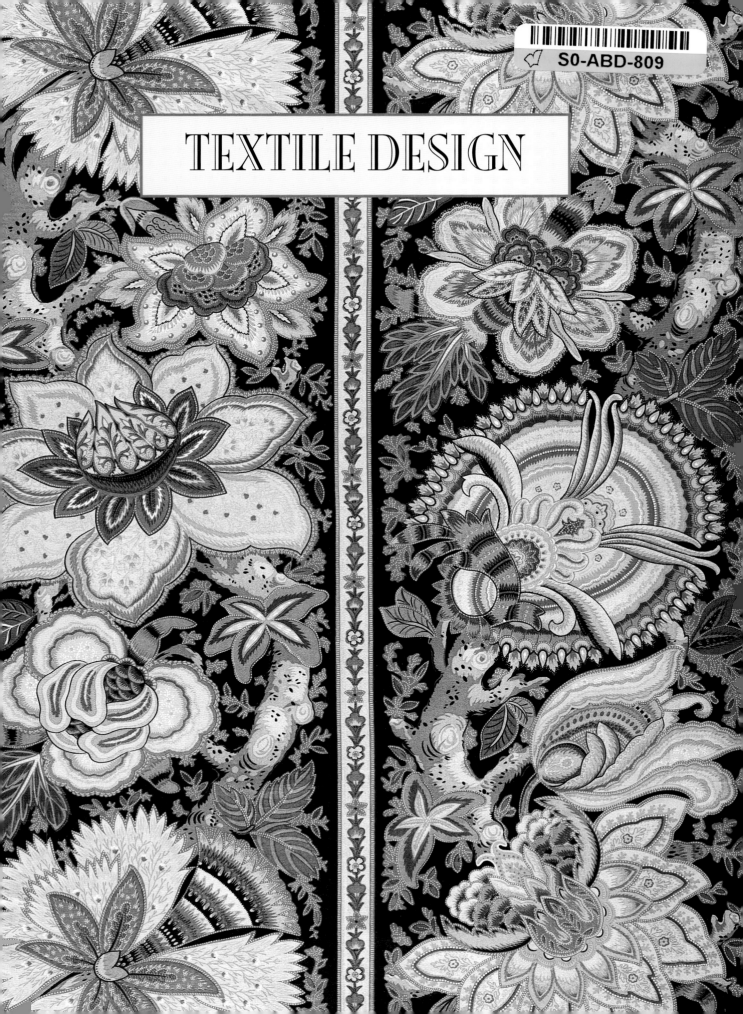

TEXTILE DESIGN

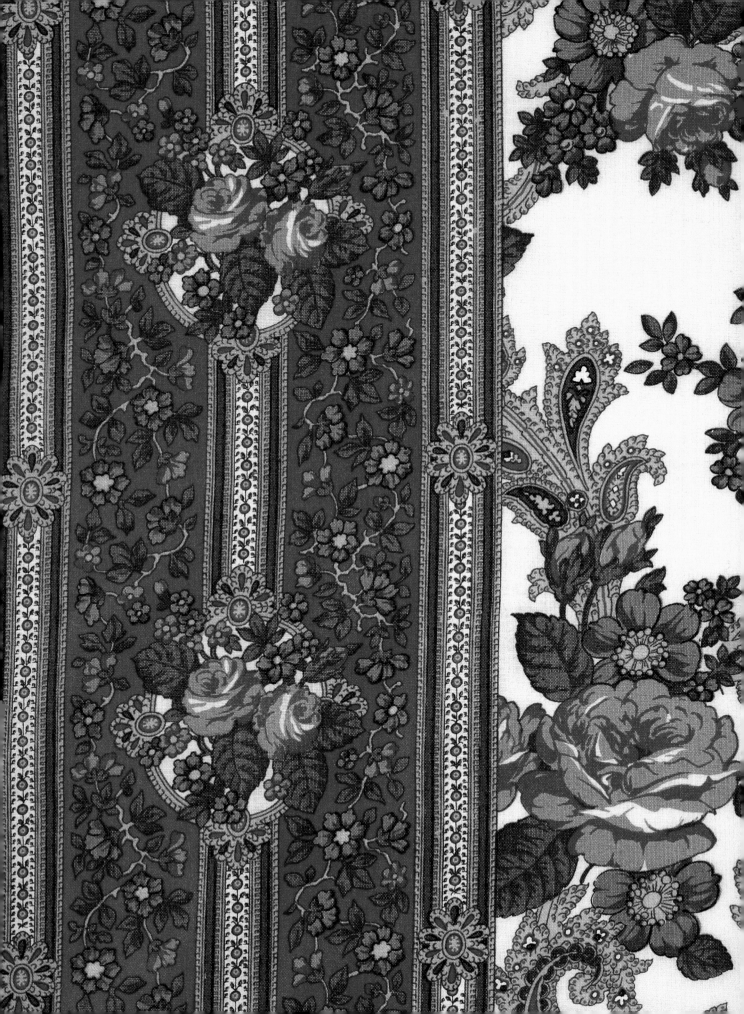

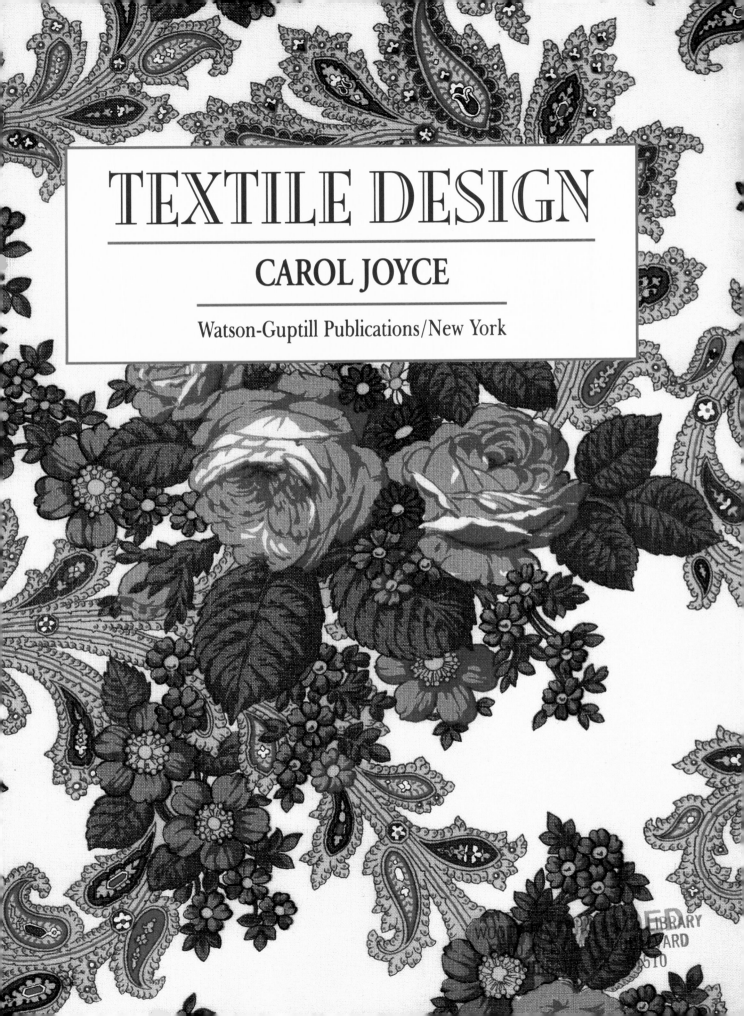

TEXTILE DESIGN

CAROL JOYCE

Watson-Guptill Publications/New York

TO MY BROTHER, VINCENT BECK

Jacket image: "Favenay," a classic country French chintz pattern. Refer to page 64 for a discussion of this type of design. *Pierre Deux*

Half Title: "Colmar," a beautifully detailed chintz stripe with stylized Persian motifs. *Clarence House Imports, Ltd.*

Title page: "La Vieille Varsovie," an elaborate border design with a field of roses and paisleys for home furnishing. *Clarence House Imports, Ltd.*

Page 8: "Art Moderne," a home furnishing design inspired by cubism. *Clarence House Imports, Ltd.*

Notes on the textiles;
All Nicole Miller designs are copyrighted by law.
All Cloth Company designs were styled by Leon Hecht.
All uncredited designs and illustrations are copyright © by Carol Joyce.

Senior Editor: Candace Raney
Edited by Joy Aquilino
Designed by Areta Buk
Graphic production by Ellen Greene

Copyright © 1993 by Carol Joyce

Published in 1993 in the United States
by Watson-Guptill Publications,
a division of BPI Communications, Inc.,
1515 Broadway, New York, N.Y. 10036

Library of Congress Cataloging-in-Publication Data

Joyce, Carol.
    Textile design: the complete guide to printed textiles for apparel and home furnishing / Carol Joyce. Pbk. Ed.
        p.   cm.
    First published under title: Designing for printed textiles.
    Englewood Cliffs, N.J.: Prentice-Hall, 1982.
    Includes index.
    ISBN 0-8230-5326-1
    1. Textile design. 2. Textile printing. I. Joyce, Carol.
    Designing for printed textiles. II. Title.
    NK9500.J65   1993
    746.6—dc20

92-38380
CIP

Printed in Hong Kong

First paperback printing, 1997

1 2 3 4 5 6 7 8 9 10 / 07 06 05 04 03 02 01 00 99 98 97

Carol Joyce has designed printed fabrics for many major American apparel and home furnishing textile manufacturers. She has taught the textile design course at The School of Visual Arts in New York for over twenty-five years.

ACKNOWLEDGMENTS

I would like to thank my husband, Bob Joyce, for his expert editing and moral support.

Special thanks to Maurice Sherman, who photographed so beautifully all the textile designs and fabrics for the book, and to Steve Levinson for his expert computer work.

I also want to express my appreciation to Ruth Soffer, Frank Delfino, Joan Gampert, Lynn Johnson, and Sheila and Lee Stewart for their advice and artistic contributions; to Bjorge Arnarsdottir and Ada Yonenaka for their photographic contributions; and to Shannon English, Laura Skrobe, and Maggie Soffer for their general help.

For their thoughtful assistance, thanks to Susan S. Freedman, Leon Hecht, Holly Henderson, José Rusch, Linda Greiff, Kenji Takabayashi, Simon Poulton, Janet Roller, Glenda Heffer, Pam Maffei, Ann Coleman, Judith Straeten, Joey Magee, Kathleen A. Rhodes, Mary Pat O'Rourke, Nicole Miller, Susan Toplitz, Jenny Kee, Theresa Ruck, Jay Yang, Anthony Noberini, Judy Clancy, Jack Prince, and Jonathan Ned Katz.

The following companies were most cooperative in helping me gather material for the book; Bloomcraft, a division of P. Kaufman; Boussac of France; Brunschwig & Fils, Inc.; Cameo Interiors; Cannon Mills; Clarence House Imports, Ltd.; The Cloth Company, a division of Cranston Print Works Co.; Deerwood Design Studio; Jack Lenor Larsen, Inc.; Liberty of London, Inc.; Martex for West Point-Pepperell; Malden Mills Ind., Inc.; Printmakers International, Ltd.; Sheridan; Schwartz-Liebman Textiles; Schumacher; Souleiado for Pierre Deux; Sublistatic International; and American Textile Manufacturers Institute.

CONTENTS

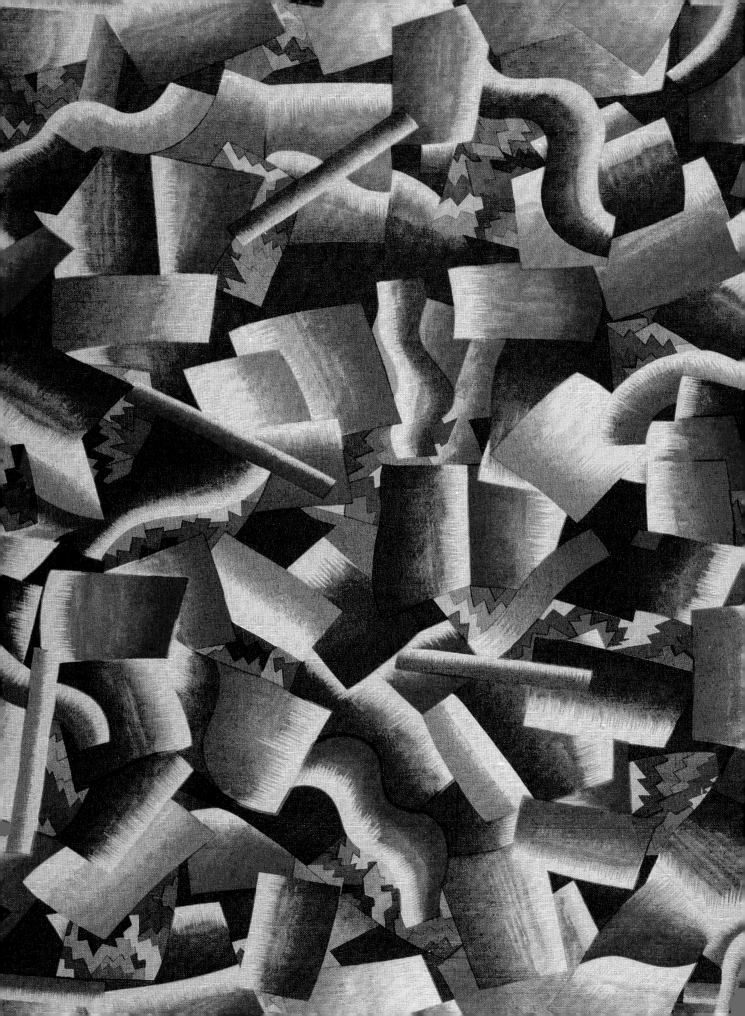

INTRODUCTION

Fabric design is one of the most enduring and functional of the decorative arts. Dating back to when primitive people first used patterned cloth, fabric enhanced by beautiful design has enriched life in almost every known society. Printed textiles are so much a part of modern life that most people are not fully aware of their myriad uses. While more than a billion yards of printed fabric are produced in the United States every year, it is difficult to estimate the number of designs that are used in their production.

A textile design begins as an idea on paper and ends printed on cloth. Happily, it serves both a useful and an aesthetic function. The designer's job is to combine her or his skills, taste, and imagination to produce good designs. This book is a complete course in the creation and preparation of designs to be commercially printed on fabric, and covers all aspects of studio and freelance work for apparel and home furnishing.

Since the early 1980s, the computer revolution has affected the professional practices of the textile/surface design industry, and there have also been many important new developments in the printing process. However, the three skills required by the textile designer—designing, creating colorways, and doing repeats—must still be learned in the traditional way, as is shown in this book. These skills are required for both apparel and home furnishing, but particularly in the home furnishing market, where fine handpainted designs are most desirable.

Fashion, styles, and, therefore, textile patterns change from season to season, year after year. To achieve longevity as a designer one must combine talent, skill, and hard work. As a designer and teacher of many decades' experience, I maintain my enthusiasm and inspiration through the study of the art of the varied cultures of the world that are so accessible to us today. I am a fervent believer in using this great resource as reference material, and I selected the more than two hundred color illustrations not only to show the broad range of contemporary textile design but to provide a creative source for designers and professionals in allied fields.

I also believe that designers who are interested in a career in textile design should arm themselves not only with the necessary technical skills but also with the knowledge that chapters such as "Special Design Techniques," "The Role of Computers in Textile Design," and "The Printing Process" can provide.

It is my hope that this book will be used as a learning aid by textile design students and as a comprehensive home-study guide by those desiring to learn on their own. I am confident that it will also prove valuable to professionals in related fields, such as fashion and interior design, and to artists and craftspeople who wish to broaden their artistic and commercial skills.

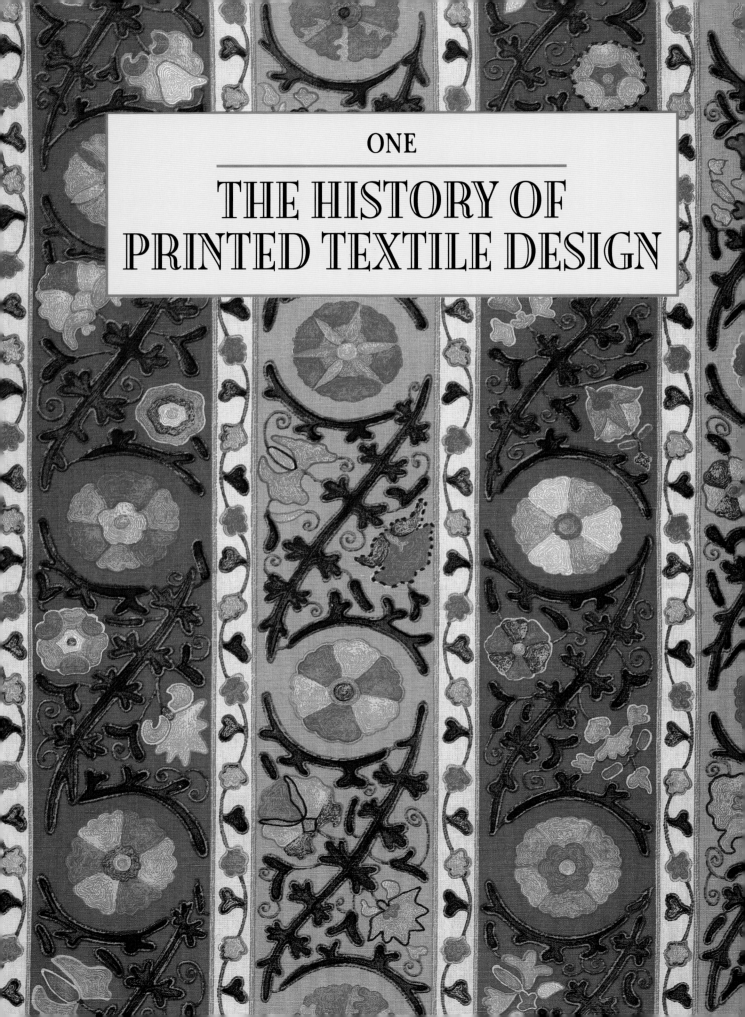

ONE

THE HISTORY OF PRINTED TEXTILE DESIGN

"Dzhambul," a home furnishing stripe adapted from a nineteenth-century Indian embroidery. *Courtesy Brunschwig & Fils, Inc.*

The history of printed textile design is a long and fascinating one. As early as 3000 B.C. patterned cloth was widely used by primitive people. A thousand years later, clothing decorated with stamped patterns was being worn in Egypt and Peru. Examples of printed fabrics survive from many different cultures and periods: Greece during the fourth and fifth centuries A.D., Europe in the twelfth century, and the African kingdom of Benin (now part of Nigeria) in the thirteenth century. In 1712, George Leason founded the first cotton printing works in North America in Boston, Massachusetts. Although manmade fibers were first developed at the end of the nineteenth century, for more than 7,000 years the history of textiles can be traced by the development of the four major categories of natural fibers: flax, wool, cotton, and silk.

"Compagnie Des Indes," an adaptation of a nineteenth-century Indian coverlet. *Clarence House Imports, Ltd.*

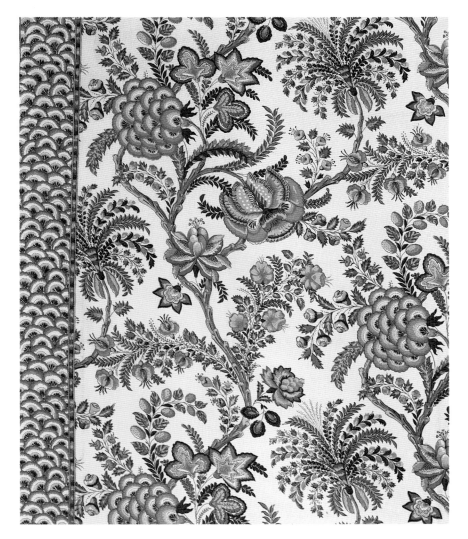

PRINTED TEXTILES: HISTORICAL DEVELOPMENTS

DATE	REGION	MILESTONE
5000 B.C.	Egypt	Flax is used by the early Egyptian cultures along the Nile to make linenlike fabrics.
4000 B.C.	Mesopotamia	Neolithic cultures probably use wool, as they are known to have domesticated sheep. However, the earliest dated findings were made on the banks of the Euphrates River in present-day Iraq.
3000 B.C.	India; Peru	Cotton is developed almost simultaneously in these two unconnected parts of the prehistoric world.
2640 B.C.	China	Silk is first cultivated and woven. By 1400 B.C. silk production in China was at its height.
2100 B.C.	Egypt	Tomb paintings show costumes stamped with orderly, repeated designs.
2000 B.C.	Peru	Clay cylinders are used to print border patterns.
1500 B.C.	Mexico; Peru	Tie-dyeing, batik (a wax resist technique), and block and small roller printing are developed; a finish for glazing cotton fabrics is also perfected during this period.
1200 B.C.	Java	Batiks are used for religious ceremonial purposes. While it is likely that batik was used in China and India well before this period, the Indonesian island of Java is where batik printing reached its height.
450 B.C.	Greece	Animal figures are painted on clothing in pigment colors.
A.D. 500	Japan	Batik, stencil printing, and tie-dyeing are used extensively.
500–600	Persia	Patterned cloth is printed in red, black, and powdered gold.
1100	Europe	Fabric printing is done at various levels in several countries.
1200	Nigeria	Printed cotton cloth is used in the kingdom of Benin.
1300–1600	Europe	The era of great weaving, which includes tapestry, damask, and silk embroidery, is at its height. Fabric printing declined during this period.
1676–1771	Europe	Cloth printing works are started during this period in England, Holland, Germany, Switzerland, France, Ireland, and Scotland. Noted among these is the factory at Jouy, France, founded by Oberkampf in 1759, where the famous Toile de Jouy fabrics are designed and printed.
1712	U.S.	George Leason establishes the "Calico Printing Works" in Boston, the first fabric printing manufacturer on the continent. During the next 150 years, more than seventy print works are established throughout New England and the mid-Atlantic states.
1785	England	Industrialized roller printing is developed by Thomas Bell.
1802	England	The first resist method of textile printing is developed.
1900	England	William Morris designs and prints fabrics and wallpaper in the art nouveau style, which are greatly admired and influential in the U.S. Today he is considered the forerunner of modern design in textiles.
1929	France	The age of synthetic chemical fibers begins with the introduction of rayon, the so-called silk substitute. Although its development began in 1884, it was finally perfected in 1929.
Late 1930s	U.S.	Nylon is developed.
1941	U.S.	Polyester is discovered.
1948	U.S.	Producing 50 percent of the world's rayon, the textile industry becomes the second largest industry in the U.S.
1950	U.S.	Acrylic fabrics are introduced commercially.
1953	U.S.	Dupont introduces Dacron, the first commercially successful polyester.
1959	U.S.	Lycra, an elastic stretch fabric, is developed, changing the swimwear industry.
1964	U.S.	The first permanent press garments are produced and are well received by the public.
1968	U.S.	For the first time in history, manmade fabric consumption surpasses that of natural fibers, mostly due to the development of polyester and synthetics.

Because no written records survive, historians and archaeologists cannot establish precise dates of the origins of ancient patterned textiles. On the opposite page is a brief overview of the historical developments of printed textiles.

CONTEMPORARY PRINTED TEXTILE DESIGN

Printed fabrics touch many aspects of our lives. Textile designs appear on a wide range of women's, men's, and children's clothing, including blouses, shirts, skirts, dresses, and jackets; ties, scarves, and other accessories; undergarments and sleepwear such as lingerie, shorts, and pajamas; as well as evening clothes and swimwear. We also live with printed designs in every room of our homes, in many different applications, such as upholstery, drapery, and wallpaper (referred to as *decoratives*); and sheets and pillowcases, comforters, towels, shower curtains, tablecloths, and napkins (known as *domestics*).

The textile designs that illustrate this book reveal the scope of the imagination and skill of contemporary textile designers. However, no work of art, including a textile design, can be created in a vacuum. While each design may approach its theme or motif in a distinctive way, all require a source of inspiration or reference material. Of course, a textile designer should not simply copy his or her source material, although in some cases the genesis of a current design is easily recognizable; in many others, the transformation from reference material to new design is remarkably inventive and subtle.

The best new designs, influenced by both traditional and contemporary ideas, motifs, colors, and layouts, reflect new patterns and trends; these designs in turn significantly influence the American and international fashion and home decorating markets. Textile designers today draw inspiration from a multitude of sources. The proliferation of exhibitions and published materials from all over the world make almost every culture and its artistic traditions easily accessible.

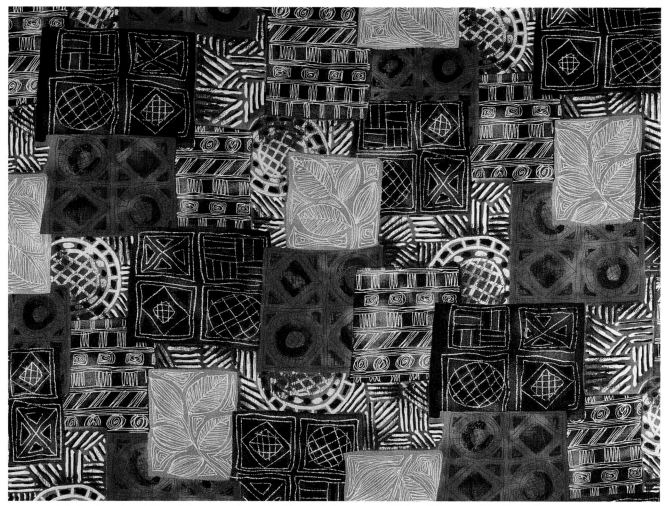

An apparel design based on African folk geometric motifs. *The Cloth Company, a division of Cranston Print Works Co.*

Several fine arts movements have influenced textile design, including neoclassicism, art deco, art nouveau, the Bauhaus, the arts and crafts movement, chinoiserie, cubism, expressionism, ethnic, folk, and pop art. Many individual fine artists have also inspired textile designers. Further evidence of this relationship are the fine artists who themselves have designed printed textiles, including Henri Matisse, Raoul Dufy, Paul Klee, Charles Burchfield, Sonia Delaunay, David Hockney, Marie Laurencin, John Piper, Henry Moore, Graham Sutherland, Andy Warhol, and Keith Haring.

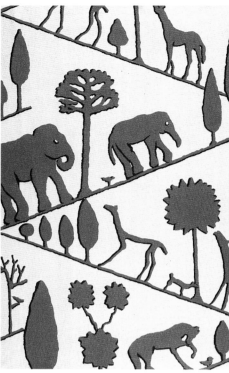

"Giacometti's Zoo," a home furnishing design inspired by Swiss artist Diego Giacometti. *Clarence House Imports, Ltd.*

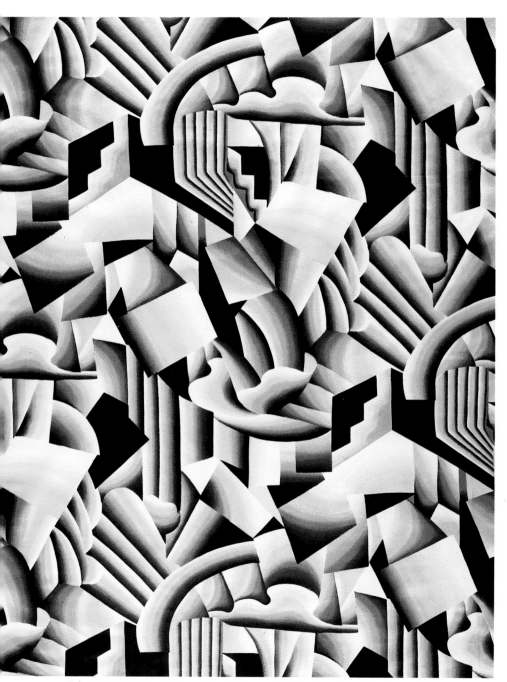

"Léger," a home furnishing design influenced by the French painter Fernand Léger. *Clarence House Imports, Ltd.*

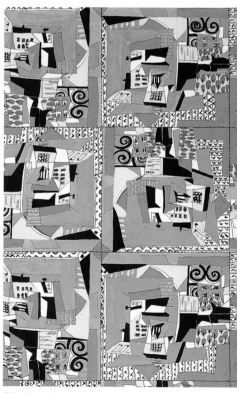

"Patchwork Picasso," an apparel design adapted from a 1920 Picasso painting. *Copyright © Joan Gampert, designer*

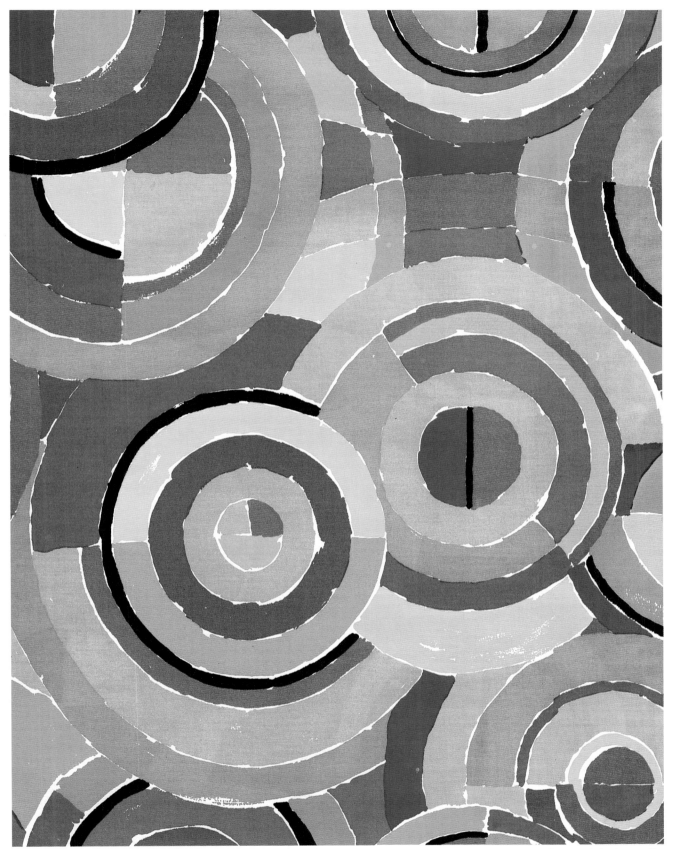

"Circle Games," a bright bedding design inspired by the work of the Russian-French artist Sonia Delaunay. *Martex for West Point-Pepperell*

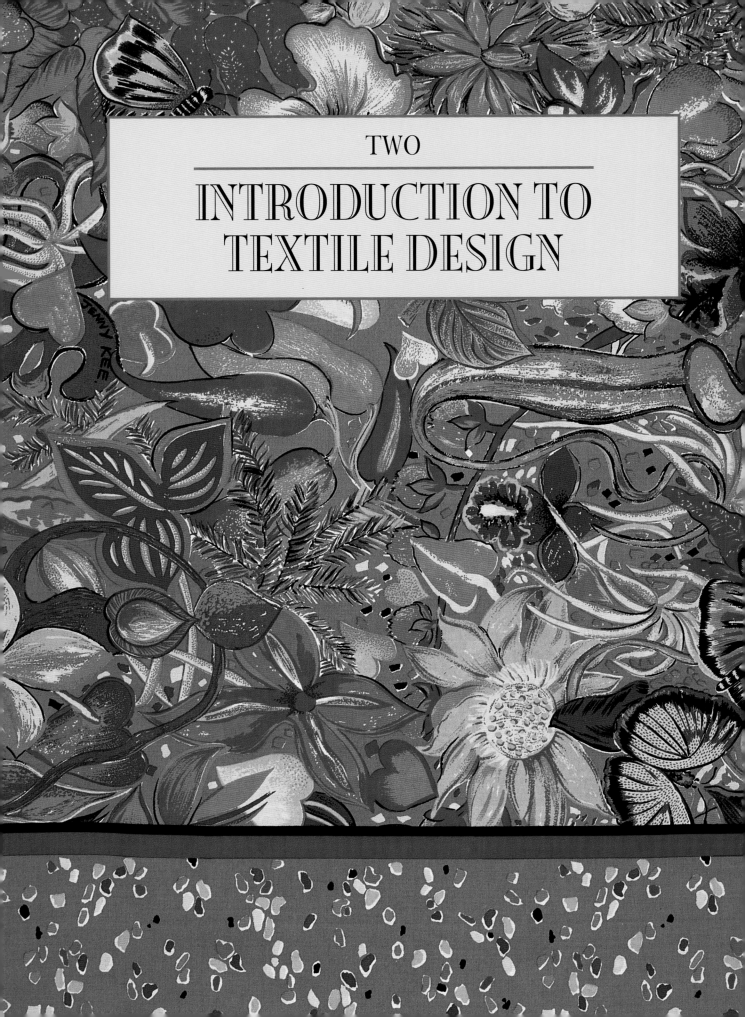

TWO

INTRODUCTION TO TEXTILE DESIGN

"Rainforest," a bright tropical floral pillowcase done with a loose but controlled hand. *Jenny Kee Australia*

In order to work in the textile design field, a designer must develop and master three skills: designing, working with color, and doing repeats. Although an individual may specialize in and be hired exclusively for any one of these skills, a designer should be proficient in all of them. Most positions, both salaried and freelance, whether for a converter or a studio, require such training. Every designer must put together a good portfolio for either the apparel or home furnishing markets, and the stylist or design director reviews it to assess whether a designer's work will meet his or her studio's needs. The textile design business is complex and demanding; developing professional work habits and making intelligent business decisions can be challenging and profitable for both the beginner and experienced designer.

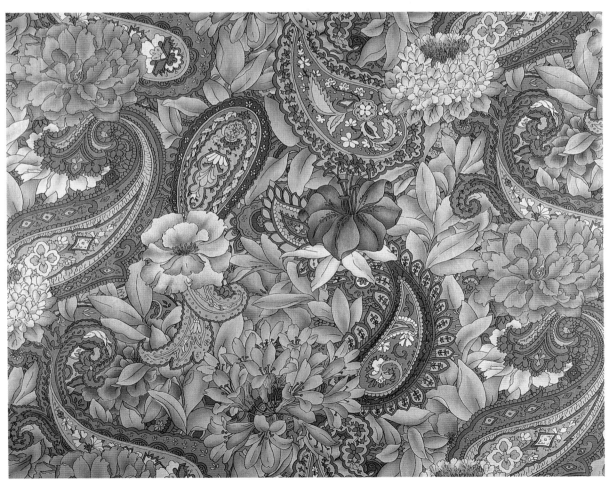

"Capri," a sheet design of florals and paisleys. *Stylepoints Collection, Cameo Interiors*

DESIGN

A textile design begins with an idea or theme. The designer then selects the appropriate reference material for developing the idea, and combines it with imagination, layout, and color sense to create the design (see Chapter 6, "Design and Layout").

COLOR

The selection of a design's colors is very important. A mediocre design can be greatly improved by good color choices; conversely, a really good design can be ruined by bad color (see Chapter 7, "Working with Color"). Usually a set of three or more *colorways* (sections of a design painted to show a pattern in various color alternatives; also called *colorings* or *color combinations*) is created and printed along with each pattern.

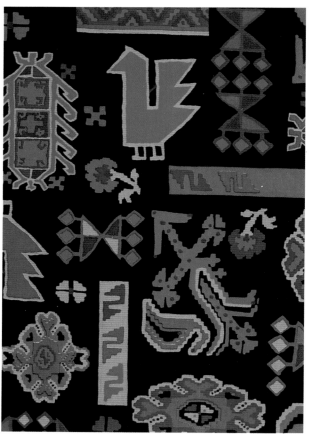

A set of three colorways derived from Mexican folk art motifs. *Designed by Sheila and Lee Stewart, Lee Stewart Associates Incorporated*

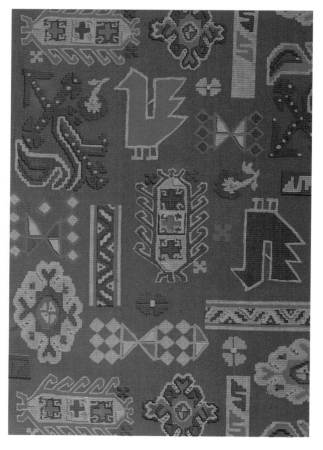

REPEATS

A *repeat* is the final version of a design, worked out and painted to meet the exact specifications of the printing process. The rendering of the design in this predetermined measurement shows how the pattern will be printed over and over again in a continuous flow, without apparent interruption. When the repeat is finished it is sent to the textile printing plant, where a separate screen or roller is prepared for each color, and the design is then printed on fabric. Refer to Chapter 8, "How To Put a Design in Repeat," and Chapter 11, "The Printing Process," for more detailed information.

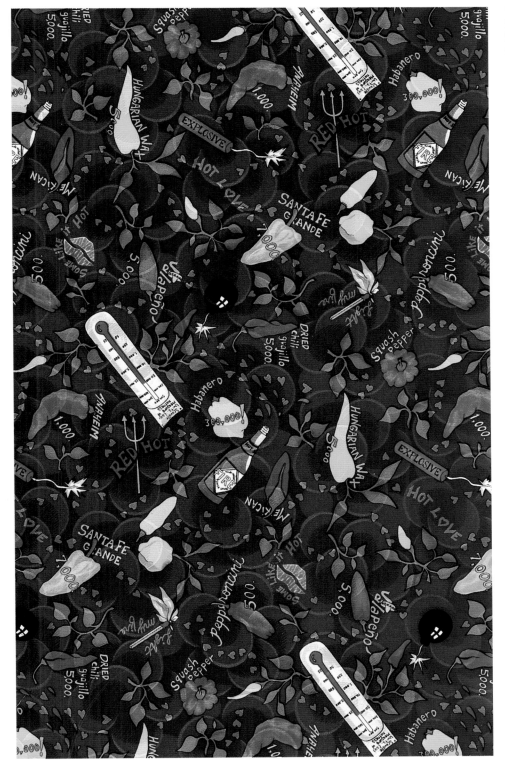

Try to find the half-drop repeat in this conversational design in a tossed layout. *Copyright © Nicole Miller*

THE BUSINESS OF TEXTILE DESIGN: WHAT DESIGNERS SHOULD KNOW

There are two broad categories of printed fabric designs: apparel and home furnishing. Apparel designs are for those fabrics that are meant to be worn; home furnishing designs are those that are used in the home or elsewhere for interior decoration. Within each of these categories, there are two main sources of work for textile designers: converters and design studios.

CONVERTERS

A converter is a company that converts *gray goods* (also called *greige goods)*, or raw fabric prior to bleaching, dyeing, or printing, into printed fabric. The converter assumes responsibility for the operations involved, from purchasing the gray goods to shipping the finished printed fabric to clothing manufacturers.

Most converters have one or more studios that employ designers, colorists, and repeat artists. Large apparel converters often maintain several studios, one for each type of clothing (women's wear, men's wear, swimwear, and so on), while large home furnishing converters have separate studios for domestics and decoratives. The largest converting houses have both apparel and home furnishing studios, and therefore maintain a sizable staff of textile artists. Small converters may have only one or two designers. Many

converters hire designers and colorists and purchase designs created on a freelance basis.

A design job with a converter is salaried, and the company owns everything its employees do during working hours. The position may include responsibility for design, colorways, and repeats, although some companies also hire people to work exclusively as colorists and repeat artists. When interviewing for a design position, always make sure that you know exactly what the job entails.

There are some advantages to working at a salaried position that are not available to freelancers. Most companies offer their salaried employees such benefits as health insurance plans and paid vacations and sick days. The

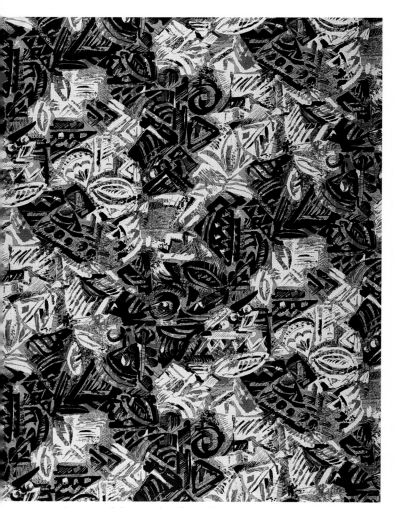

An apparel design taken from African geometric motifs. *The Cloth Company, a division of Cranston Print Works Co.*

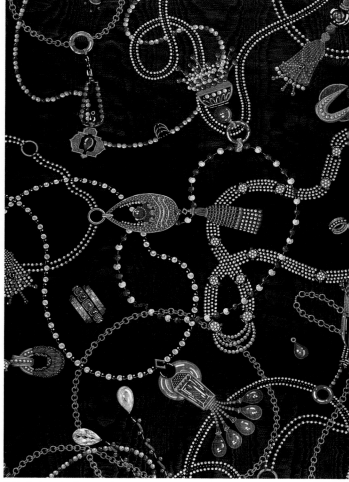

"Bimbeloterie," a novelty conversational home furnishing pattern with a moiré background. *Clarence House Imports, Ltd.*

larger converters often have profit sharing and pension plans. They also offer the possibility of advancement into a better position, such as assistant stylist or stylist (discussed later in this chapter), as well as the opportunity of going to the mill and learning how to take charge of printing the patterns (see Chapter 11, "The Printing Process").

During a company's busy seasons, the opportunity to do freelance work for the company may arise. This work is either done at home or on an overtime basis at the studio, and fees are either based on an hourly rate or charged by the job, according to current freelance rates. It is to the company's advantage to have an inside designer who is familiar with its needs do its overtime work, so whenever possible negotiate for freelance rates, which tend to be higher. (Consult the *Graphic Artists Guild Handbook: Pricing and Ethical Guidelines*, listed in the Resources.)

Fearing that their line may be copied or disclosed in some other way, many converters make it clear from the start that you will jeopardize your job if you work for other converters, and some require signed statements to that effect as a condition of employment. If you already have established freelance relationships with other converters, or if you would like to pursue freelance work in the future, it is wise to develop a code of ethics that is workable for you and acceptable to your employer. If you have any questions about signing any restrictive statements for a salaried position, talk to experienced designers and consult the *Graphic Artists Guild Handbook*.

When you apply for a design job with a converter, expect that some companies will request that you paint two or three colorways for a design of their choice as a test of your skills. Although this is more or less standard, try to negotiate a fee for this work or, at

the very least, have it returned to you so that you can incorporate it into your portfolio.

The Stylist or Design Director. At a converter, the stylist or design director "styles the line," or selects the designs and colors to be printed in each season's line of fabrics, delegates work to the designers, oversees the day-to-day operations of the studio, and is directly responsible to company executives. The stylist is also responsible for supervising *strike-offs,* which involves approving or

making final changes or corrections on the first yardage of a pattern printed at the mill. An assistant stylist works as a designer, manages the studio when the stylist is otherwise engaged, and is trained to help supervise strike-offs.

DESIGN STUDIOS
At most textile design studios, designers work on a freelance basis, with the studio acting as agent and paying only for designs that are sold. In addition to providing a sales force and direction concerning the types of designs

"La Roseraie Interieure," a traditional chintz rose pattern for home furnishing. The coordinate for this design is on page 104. *Clarence House Imports, Ltd.*

its customers require, a large studio may provide a designer with workspace. Some designers use a studio as their agent but work at home, though fees and commission are the same in both circumstances. It is possible in some design studios to hold a salaried position, or to make other financial arrangements, such as commissions on sales plus some salary.

A design studio sells its designs either by sending its salespeople out to show its collection to potential customers, or by having clients visit the studio to shop for designs. When a design is sold and delivered, the studio bills the customer and takes a commission on every piece of work it sells. There are standard recommended prices for designs, colorways, and repeats listed in the *Graphic Artists Guild Handbook*. For many decades the standard studio commission has been 30 to 40 percent; some

studios now take up to 50 percent, but this practice is discouraged by the Graphic Artists Guild. In any event, a freelance designer owns the copyright to all of his or her original designs until they are sold to a customer. If necessary, the designer can borrow the unsold designs at a prearranged time to make up a portfolio to use while job hunting.

A design can be sold either as a sketch or as a design in repeat. Usually, a designer will put his or her own designs into repeat; if one of the studio's repeat artists is used, the repeat fee is deducted from the designer's share of the money. However, in some cases the customer is billed for the design and repeat fees separately.

Whether working in the studio or at home, a designer must try to be disciplined about keeping regular hours (mutually agreed on, if work is done at the studio),

and should work at a reasonably steady pace. This assures the best chances for future sales, since a studio will have a continued interest in the artistic development and sales of its reliable designers. If working from home, for instance, you might arrange to deliver your designs once a week and at the same time pick up directions for the following week's work. This ensures a steady work pace and regular contact with the studio.

Freelance sales can be good one week and nonexistent the next, which presents psychological as well as financial problems. Because of the inconsistencies in this type of work, designers must be patient and give their freelance work time to develop, evaluating their progress on a quarterly or semiannual basis and perhaps pursuing another source of income while developing a steady rate of sales.

"Maceta," three coordinate bedding patterns adapted from Mexican motifs. *Martex for West Point-Pepperell*

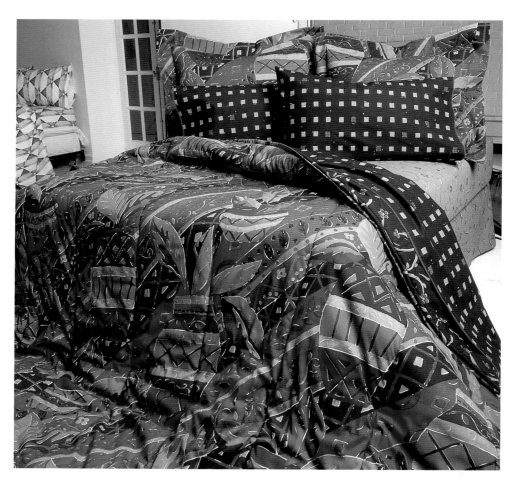

The studio often provides special-order work for which payment is assured, which is of some financial help. It is also permissible for designers to work for other contacts if there is no conflict of interest. For example, a designer may accept work from a studio that designs for apparel if his or her primary source of work is for home furnishing. However, some studios and agents require their designers to sign an exclusive contract restricting work with other studios. Before agreeing to this, refer to the *Graphic Artists Guild Handbook* and discuss the contract with knowledgeable persons in the field.

For income tax purposes, it is essential that a designer keep records of all designs sold or otherwise completed. Each piece should have a number or facsimile and should be dated for delivery and payment.

THE AGENT OR REPRESENTATIVE
There are a number of individuals who will act as your agent to sell your designs for a commission but do not have workspace to offer you. They work from home, offices, or showrooms. In an arrangement with such an agent, you work at home and the agent gives you directions for designs, sells the designs, bills the customers, and pays you after collecting the amount due. These agents usually charge the same commission as the design studios, currently around 40 percent. It is important to make certain of the percentage they will take and the length of time it will take them to pay you after the delivery of the finished work. (These are the two things I hear the most complaints about from students.) Once again, check with someone in the field or call the Graphic Artists Guild to make sure the agent you are considering is reputable, and to review any contracts before signing them.

FREELANCE: ACTING AS YOUR OWN AGENT
It is possible, of course, to act as your own agent, selling your designs and doing freelance colorways and repeats. The biggest advantage in acting as your own agent is, naturally, that you eliminate the agent's commission on sales while charging the same price the agent would. The disadvantage is having to deal with the problems that arise with customers, such as arbitrary changes in the work, disagreements about instructions, picking up and delivering work (perhaps several times if changes are being made), making new contacts, and collecting payments, all of which can be time-consuming and emotionally draining. It is best to work through a studio or agent until you are established and have made good contacts in the field, and developed confidence in yourself.

BUSINESS TIPS FOR FREELANCERS
- Make *all* agreements in writing. Also, confirm all design, color, layout, and repeat instructions in writing to protect your interests in the event of a dispute upon delivery of the work.

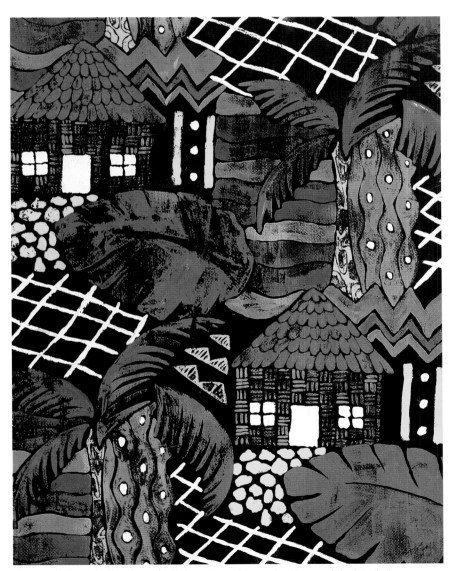

"Tropical Village," a beach towel design done with a painterly woodblock technique.
Copyright © Susan Toplitz, designer

- Don't be afraid to ask as many questions as are necessary to make the job clear in your mind.
- While it is permissible to use a design for inspiration or as reference material if you sufficiently change it to create a new design, do not "knock-off," or copy outright, any design created by another artist unless it is in the public domain, even if the stylist or client requests it.
- If you are not familiar with a client, you should discourage them from holding your designs or portfolio for more than a day. Some artists permit holding for only a few hours. Use a holding form whenever possible. (Refer to the *Graphic Artists Guild Handbook* for more details.)
- Customers will ask for reduced prices when they purchase several designs at one time. A designer should permit this arrangement only in special cases; for example, with the potential for some future benefit.
- If a customer cancels a job through no fault of the designer, a kill fee is due, which is based on the total time spent on the job. Use tact and common sense to negotiate.
- Additional fees may be charged when the client requests changes that were not part of the original agreement.
- Try to have your original art returned to you, and request printed fabric for your designs whenever possible. It is essential that you continue to add new pieces to your portfolio for future job seeking.

THE PORTFOLIO

A good portfolio is the key to getting the job you want, whether salaried or freelance. Your portfolio will be judged first by your *hand*, or technique, which is the care and clarity of your line and painting. A "tight hand" is most desirable, and means that the painting and line work are clean-edged, professional-looking, and meticulous. A "loose hand" is one that incorporates a controlled but freer painting technique. Experienced designers can work in both techniques—and any in between—equally well. Second in importance to a designer's hand is his or her color sense.

The designs in your portfolio should, of course, be as beautiful as possible and have a good overall look. A complete portfolio should include twelve to fifteen designs, which reflect a variety of

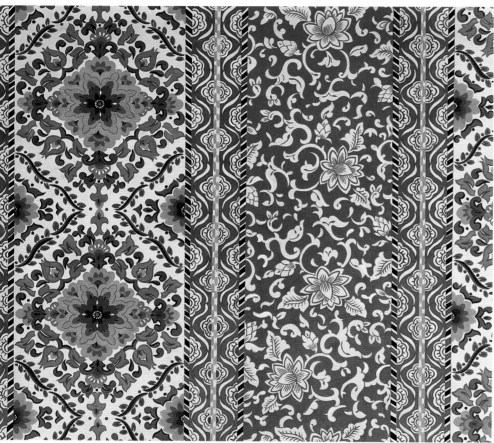

"Chan," a bedding stripe of Persian motifs beautifully painted with a tight hand. *Copyright © Lynn Johnson, designer*

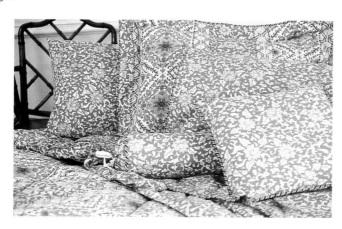

"Chan" shown with its sheet coordinates. *Copyright © Lynn Johnson, designer*

themes, layouts, and trends, both classical and current, and demonstrate your technical skills, layout ability, and color sense. At least two or three designs should have a set of colorways accompanying them, and two or three coordinate designs mounted together look great. Based on the designs you include in your portfolio, the stylist will assess whether, with direction, your work will satisfy the studio's needs.

PREPARING YOUR PORTFOLIO

It is not necessary to have an elaborate presentation for showing your portfolio. The portfolio should be clean, neat, and arranged for easy handling by the interviewer. The designs should be presented the same way they are shown in a studio: squared off with a triangle, neatly cut, then matted on white mounting paper. This method of presentation makes it easy for the interviewer to flip through the portfolio. Two sizes of mounts can be used: large (for medium to large designs) and half-size (for smaller designs). Do not paste the design onto the mount. Instead, tip the design onto the mount with double-faced tape on its top center and upper corners, and center it on the mount. This leaves the designs loose on the bottom, which prevents creasing when they are rolled up for storage or transport, and makes the designs easy to remove for remounting. Very large designs that do not fit on mounting paper can simply be rolled up and carried separately in a cardboard tube. If your designs are on waxed rice paper, which can tear easily, put invisible tape along all the edges on the back. Masking tape can be used on opaque papers for this same purpose.

Put your name and address on the back of your designs and/or mounts. You can purchase a rubber stamp for this purpose. Designs with a set of colorways should be mounted with the design on top and the colorways below. If the colorways are too large to fit on the same mount, they can be mounted separately or placed beneath the design, partly showing. For transporting your portfolio, large manila envelopes with handles and vinyl and plastic carrying cases are both inexpensive and easy to find.

It is a good idea to show one or more of the designs in your portfolio in repeat. However, when you first begin job hunting, it is possible that most of them will not be in repeat. If this is the case, when an interviewer asks about your repeat skills be frank and say that you will need a little extra help on the first one or two. Most employers understand this, since it would be impossible to be an expert repeat artist on one's first job. After you have successfully completed your first couple of repeats, you will feel like an old pro.

LOOKING FOR A JOB

Your portfolio is all set and you are ready to look for a job. The following is a partial list of employment sources:

- The classified advertisements in major newspapers. Look under "Textile Designer," "Designer," and "Artist."
- Professional employment agencies. This type of firm usually charges a fee, but it may be worth a try. Professional recruiters always charge the employer the fee, so it is best to try them first.
- Converters and textile design studios listed in the yellow pages of the telephone directory. Call and ask to speak to either the personnel department or the studio stylist.

- Friends or contacts who work in the textile industry. You will find that most people are helpful. While there may not be a position open where they work, many can direct you elsewhere if they like your portfolio.
- The state employment office. Check to see if they list textile design jobs.

Do not get discouraged if it takes you a while to develop leads. In most cases, designers with good portfolios eventually find work. Some people get placed quickly and others, even those with good portfolios, may take some time to find a job, perhaps because of a slow season, bad timing, personality problems, and so on. Keep trying.

INDIVIDUAL ENTERPRISES

Some readers may be interested in developing their own textile craft items or products and finding ways to market them. If you design one-of-a-kind items, research the art galleries and craft shops in your area as possible sales outlets. Also, many museum and gallery exhibits feature textile arts: fabrics that are woven, painted, stenciled, and so on. Investigate boutiques and department stores for sales possibilities, but call first and make an appointment with the buyer to ensure that someone with decision-making authority will see your work. There are also many local and regional arts and crafts fairs at which you can display and sell your work. An entrance fee is required at most fairs, and some of them stipulate that your work be accepted by a panel of judges.

If your one-of-a-kind item becomes successful, be prepared to take orders and duplicate it, perhaps with some differences to maintain its individual look as well as your own interest.

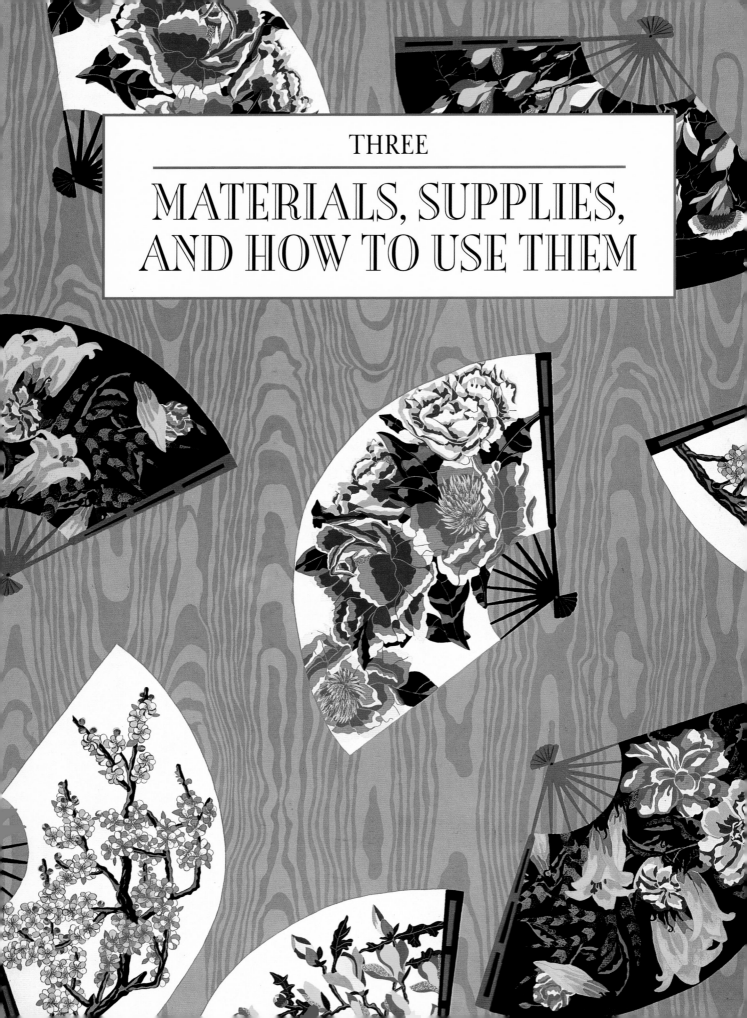

THREE

MATERIALS, SUPPLIES, AND HOW TO USE THEM

The rendering of a textile design is a synthesis of ideas, materials, and technique. These three elements provide a firm foundation for the expression of a designer's creativity and imagination. The choice of supplies is determined by the look you want to achieve in a particular design. Always choose the most sensible and appropriate materials to get the desired effect in the most efficient way. Many new items appear on the market that are tempting to buy. A few of them work but most are disappointing, so be cautious and first learn to use the supplies recommended in this chapter. Experimenting with these basic materials on a variety of designs is the best way to discover what works best for you.

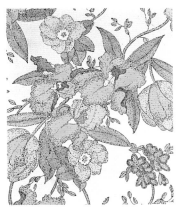

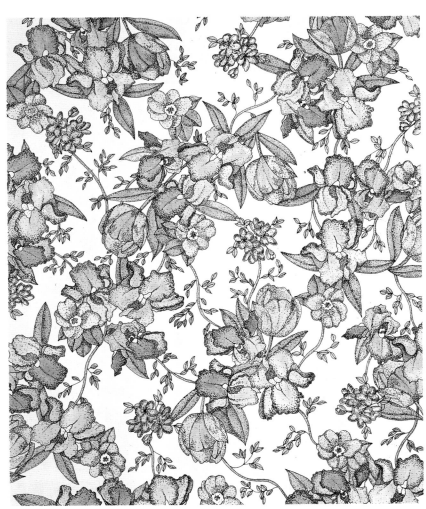

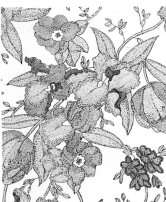

A delicate lingerie floral design with two colorways done in dyes on waxed rice paper. The fine outline and stipple were drawn with a 000 rapidograph. *Copyright © Glenda Heffer, designer*

PAINTS

Two types of paint are used in textile design, both of which are water based. *Gouache* and *tempera* are opaque, which means that one color can be applied over another without either bleeding or changing. *Dyes* or *concentrated watercolors* are transparent, which means that one color applied on top of another will form a third.

GOUACHE AND TEMPERA

Gouache and tempera are the two basic opaque paints used in textile design. While gouache is made with a preparation of gum and tempera is made with egg, both are water based and can be used interchangeably, as both produce a flat, dull, opaque finish. Winsor & Newton gouache is considered the best available, and is the opaque paint of choice for many designers. However, tempera is cheaper and is an adequate substitute for gouache. Both paints cover pencil sketch lines, and although light colors such as white and yellow tend to bleed when painted on top of darker colors, this can be remedied by simply adding another coat of the lighter color.

Gouache and tempera must be mixed thoroughly with water, and thinned just enough to achieve a creamy consistency. If too much water is used, the paint will be so thin that the paper underneath will show through. If not enough water is used, the dried paint will tend to chip, especially if two or three coats are used. Also, it is difficult to render fine details with thick paint. When opening a new tube of gouache or bottle of tempera, you may notice an oily film on top. Pour this oil off and thoroughly stir the remaining paint before mixing it with water.

Gouache and tempera can be used on all the papers and painting surfaces recommended in this chapter. Listed below are what I consider the minimum number of basic colors a designer needs. Many other colors can be purchased, but with a set of either gouache or tempera, or a combination of both, you can mix and match virtually any color (see Chapter 7, "Working with Color").

Gouache. Use Winsor & Newton Designers' Gouache (in tubes) or any other reasonably similar brand, such as Grumbacher, Pelikan, Talens, or Turner.

1. Flame Red
2. Sky or Cerulean Blue
3. Lemon Yellow
4. Orange
5. Daffodil or Tiger Yellow
6. Permanent Green Middle
7. Bengel Rose (Grumbacher brand is the best)
8. Turquoise
9. Brown
10. Lamp Black or Jet Black (tempera may be substituted)
11. White (tempera may be substituted)

Tempera. Use Rich Art Tempera (in jars) or any other reasonably similar brand.

1. Vermillion
2. Light Magenta
3. Spectrum Green
4. Spectrum Orange
5. Spectrum Yellow
6. Van Dyke Brown
7. Turquoise
8. Spectrum or Azure Blue
9. Prussian or Ultramarine Blue
10. Poster Black
11. Poster White

DYES OR CONCENTRATED WATERCOLORS

Transparent dyes come in bottles, and are labeled "Brilliant Concentrated Watercolors" or "Radiant Concentrated Watercolors." Being transparent, these dyes are the opposite of opaque tempera and gouache paints. The dyes can be mixed together to create a variety of beautiful shades, and light shades are made by mixing the dyes with water. Dyes are concentrated and very brilliant, and for this reason caution must be used when mixing a color, as adding even a very small amount of one dye to another can quickly change the color. Dyes can be used on most white or light-colored drawing papers; because they are transparent, dyes do not show up on dark grounds. They are particularly brilliant when used on waxed rice paper, which is also transparent. A design painted with dyes on waxed rice paper and mounted on white paper appears very bright, airy, and luminous, but remember to add a few drops of Luma Wax Grip or Braun Non Crawl, which are color media that allow the dyes to adhere to the paper properly and prevent beading (see "Color Mediums: Wax Grip and Non Crawl," later in this chapter). Although dozens of dye colors are available, the colors listed below will enable you to mix and match most of the shades you will need. A touch of dye mixed with white or other gouache paints can be used to heighten a shade's brilliance.

Dyes or Concentrated Watercolors. Use Luma, Dr. Ph. Martin's, or any reasonably similar brand.

1. Tropic or Hot Pink
2. Cerulean Blue or True Blue
3. Daffodil or Tiger Yellow
4. Lemon Yellow
5. Flame Red or Vermillion
6. Orange
7. Grass Green
8. Sepia
9. Turquoise
10. Ultramarine Blue
11. Black

TIPS FOR APPLYING DYES
- Don't let the dyes intimidate you. Although they tend to be unpredictable, with practice you will learn to control them.
- Concentrate on one area of a design and work rapidly,

smoothing out the dyes while wet, so that overlapping strokes are not apparent.

- When you need to refill your brush, stop painting where the interruption will be least noticeable, such as a narrow space between motifs. This will allow you to pick up the color and continue painting with a minimum of obvious overlap.
- When you pick up an edge to continue painting, it helps to feather your brush, or use the tip of your brush with a very light touch where you're making the connection. You can also try to blot up the overlap of dye very lightly with a tissue or with the tip of your finger.
- If puddles of dye appear on the paper, work with a drier brush by either removing the excess dye on the side of the palette or on a piece of scrap paper. Do not load your brush with dye unless you are painting a large area.

- When painting large areas, use the full width of the brush by applying pressure on it. This will give you the maximum coverage with one stroke and minimize overlaps.
- Use the right size brush for the space you are painting: No. 3 or 4 for small areas, and No. 7 or 8 for large areas.
- Don't make picky little strokes. Try to cover both large and small areas with as few strokes as possible. Always smooth out the dye quickly while it is still wet.
- To avoid having to stop and remix and match colors, mix enough of a color to complete your design.

PAPERS AND OTHER SURFACES

There are several painting and sketching surfaces available to the textile designer—textured, smooth, transparent, and opaque.

Papers with very slick surfaces should usually be avoided, as they do not absorb paints well.

DRAWING PAPER

Tweedweave or Georgian is a white or off-white paper with a slightly textured surface that takes dye, tempera, and gouache very well. Strathmore Bristol and Fabriano drawing papers are also good painting surfaces. These papers come in large sheets which can be cut down to smaller sizes, and are available in one-, two-, or three-ply (light to heavier weights). Papers of equal quality can be substituted for these brands.

DRAWING PADS

A drawing pad of white Bristol or a similar paper with a slightly textured surface is inexpensive, and can be used for small to medium designs as well as for test sketches in all paints. It is also smooth enough for pen and ink. A 14 × 17 inch pad is usually adequate.

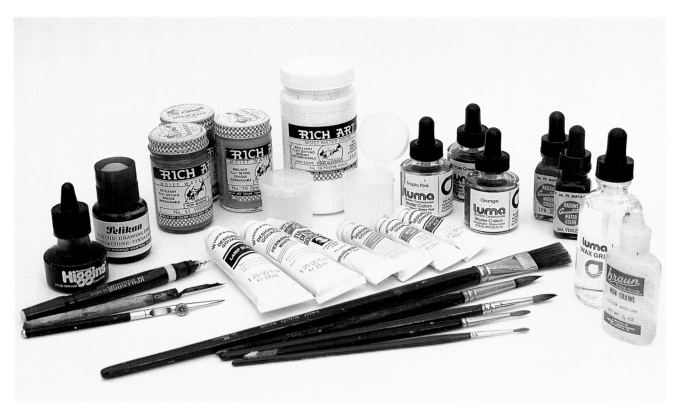

A variety of supplies, including (back row, from left) Higgins and Pelikan inks, Rich Art Tempera colors, small plastic mixing jars, Luma and Dr. Ph. Martin's watercolor dyes, Luma Wax Grip and Braun Non Crawl; (middle row) rapidograph, crow quill, and ruling pens, and Winsor & Newton and Turner's Designers' gouaches; and (front row) a variety of brushes, from a No. 2 to a 1-inch ground brush.

MASA WAXED RICE PAPER

Waxed rice paper is rice paper that has been treated with a smooth coat of wax, which makes the paper completely transparent. Pencil lines cannot be erased on waxed rice paper; therefore, when using this surface, work out your design on tracing paper first. Tape the waxed rice paper on top of the tracing paper, mix your colors, and you are ready to paint. If you want to rework a design, either to improve it or change the colors, simply place waxed rice paper on top of the existing design and make your corrections as you paint.

Both dyes and opaque paints can be used on waxed rice paper. As mentioned earlier, when a design is painted with transparent dyes on waxed rice paper and placed on a white mount, the colors appear exceptionally clear and luminous, and these designs have a much lighter quality than those painted in opaque gouache or tempera. Once again, remember to add a few drops of Wax Grip or Non Crawl to the dyes so that they will properly adhere to this surface.

COLORED PAPERS

Many papers with slightly textured surfaces are available in colors that can be used as backgrounds for gouache or tempera designs. One such paper is Canson Mi-Teintes. The heavier weight is better, as warping and puckering occur on papers of lighter weights. For designs that require special techniques, watercolor papers with heavier, textured surfaces are available. Dyes, of course, being transparent, cannot be used unless the paper is very light in color.

PLASTI-VELLUM PAPER

Plasti-Vellum paper has a clear, white, transparent surface. For textile designs Plasti-Vellum is the preferred product, and should not be confused with other vellums intended for tracing or drafting. Place Plasti-Vellum over the tracing paper on which your motifs or designs are drawn, and you are ready to use gouache paints, pen and ink, or dyes. As with waxed rice paper, add Wax Grip or Non Crawl to your dyes for this surface.

TRACING PAPER

A 19 × 24 inch, medium-weight pad of tracing paper is appropriate for most designs. Rolls are also available, for extra-large designs. The weight should not be too thin, to avoid tears when rubbing the tracing down while transferring the design from the tracing paper to the drawing paper; or too heavy, as you must be able to see through it clearly.

SARAL TRANSFER PAPER

Transfer paper is used to transfer a single motif or a whole design from tracing paper to drawing paper. The transfer paper is placed, *carbon side down,* on the drawing paper. The tracing paper, which has the motif or design on it, is then laid on top. The motifs on the tracing paper are retraced in pencil, and transferred through the transfer paper to the drawing paper underneath. Heavy pencil lines are hard to erase, so use a light touch when retracing, and use a plastic eraser if needed.

Saral Artists' Transfer Papers, made especially for transfers to paper, are available in a wide range of colors. White or yellow can be used on dark-colored grounds; graphite is good for light-colored grounds. When planning to paint pale colors on a light or white ground, work with a light-colored transfer paper so that the lines will be easier to erase after the colors have been applied. The use of transfer paper is sometimes a preferred alternative to the rubdown method described in Chapter 6, "Design and Layout." The advantage of the rubdown method is that the tracing paper is transparent, which makes it easy to position and to check your work as you proceed. Transfer paper eliminates the rubdown process, which is tedious and time-consuming.

ACETATE

A sheet of plain or treated acetate is invaluable for testing designs and colors before beginning your final painting. Colors can be washed off, and the sheet can be used over again. Some studios find it convenient to use acetate for colorways and other design work. Treated acetate, which has a prepared surface that is nonresistant to paint, is preferable. Plain acetate will require a few drops of Wax Grip in your paint or dye.

BRUSHES

In textile design, the important features to look for in a brush are its resiliency and point. A few brushes of good quality, in a range of sizes, should be adequate for the beginning designer.

CHOOSING AND TESTING A BRUSH

Before purchasing a brush, complete these two tests: Dip the brush in water and make sure the bristles shape into a good sharp point; and test the spring in the brush by snapping the bristles back and forth with your finger. Any good art supply store will let you make these two tests. For purposes of comparison when buying other brands, ask to see a Winsor & Newton Series 7 brush. This is the best brush available for textile designing, but it is expensive, especially the larger sizes. I usually suggest to students that if they wish to invest in Winsor & Newton brushes, they should buy Nos. 1 to 4 in Series 7. For the larger sizes, Series 707, which is less expensive, is quite adequate. Of course, there are other good brands of brushes; for example, Grumbacher, Kolinsky, Rafael, Isabey, Simmons, and L. K. Hecht. The salesperson may suggest others. I recommend that beginners purchase a No. 4 and a No. 7 or 8.

Regardless of size, a brush should make a point fine enough to draw small details, which is essential in painting textile designs. Many designers use a No. 7 or 8 brush to do very fine work. The difference between using a small or large brush is the amount of paint that the brush holds. However, beginners often feel awkward using anything but a very small brush for tight work. If this is true for you, try a No. 2 or 3 brush. These small sizes are less expensive, and you can buy several to determine which size works most comfortably for you. It is also convenient to have a selection of brushes. When I work on a design, I often use five or six brushes, one for each color. For a loose technique, experiment with other types of brushes, such as those with flat edges.

The hairs on a new brush may tend to separate, making it difficult to keep a pointed tip. To force a brush into shape, lightly wet the brush and swish it around on a cake of soap. When the brush is full of lather, form the bristles with your fingers into the best point you can and stand the brush upright overnight or for a day or two. When you are ready to use your newly shaped brush, simply wash away the soap. Always work the brush into a pointed tip on a piece of scrap paper before you paint with it.

After you've finished using your brushes, always clean and rinse them well, and store them by standing them bristle end up in a brush jar or other container. Make sure their tips are protected when transporting them. Do

not use a good brush to apply bleach, chemicals, or substances that are hard to remove; save your old brushes, or buy some really inexpensive ones for those purposes.

If a brush has a single hair at its tip that is annoying you when you paint, do not try to cut it off because you will most probably cut into the other bristles. The proper way to get rid of the hair is to burn it off quickly with a match. Wet the tip slightly and shape it into a very sharp point. Hold the brush up to the light, keep the hair in sight, and pass the flame very quickly over it so it just catches the tip and burns off the hair. Repeat the process, if necessary. If possible, ask an experienced person to do it for you.

USING YOUR BRUSHES

When you start painting, have a piece of scrap paper on hand on which to test your colors and to work the brush into a point before painting. Rest your arm on the table and hold the brush firmly, about 1 1/2 inches above the tip. The brush will respond to the amount of pressure you put on it; you control the delicacy or thickness of a line by applying more or less pressure to the brush. With more pressure, the paint spreads and covers a larger area. A fine line can be made with a light touch, using just the tip of the brush. Do not try to paint a large area with a small brush.

The amount of paint on the brush is also important. Do not overload your brush for the area you are painting. If you are using dyes, an overloaded brush will result in puddles of color that must be quickly picked up with a tissue or brush. If you use too much gouache on your brush, you will have great difficulty in pushing the paint around and maintaining a fine line. Too much gouache will result in cracking or chipping after the

paint has dried, especially if a second or third coat is applied.

PEN AND INK SUPPLIES

There are several types of pens used in textile design; among them are technical pens or rapidographs, ruling pens, and the crow quill pen point.

Smooth papers are best for pen and ink work, although papers such as Tweedweave and others with slight textures can be used. Waxed rice paper causes problems for many beginners because the pen tends to get caught on the paper. As students learn to work more confidently with the pen, using a light touch on the surface of the paper, most of them overcome this problem.

TECHNICAL PEN OR RAPIDOGRAPH

A technical pen comes fitted with an ink-filled cartridge. The ink flows out evenly as you draw, producing a clear, fine line. For textile design, a variety of points—from No. 000 (very fine) to 2.5 can be used with one pen, but it is inconvenient to have to change points often. Since the points cost almost as much as the whole pen, most people purchase and work with several pens, each fitted with a different point size, to accommodate different designs. The biggest problem with technical pens is that they clog easily, so carefully follow the manufacturer's instructions for their care and cleaning. Several brands— Koh-I-Noor, Faber-Castell, LeRoy, and Mars-Staedtler technical pens—are both inexpensive and fairly easy to use.

Other pens that can be used to outline designs are the Wrico dotting pen (also used for the stipple dot technique described in Chapter 9), and permanent ink drawing pens such as the Pilot Ultrafine Point and the Eberhard Faber Design Marker.

RULING PEN

A mechanical pen used for ruling straight lines, a ruling pen has two sides that open and close by turning a small screw. Ink, paint, or dye is placed between the two sides with a brush or pen point, and the screw is tightened to the width of the line desired. The ink flows out as the line is drawn against a firmly held ruler or triangle. You can buy rulers with raised backs or, as many designers do, tape two or three coins on the back of the ruler to raise it above the surface of the paper so that when the tip of the pen moves against the ruler, the fluid will not smear.

When a thick line is desired, it is best to draw two thin lines next to each other and fill in the space between them with either the ruling pen or a brush. Gouache and tempera should be watered down to the consistency of India ink so that the paint will flow evenly out of the ruling pen. If the fluid dries in the pen and does not flow out, dip the pen in water and thoroughly clean it with a tissue, then fill the pen with fresh ink or paint. Make sure that you wipe the sides of the ruling pen before you begin drawing. Ruling pen lines are used for stripes, geometrics, and other designs that incorporate motifs with neat straight edges.

When a job requires many ruling pen lines, it is helpful to set up a board or table with a straight edge and use a T-square. You can zip right along with your ruling pen, moving the T-square from one position to the next.

CROW QUILL PEN POINT

Designers should learn to use the old-fashioned crow quill pen point in a holder, which gives great flexibility in drawing fineline designs. For instance, when changing inks, you only need to clean off the point and dip it into the new color. When the pen point clogs up, simply swish it in water and wipe it off carefully with a tissue. Another method is to scratch off the caked ink with an X-Acto knife or a single-edged razor blade.

The price of the point is nominal, and the point will last a long time if you take care of it. One holder can be used with all point sizes. I recommend a Joseph Gillot pen point No. 659, which is very fine but hard enough so that when you draw a circle the nib does not separate. Buy other brands and test them.

As when using a brush, the pressure put on the point determines the thickness of the line. Most fineline textile designs require an even outline. Practice the following pen technique, particularly when drawing flowers, for a good, even line: Rest your arm comfortably on the table, get a firm grip on the pen holder about 1 to 2 inches above the nib, and keep a steady pressure on the point as you move it smoothly along the paper's surface. If you dig the nib into the paper, the point will tend to separate and the ink will spatter. It will also cause the width of the line to vary.

INK

Any good-quality waterproof or permanent ink may be used for designing. Nonwaterproof ink will smear, particularly when dyes touch it.

OTHER SUPPLIES

The textile designer needs a variety of auxiliary products to trace, paint, and present his or her work: palettes, rulers and triangles, markers and mechanical pencils, erasers, liquid mediums and masks, and other labor-saving materials for special design techniques.

PALETTE

Several kinds of vessels are available for mixing paints. Small covered jars made of plastic or glass are useful. Plastic egg crates and ice cube trays are good, inexpensive alternatives. Other palettes, made of plastic or porcelain, have six or eight wells in which to mix paints. When using these you must cover the colors tightly with tape or plastic wrap when you stop painting for the day. Put one or two drops of water in leftover gouache or tempera mixtures before covering them to compensate for any evaporation that may occur. There is nothing more annoying than starting your work and discovering that your paints have dried up. If this happens, add a few drops of water—just enough to cover the paint—and in a short time, the paint will loosen up as you mix it. Be sure to sop up any excess water *before* mixing to avoid making the paint too thin.

RULER

A steel ruler (18 inches for apparel designs, 36 inches for home furnishing designs), preferably one with a raised cork backing, is the best type for design work. Accurate measurement plays an important role in layouts and repeats, so learn to rely on your ruler. Many of my students think that $1/2$ inch and $1/4$ inch are the same thing. Obviously they are not the same measurement, and $1/4$ inch makes a big difference when you are laying out a set design or measuring a repeat.

TRIANGLE

A 12-inch plastic triangle, 45 to 95 degrees, can be used for both large and small designs. I usually start a design by squaring off my paper with a triangle, leaving a few inches on the top and left side. This serves two purposes:

First, it gives the design an enclosure on the top and left side; it is usually not a good idea to work to the very edge of the paper because this leaves no space to extend the design if necessary. Second, the right angle forms a horizontal and vertical line from which a stripe or any set layout can be measured.

TRACING AND MECHANICAL PENCIL

Neat, clean tracings are essential to well-rendered designs. Tracing pencils in a range of sizes—Nos. 2H, 3H, and 6H or HB—as well as a mechanical pencil with the same number leads should be included among your supplies. Test several pencils and select the best lead for your hand, using No. 2H as a starting point. If the lead is too hard, the design will be difficult to see when the tracing is rubbed down. If the lead is too soft, the tracing and rubdown will become sloppy. Keep your tracing pencil sharp to attain maximum clarity of detail. A sandpaper block or small pencil sharpener should always be nearby when you work.

FELT-TIP MARKERS

Felt-tip markers are available in a wide variety of colors and widths. Make sure that the markers you purchase are either permanent or waterproof. If you use a nonwaterproof marker to outline motifs, smearing will occur when dyes are applied. To test the marker, simply draw a line on a piece of paper, wet your finger, and run it over the line; if it smears, do not buy that marker.

ART GUM, KNEADED, AND PLASTIC ERASERS

Make sure your eraser is clean before you use it. Use a light touch with art gum when erasing pencil lines on gouache grounds so that you do not smear the

colors. Plastic erasers work well removing Saral transfer paper lines, and a kneaded eraser is good for general use as it does not shed.

RUBBING SPOON

An ordinary spoon will work very well for rubbing down tracings. Put your thumb in the bowl of the spoon and use the edge to rub down the tracing. You can also use a dull-edged knife or purchase a rubbing bone.

COLOR MEDIUMS: WAX GRIP AND NON CRAWL

Luma Wax Grip and Braun Non Crawl are liquid mediums that, when added to dyes or paints, enable them to adhere to slick surfaces. Mix a few drops of Wax Grip in your color when painting on waxed rice paper, acetate, or any other surface that resists paint. A few drops of ordinary liquid household soap, such as Ivory or Palmolive, can also be used as an adherent. It is a good idea to try both Wax Grip and soap to decide which works best on a particular design.

BLEACH

Bleach is used for creating special effects when designing with dyes, and for making corrections and touch-ups. (See Chapter 9, "Special Design Techniques," for detailed information on using bleach.) Clorox is the strongest bleach available.

PRO WHITE

Pro White is an opaque white watercolor paint that covers dyes without bleed-through. It can be used to cover mistakes and make corrections, or to add touches of white to designs. Pro White is particularly effective in small areas; large areas covered with it can look messy. Pro White can also be used in place of white gouache or tempera.

LIQUID FRISKET

Liquid frisket is a thick, gray liquid that can be applied to specific areas of a design to mask them off from the rest. This technique allows the designer to paint over areas that are masked off, with the areas beneath remaining unaffected. Note, however, that the edges of the motifs tend to blur when the liquid frisket is peeled off. Because of this, liquid frisket is most appropriate for freely rendered designs, rather than tight ones.

Do not use a good brush to apply liquid frisket, and immediately wash the brush you do use. If necessary, clean the brush first with rubber cement thinner, then with soap and water.

Several brands of liquid frisket are available, including Art Maskoid and Luma Liquid Mask Frisket. Frisket is also available in sheets with adhesive backing. Use an art knife to cut the sheet into the shape and size of the area to be covered. The excess frisket is then peeled off the design before painting.

LIGHT BOX

A light box is a viewing and tracing device, which basically consists of a plastic or wooden box fitted with a glass top that is lit from below. Designs, tracings, photocopies, and other references are placed on the glass, with your drawing or tracing paper positioned on top. With the light shining from beneath, you can sketch, trace, or paint directly on your final paper for designs, colorways, and repeats. This eliminates the rubdown or tracing process.

You can create your own light box when you're away from your studio or work area by placing a light under any glass-topped table or piece of glass supported from underneath.

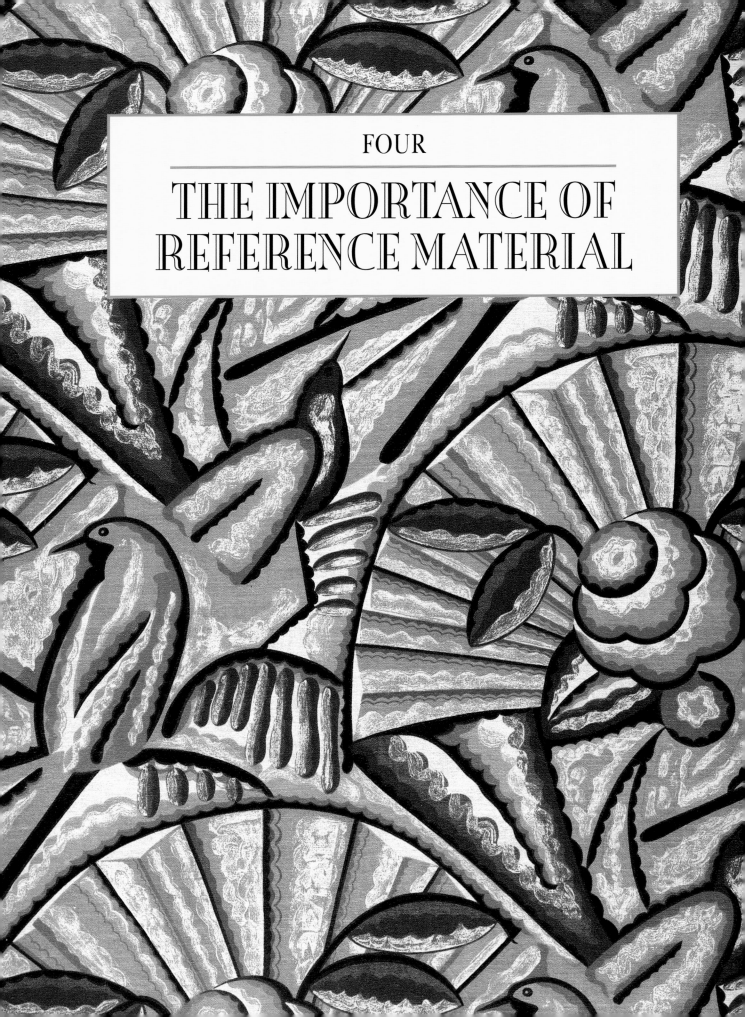

FOUR

THE IMPORTANCE OF REFERENCE MATERIAL

"L'Oiseau De Passage," a fan and flower pattern typical of French art deco style, circa 1920. *Clarence House Imports, Ltd.*

The importance of good reference material—both its collection and use in design—cannot be overemphasized. A designer's career can easily span two or three decades, during which time thousands of designs may be worked on. Design trends in style, theme, color, and technique change constantly; in order to keep up with these changes, you must be alert for all kinds of reference material. Every artist's studio is filled with photographs, postcards, artifacts, and clippings from all over the world, providing inspiration from cultures past and present. The ways that designers use their reference materials can vary a great deal. Sometimes the relationship between the finished design and its reference is virtually unrecognizable; in other instances, the connection is quite obvious.

"La Fleur," inspired by a 1920s art deco pattern. *Clarence House Imports, Ltd.*

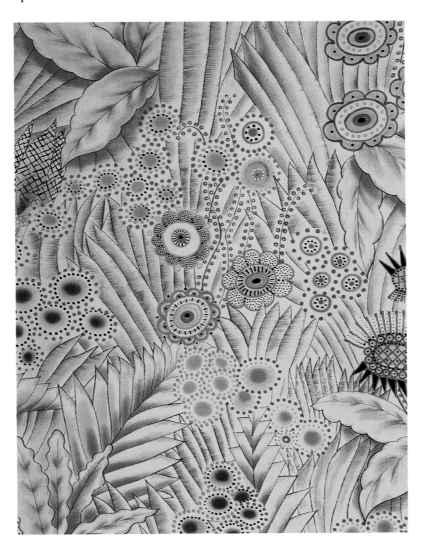

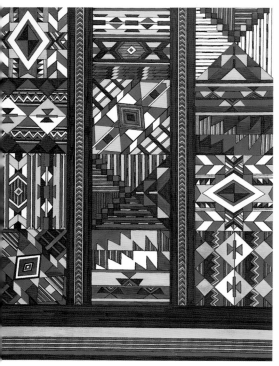

A modern design for a beach towel inspired by Native American geometric designs. *Copyright © Glenda Heffer, designer*

A designer uses reference material in an original way when he or she changes or combines past designs or styles, and comes up with a fresh approach. For example, in designing a pattern that tosses an old-fashioned Victorian bouquet on top of a geometric art deco background, a designer unites two distinct pieces of reference material to create an original look. It is not a good idea to copy a piece of reference material for a design without adding your own original touches. For one thing, other designers may also use the same reference material. You may be lucky enough to occasionally find a rare, original, or old piece of reference material that you can be reasonably certain no one else has. In such a case, only minimal changes need be made in the original material when adapting it for your design.

UNIQUENESS AND ORIGINALITY

My students are always worried about being able to express their design sense and adapt reference materials in original ways. To allay these fears, I have conducted the following experiment many times in class: The students, perhaps thirty in all, are given specifications for a floral design, including the layout and the kind, size, and color of the flowers. To make it even more specific, I draw the design on the blackboard. Each student must then work out a design according to those specifications. Although my students expect to see thirty very similar designs, each is invariably different. My advice: Do not worry about being unique and original; your own particular set of aesthetic values will enable you to be inventive and creative.

Another modern Native American geometric pattern for apparel. *Copyright © Lisa Townsend, designer*

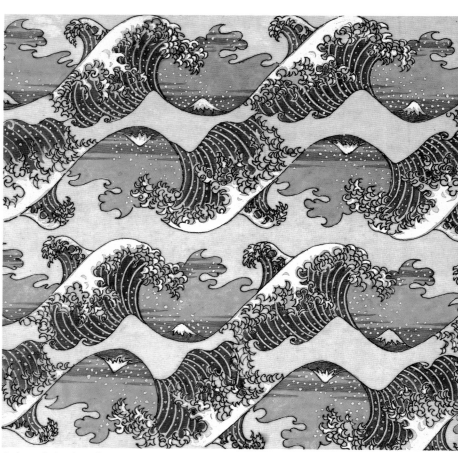

A sheet design based on a nineteenth-century Japanese woodblock print, "The Great Wave," by Hokusai.

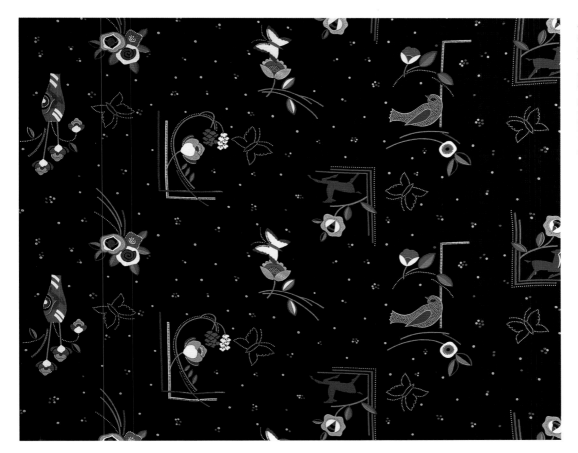

A design for apparel showing an art deco influence. The coordinate pattern *(below)* has the same motifs, smaller in size, in a packed all-over layout. *The Cloth Company, a division of Cranston Print Works Co.*

DEVELOPING YOUR EYE

A textile designer—or any artist, for that matter—must continue to develop his or her sense of design, layout, and color, devoting time and energy to researching and looking at many different kinds and sources of art, from current design magazines to antique Chinese porcelains, for example.

A piece of art can be appreciated on several levels— for instance, for the emotional reaction it evokes, or for the artist's skill. Art can also be seen through a designer's eye; that is, to extract from the work the various elements that can be translated into design. By consciously training yourself to look at art in this way, you are not only developing your eye but also mentally storing away visual ideas and concepts that can be called on when needed.

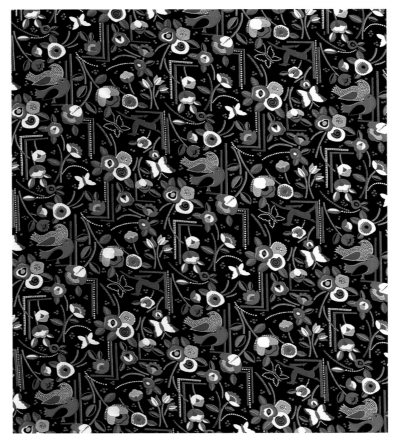

You are also teaching yourself to see spatial relationships (layout), color relationships (the way colors react with one another), and design ideas and concepts.

WHERE TO FIND REFERENCE MATERIAL

Reference material can be gathered in several ways and from a variety of sources: by clipping articles or illustrations from newspapers and magazines; by collecting books, brochures, and fabric swatches; and by visiting museums, art shops, department stores, and galleries. A good designer is also interested in culture, art, politics, and current events in general. Almost every point of connection can become a source of inspiration for design.

MAGAZINES AND BOOKS

Because they are current and have excellent color illustrations that can be clipped and filed away, the many fashion and home furnishing magazines on the market serve as particularly good sources of design reference. They can be subscribed to or bought at newsstands, stationers, and book stores. Magazines published in Europe and distributed in the United States tend to be expensive; I advise that you thumb through them first and purchase only those issues that contain a large amount of usable reference material.

In recent years, there has been a proliferation of art books of particular value to designers, on such subjects as ethnic and folk arts, priced from a few dollars to several hundred.

NEWSPAPERS

Daily newspapers are another good source of current reference material. Many contain special sections on fashion, home furnishings, art, and design, with articles covering fashion shows

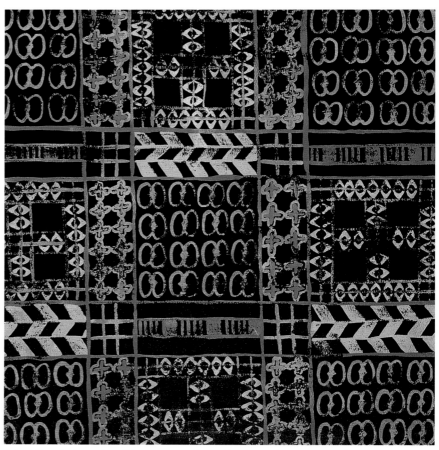

A bedding design using African geometric motifs. *Copyright © Susan Toplitz, designer*

in Paris, Rome, New York, and other cities, and on the latest trends in home decorating. These stories give clues to the styles, designs, and colors that will be at the forefront of textile design. Newspapers also review books and shows relating to art and design, and list galleries, museums, and auction houses that exhibit and sell art and antiques.

The one industry newspaper that all converters and design studios subscribe to is *Women's Wear Daily,* which furnishes the fashion and fabric design world with the latest news. Another important weekly news publication, *HFD—Retailing Home Furnishings,* covers trends in home furnishings, including textiles. While both of these publications are available by subscription, if you have contact with a studio or a converter you might be able to review their copies.

MUSEUMS

Museums provide a major source of inspiration and reference for artists and designers. For example, museums have mounted exhibitions of Navaho rugs, Indonesian batiks, early American quilts, Chinese embroideries, African textiles, Japanese stencils, and Guatemalan weavings, to name just a few of the subjects of particular interest to textile designers. Such exhibits are listed in and often reviewed by newspapers and art magazines. Monographs or catalogs with informative texts and images are usually published to accompany exhibits. Always check museum shops for postcards, reproductions, and books; they provide new and excellent reference material for your collection.

Many museums throughout the world also maintain special

textile collections, which are invaluable sources of reference material. In most cases, you must make an appointment to see the collection; when doing so, specify the type, period, and country of origin of the reference you are researching. Also inquire about the museum's facilities; for instance, their collection may include fabric samples, a library of reference books, and a picture collection. If there is a photocopy machine on the premises, most museums will allow to you to make copies for your reference file. (Refer to the Resources for a listing of museums in the United States that house major textile collections.)

DEPARTMENT STORES

Department stores (as well as smaller boutiques) are like contemporary fashion museums. Regular visits are a must, and it doesn't cost anything to go in and sketch a few ideas. The latest design trends in a wide variety of apparel and home furnishings are all there for you to use as source material. Stylists often send designers on store trips to stimulate new directions in color and design.

FABRICS AND SWATCHES

Fabric shops and some department stores sell fabric by the yard. You can purchase one or one-half yard of a pattern, or ask for a sample swatch. This is a good, inexpensive way to study different techniques, colors, and layouts, and to find inspiration for your own designs. It is also useful to copy these fabrics to help develop your hand. If your copy is good enough you may include it in your portfolio, alongside the original swatch of fabric.

CARDS AND REPRODUCTIONS

Postcards, greeting cards, and art reproductions are inexpensive, easy to handle, and convenient to store. Look for florals, folk art, conversationals, and other decorative motifs when you visit card shops, book and department stores, and, in particular, museum shops. For example, I recently purchased two sets of cards in beautiful colors depicting Japanese and Guatemalan textiles at the Cooper-Hewitt Museum shop in New York City. Museum sales catalogs also contain a good selection of cards and other reproductions that can be purchased by mail.

GALLERIES, AUCTION HOUSES, AND OTHER SOURCES

Many designers don't realize that visiting their area art galleries and auction houses is a good way to expand their art background. These establishments house a constantly changing display of art and designs from all over the world. Auction dates are usually listed in newspapers, and the items for sale are put on display days before. During this period it is possible to examine, for example, contemporary and antique rugs, tapestries, quilts, embroideries, pottery, glass, porcelains, baskets, beads, jewelry, furniture, paintings, and prints. Familiarizing yourself with this variety of visual treats will sharpen your design sense. If a catalog is not available, take notes and make sketches of items that suggest possible design motifs.

Flea markets are an excellent resource for interesting and affordable reference materials. At one such flea market, a student of mine recently purchased a collection of large drapery swatches from the 1940s for a very low price. Using them as the basis for his designs, he created a successful series of wallpaper patterns.

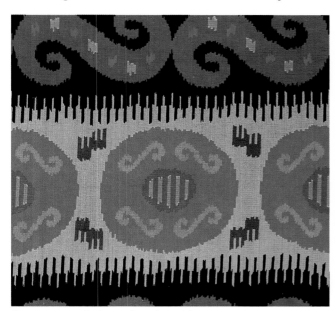

"Pomegranate," a home furnishing fabric inspired by traditional Afghani motifs. *Jack Lenor Larsen, Inc.*

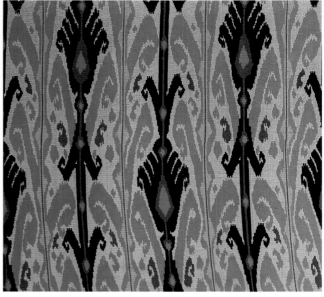

"Bukhara," the coordinate stripe pattern, is done in the same bold technique. *Jack Lenor Larsen, Inc.*

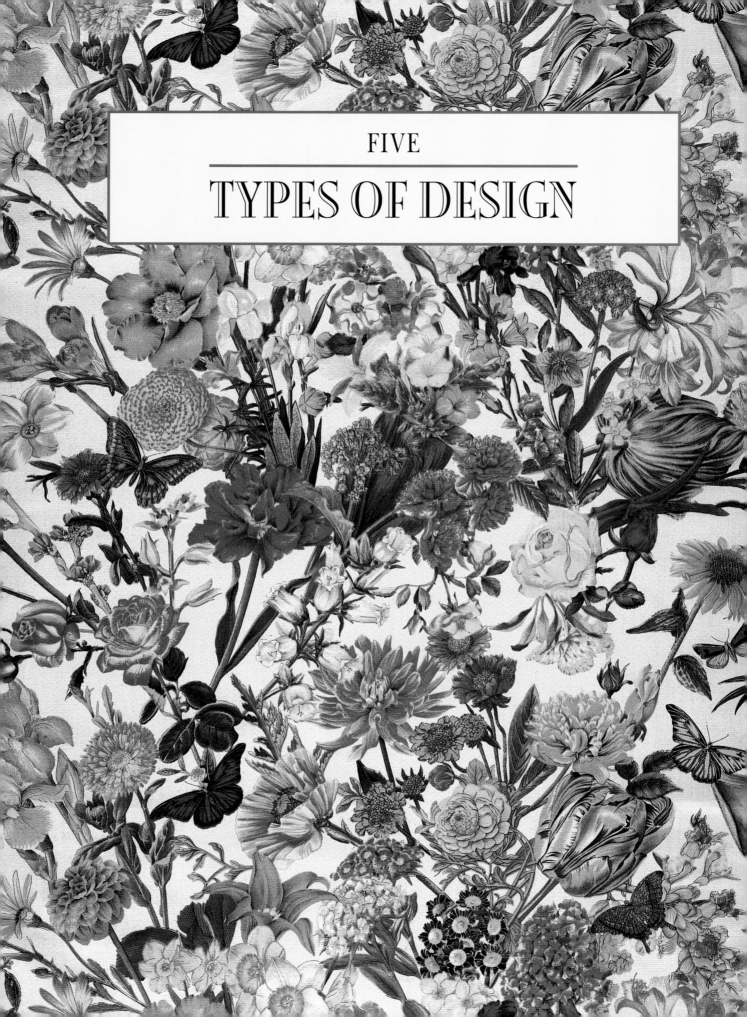

FIVE

TYPES OF DESIGN

Each new season brings requests from the fashion and home furnishing industries for different types of textile designs. The trends for these designs are developed from many sources. For example, when the ecology movement gained prominence in the 1970s, "scenic" or "landscape" patterns, illustrated with sky, birds, water, and trees, became popular. When an American president traveled to China, "Oriental" designs were called for; when a Paris couturier created a gypsy theme for his new line, "peasant" designs were in vogue. In the early 1990s, two shows at New York's Metropolitan Museum of Art influenced the textile design world: One, entitled "The Fauve Landscape," presented French art of the early twentieth century characterized by bold strokes and vivid colors; the other exhibited the work of American abstractionist Stuart Davis. Whether the designer's inspiration is a social movement or a museum exhibition, the world of design is constantly changing and responding to outside influences.

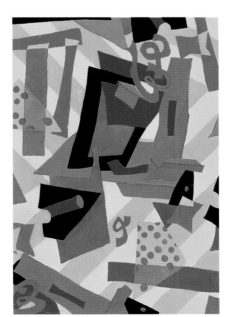 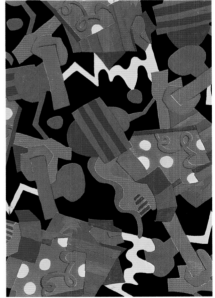

An apparel design *(left)* and its coordinate *(right),* influenced by the American abstract painter Stuart Davis. *Copyright © Joan Gampert, designer*

A good designer should always be well informed about art, politics, and other current events. However, unless he or she works as a freelance artist, a designer usually receives the design concept and—very often—the reference material from the design director or stylist. Both the stylist and the company's salespeople are in constant touch with the demands of their customers and of the textile market in general. It is the designer's responsibility to translate the stylist's concept, with the help of reference materials, into a pattern that is both salable and aesthetically pleasing.

The designs described and illustrated in this chapter will familiarize you with a variety of classic and current patterns. References are made throughout to specific types of layouts (covered in Chapter 6) and special design techniques (the subject of Chapter 9; refer to those chapters for more detailed information). The descriptions are meant to serve as a general guide to design types. Of course, each type can be combined with innovative ideas, layouts, and colors to create fresh, new looks.

A home furnishing fabric inspired by the French Fauve artist André Derain. *Copyright © Joan Gampert, designer*

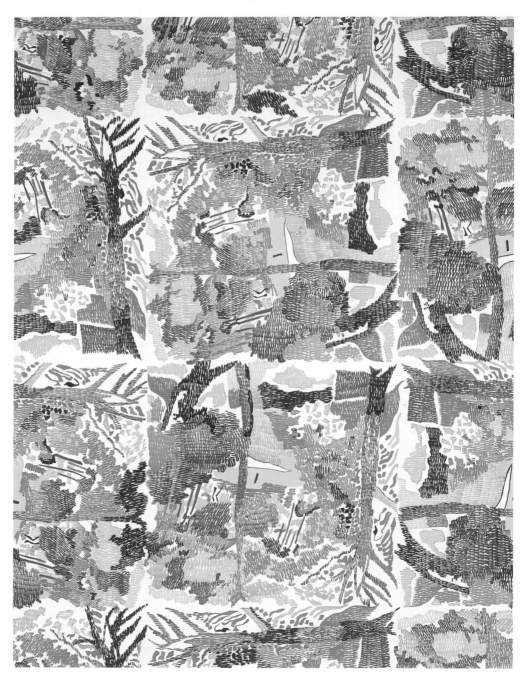

FLORAL

In all its infinite variations, ranging from the smallest fineline apparel designs to huge, freely executed drapery patterns, the floral is the most important basic textile design. It is essential, therefore, that every designer be able to draw flowers well, including stems and leaves. Most designers become good floral artists simply because they have traced and painted so many different flower motifs. A strong ability to draw flowers can inspire a wealth of creative designs: abstract, stylized, and realistic.

Many special design techniques, such as shading, stipple, and drybrush, may be used to render a realistic three-dimensional flower.

Florals are done in all layouts and all color schemes, and can be combined with other motifs and nature subjects, as well as with many interesting backgrounds.

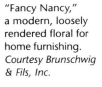

"Fancy Nancy," a modern, loosely rendered floral for home furnishing. *Courtesy Brunschwig & Fils, Inc.*

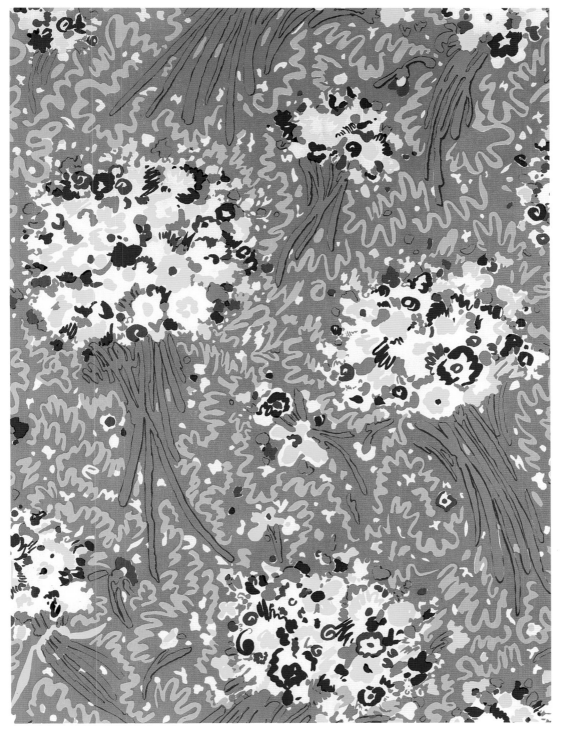

ETHNIC OR FOLK

Ethnic designs (also known as *folkloric, peasant,* and *provincial),* are inspired by the traditional popular motifs associated with specific cultures or countries. These motifs include all forms of plants, flowers, birds, animals, human figures, scenic subjects, and geometric patterns. The treatment of ethnic designs varies from country to country—often highly stylized, sometimes quite realistic, surprisingly sophisticated, or delightfully naive. Techniques such as batik and woodblock are perfect for ethnic designs. Any layout would be appropriate, including all-overs, stripes, and borders, and colors can vary widely, from very bright and brilliant on either dark or light grounds to earth tones and monotones.

Since every country or region has its own folk tradition, there is a wealth of reference material available for this type of design. Among the many ethnic looks that have been used in the American textile market are African, Chinese, Japanese, Native American, Russian, Egyptian, Indonesian, Mexican, Pennsylvania Dutch, Guatemalan, Peruvian, Persian, Indian, and Afghani.

An apparel design inspired by Ukrainian folk art.

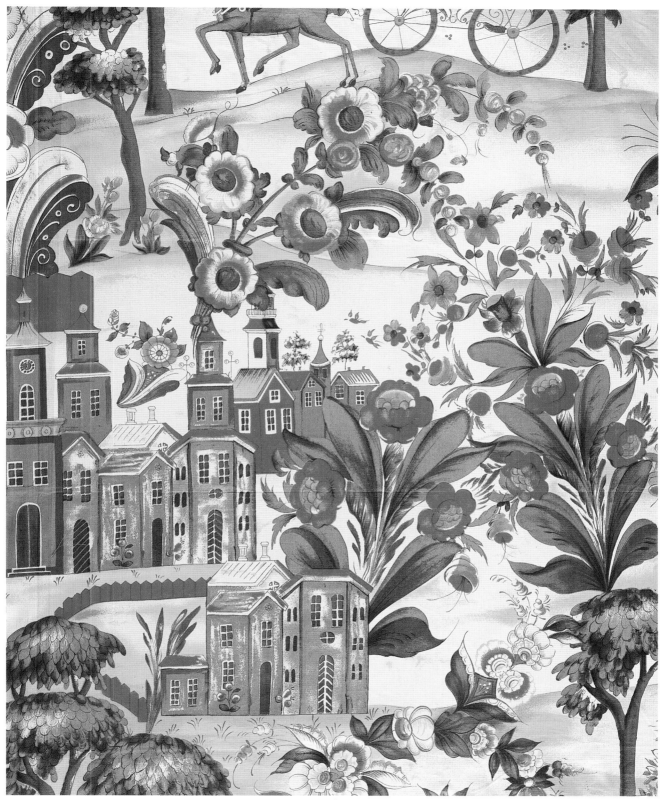

"Tsarevich," a home furnishing design influenced by Scandinavian folk painting. *Clarence House Imports, Ltd.*

MONOTONE

Monotones are designs that use only one color with white; for example, blue or red motifs on a white background. The absence of all but one color presents an interesting problem because there are no other colors to distract the eye and the background space forms a very noticeable pattern of its own. Therefore, the *coverage,* or the amount or density of design, becomes very important. It is a good idea to look at a monotone design from some distance to help see the distribution of color.

A monotone layout can be either simple or complicated, and motifs or themes can be adapted from both modern and traditional sources. A variation of a monotone occurs when the cloth is dyed a ground color first—red, for instance—and the motifs are printed in another color, such as black, on top of it. The result is a two-color design, but the printing process is the same as for a conventional monotone.

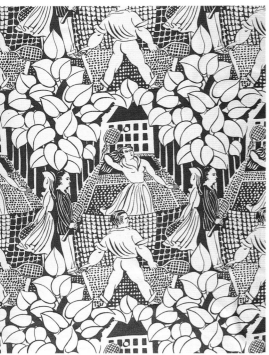

"Leçon Du Tennis," an amusing conversational monotone for home furnishing. *Clarence House Imports, Ltd.*

"Queen Anne Resist," a documentary monotone adapted from an English textile, circa 1760–1770. *Courtesy Brunschwig & Fils, Inc.*

PATCHWORK

Patchwork designs are named for and derived from the early American quilts that were made by women in the eighteenth and nineteenth centuries. The traditional patchwork quilt was made by cutting scraps and pieces of different printed fabrics and sewing them together to form beautiful geometric, realistic, or random designs. To achieve a traditional patchwork look, each section of the design should appear to be cut out of a larger piece of printed fabric and pieced together. A modern look can be obtained by using freer layout and painting techniques. Another patchwork technique, called *appliqué*, involves cutting motifs out of various fabrics and stitching them on a background to create a variety of complicated geometric or realistic designs. To achieve an appliqué look, the motifs should appear to be stitched onto the background.

Patchwork designs do not necessarily have to be based on traditional American motifs; they can easily be created from Asian, African, or any other ethnic themes. Although the colors in these designs are often bright, many subtle color combinations can also be used. Why not a beautiful monotone patchwork? The size of these patterns can range from small (for apparel) to large (for home furnishing), with layouts from very set to free-flowing.

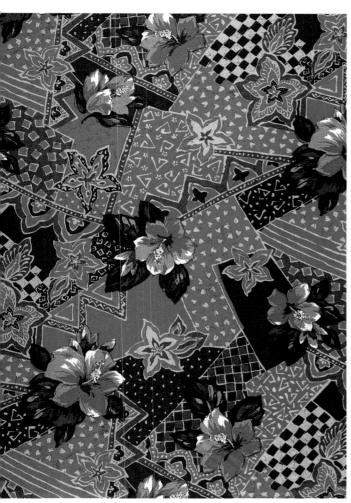

A loosely rendered contemporary patchwork for apparel, enhanced by bold flowers tossed on top. *The Cloth Company, a division of Cranston Print Works Co.*

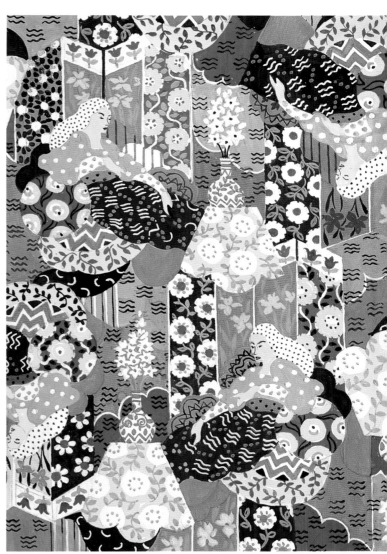

A detailed conversational patchwork for apparel.

LIBERTY

Liberty designs take their name from Liberty of London, an English textile company that was founded in 1875. Liberty's blouse-sized, carefully drawn floral patterns were later updated by American designers, and have become classics in the American apparel market. Liberty of London produces many other designs, including those of William Morris.

The classic Liberty floral design often has a fineline outline. The colors should be carefully chosen to add the most interest possible, and can range from muted to bright according to current trends. Backgrounds can be any color, from bright, to white or beige, to black. Layouts also vary, with stripes and all-overs, either packed or spaced, predominating.

Liberties require a good tight hand and should be beautifully drawn. They should be small to medium in size and, as always, the dominant floral motifs can be combined with others, such as butterflies, ribbons, and so forth.

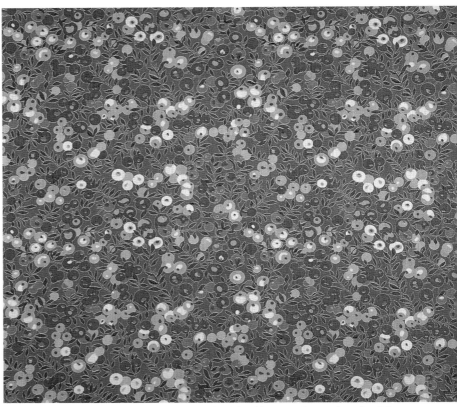

"Wiltshire," a Liberty apparel design in a packed floral layout. *Liberty of London Prints*

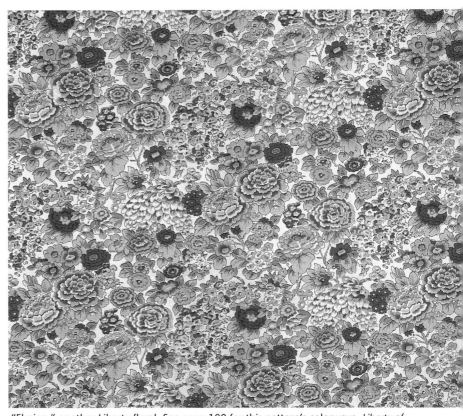

"Elysian," another Liberty floral. See page 100 for this pattern's colorways. *Liberty of London Prints*

CHINTZ

Chintz is a glazed or polished cotton, usually used for upholstery, drapery, and sheeting. The designs are beautiful florals with motifs such as trees, birds, and animal and human figures, often combining realistic and stylized motifs in the same design.

Because chintz originated in seventeenth-century India, early chintz designs had a strong Eastern influence. These were greatly favored in England and Europe, where new versions of exotic chintz patterns were created. Traditional English chintz patterns usually feature realistically rendered garden florals, muted in color and printed on antique beige backgrounds. French country chintz designs are more elaborately styled, using bright, primary colors and provincial motifs.

The layouts on chintz designs range from elaborate all-overs and stripes to very detailed borders. Background colors can be white, beige, black, or primary colors such as red, blue, and yellow. Any combination of rich or exotic colors looks well on chintz, and is enhanced by the high glaze on the fabric (a dull glaze is sometimes used). Beautiful drawing and painting are essential when designing chintz patterns.

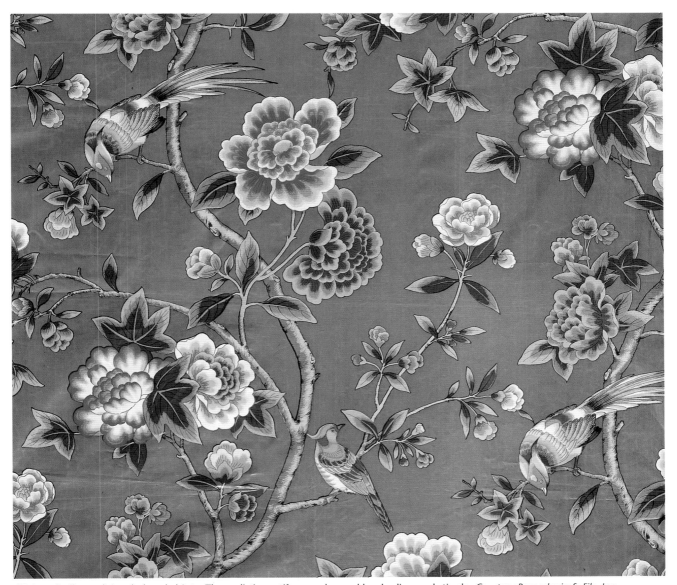

"Orientalia," a traditional glazed chintz. The realistic motifs are enhanced by shading and stipple. *Courtesy Brunschwig & Fils, Inc.*

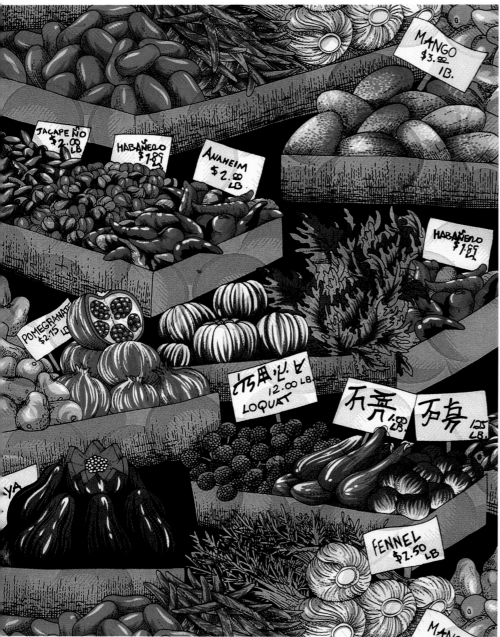

CONVERSATIONAL

A conversational is a design with realistic or stylized motifs that either tell a story or contain a message. This type of design is portrayed either by very realistic drawings or by treating the subject matter so subtly that from a distance the pattern appears to be nothing more than a color effect. Layouts can vary: all-overs, sets, stripes, borders, and so on.

Usually blouse-sized, conversationals can be campy and fun or sophisticated and high style. Care should be taken in the choice of motifs, color, and treatment to avoid mere cuteness (unless deliberately done for children's wear). A good conversational can often be worn by both women and men, and by all age groups.

An unusual, bright conversational pattern consisting of crates of vegetables. *Copyright © Nicole Miller*

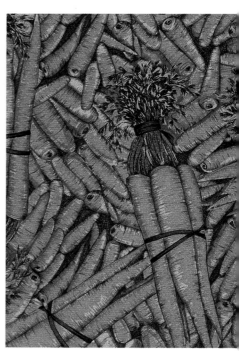

Another off-beat vegetable conversational. *Printmaker International, Ltd.*

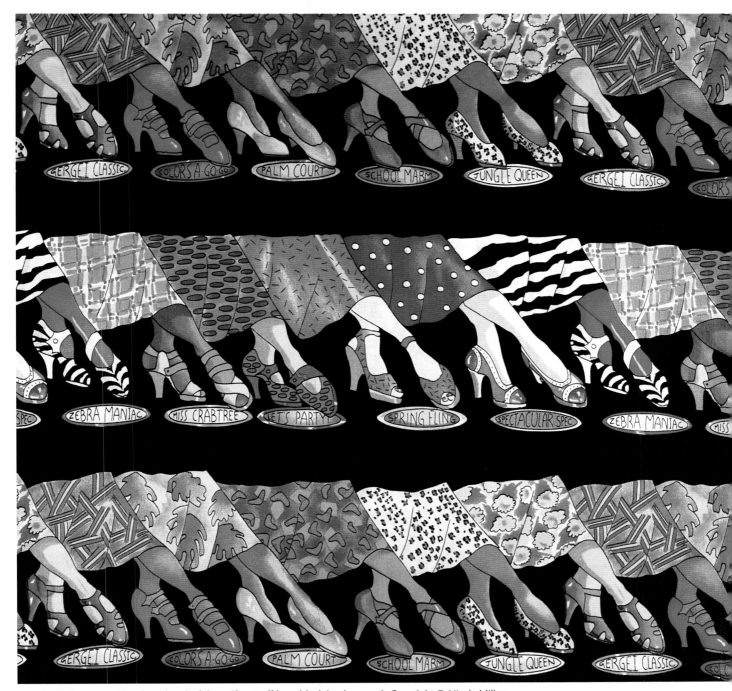

A whimsical conversational, with colorful motifs set off by a black background. *Copyright © Nicole Miller*

BATIK

Batik is a resist method of decorating fabric in which certain areas of the fabric are covered with liquid wax before it is immersed in dye. The waxed areas resist the dye; when the wax is removed the design is revealed. This procedure can be repeated many times to achieve the desired effect. In the dyeing process, a random crackle pattern emerges where the dye penetrates the cracks in the wax, giving the batik its distinctive character.

Although batik was probably first developed in China or India, Indonesia, particularly the island of Java, is most famous for this technique. Javanese women make batiks either individually or collectively in small workshops, producing designs in traditional colors (indigo blue and shades of brown) as well as modern designs in a wide range of colors. Of course, printed textile designs are painted on paper to imitate the batik look (see Chapter 9), which is then simulated by screens prepared for the printing process.

Batik motifs are usually exotic florals and ethnics such as Asian and African, and layouts can be all-overs, stripes, and borders of all kinds. Batik patterns range in size, to accommodate both apparel and home furnishing.

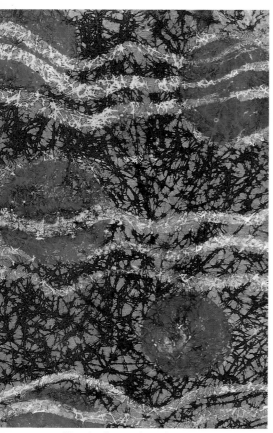

"Sunrise," a modern abstract scenic batik.

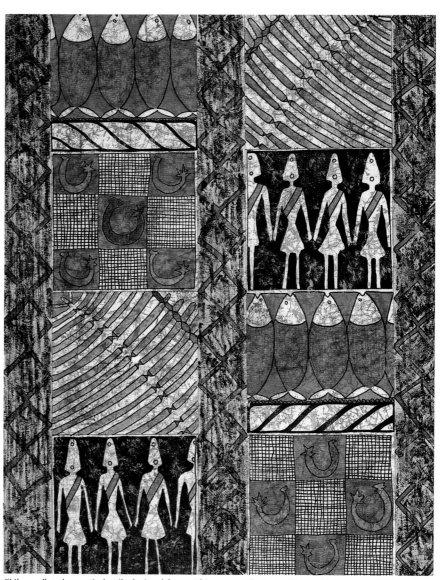

"Uhuru," a dramatic batik derived from African motifs, in traditional browns and blues.
Copyright © Frank Delfino, designer

PAISLEY

The paisley design is characterized by the palm or curved abstract figure, which is usually accompanied by elaborate symmetrical detail. It is derived from the cashmere shawls of India that were woven in Paisley, Scotland. Paisley designs are sometimes very set and conservative in layout, but can also be bold and dramatic in scale and design. Layouts are tossed, set, stripe, and border. Typical paisley colors are combinations of rich red, blue, green, and gold with brown and black, although innovative color combinations can give the classic paisley design a fresh look, for both fashion and home decorating.

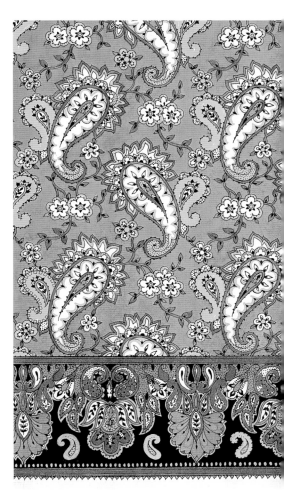

A set paisley design with a border for apparel.

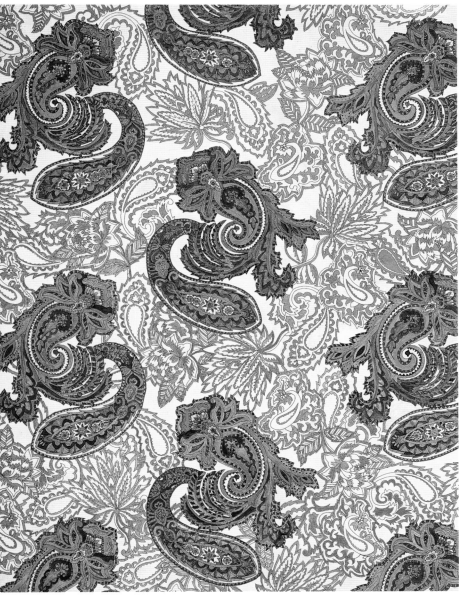

A tossed "pattern on pattern" paisley for home furnishing. *Copyright © Glenda Heffer, designer*

GEOMETRIC

A geometric design is composed of abstract shapes such as squares, triangles, and circles. Geometric layouts run the gamut from large, spaced, and free in feeling, to small, neat, mechanically set designs, and colors range from monotone to bright and bold. Geometrics are used for both apparel and home furnishing.

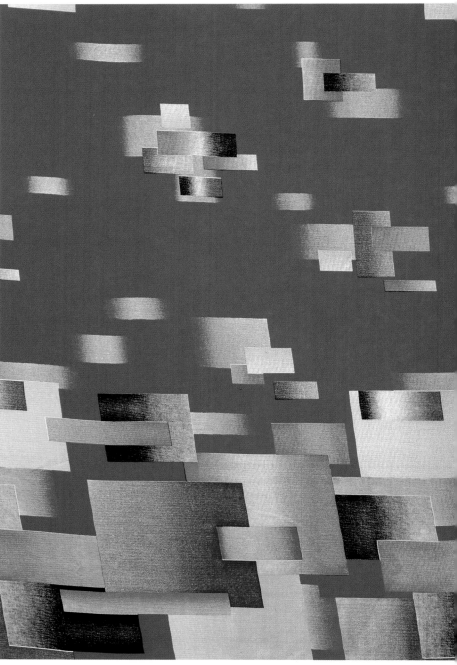

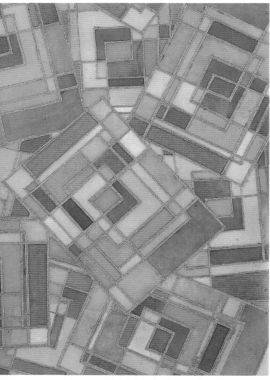

A geometric stained glass pattern for apparel. *Copyright © Joan Gampert, designer*

An unusual geometric border design done with airbrush for apparel. *The Cloth Company, a division of Cranston Print Works Co.*

FOULARD

A foulard (also known as *madder,* *tie-silk,* and *cravat)* is a small, neat design in a set layout originally used for neckties. Foulards are carefully drawn, geometrically styled floral, paisley, or Persian motifs, and are now used on a wide variety of apparel and home furnishing textiles. Traditional foulard colors include rich shades of red, blue, green, and gold, but all color combinations and backgrounds can be used. Foulards work well in all-over, stripe, and border layouts, for both men's and women's wear.

These designs must be measured and laid out with precision. Ruling pens and technical drawing pens should be used, as well as a compass when needed.

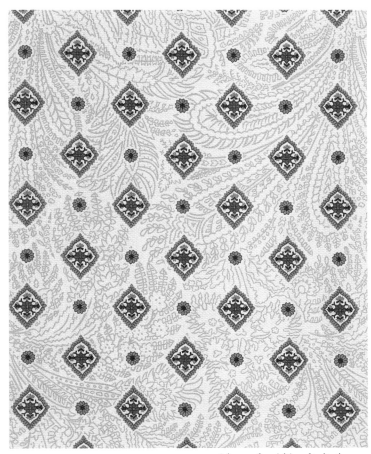

A home furnishing foulard design on top of a subtle damask paisley background.
Cohama Riverdale, a division of Richloom Fabrics Group, Inc.

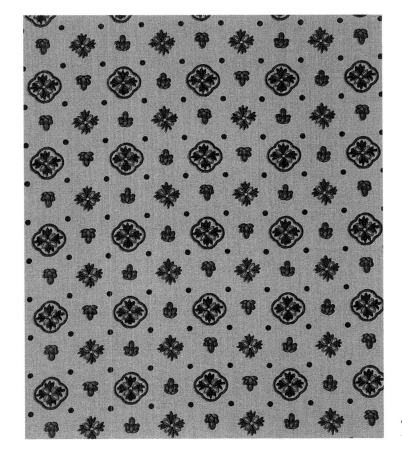

A typical foulard for apparel.
Schwartz-Liebman Textiles

ART NOUVEAU

Art nouveau was an artistic movement that started in Europe in the late nineteenth century and ended about 1920. The movement was partly a reaction against industrialization and mass-produced objects. Art nouveau design is characterized by sensuous, flowing, organic lines, with motifs taken from nature and plant life. During the art nouveau period the famous Tiffany lamps and other beautifully designed home furnishings were produced. The art nouveau influence extended to textiles, wallpaper, architecture, ceramics, fine art, and many other areas, all highly appreciated today.

Contemporary textile designers can find inspiration in the many reference books on art nouveau. Beautiful muted tones combined with bright and dramatic colors can be used, and layout and size can vary.

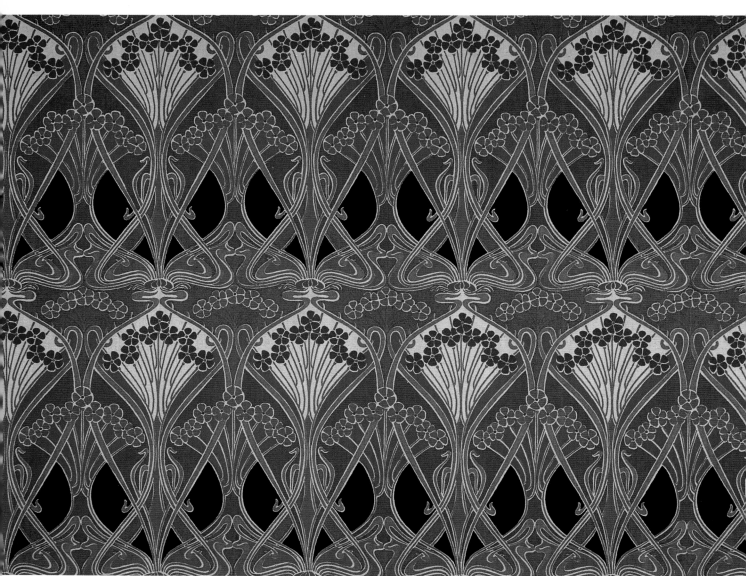

"Ianthe," a home furnishing fabric in art nouveau style. *Liberty of London Prints*

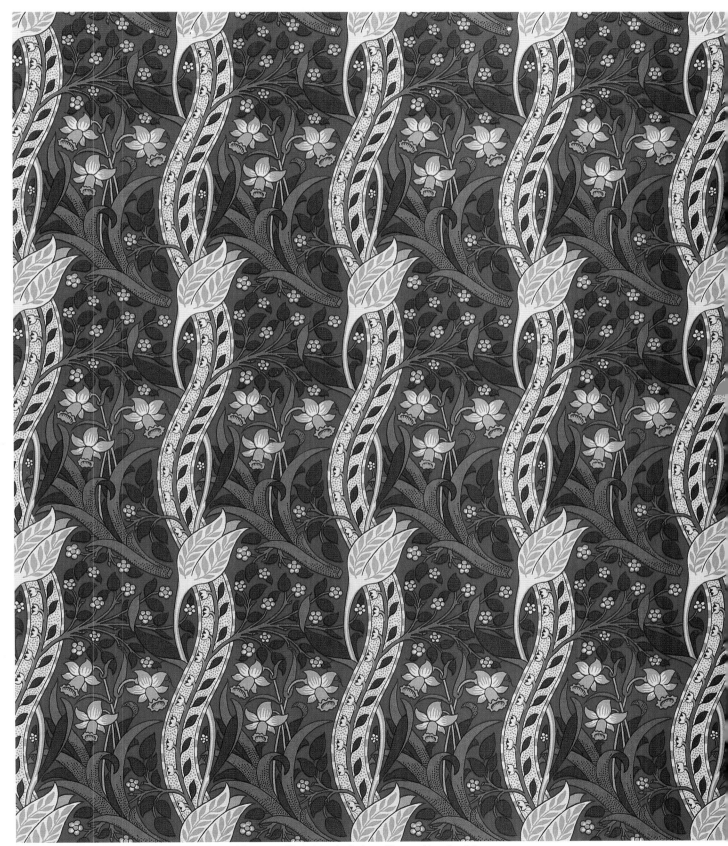

"Trent," an art nouveau drapery stripe adapted from a William Morris design. *Liberty of London Prints*

ART DECO

As an artistic style, art deco followed art nouveau, lasting roughly from 1910 through the 1930s. Much of the stimulus for art deco is derived from an acceptance of industrialization and the aesthetics of machinery, essentially stripping art nouveau of its ornament and flowing lines. Art deco design is generally distinguished by its clean, geometric lines, and motifs include flowers and other plant life, animals, human figures, and the geometric decorations of Egyptian art—all formalized, modern, and angular in execution. Fashion, architecture, textiles, painting, and ceramics were all influenced by the art deco movement.

In an art deco design, several shades of one color can be used, combined with creamy mauves, peach, grays, blues, and ecru (a yellowish beige), as well as brights on dark grounds. The size and layout of an art deco design varies according to its use.

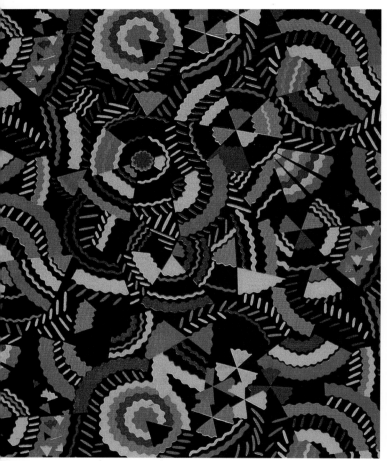

An apparel design showing an art deco influence. *The Cloth Company, a division of Cranston Print Works Co.*

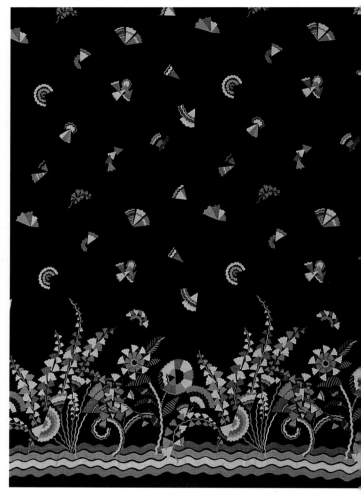

The coordinate border pattern, which uses the same art deco motifs in the field, but smaller in size. *The Cloth Company, a division of Cranston Print Works Co.*

CONTEMPORARY

Contemporary designs are usually nonfigurative, and can have either a modern, crisp look, or take a painterly approach. These patterns can vary in size, depending on their use, and all color combinations and layouts can be used.

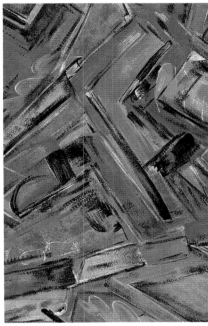

"Cartagena," an abstract brush stroke design for sheets. *Stylepoints Collection, Cameo Interiors*

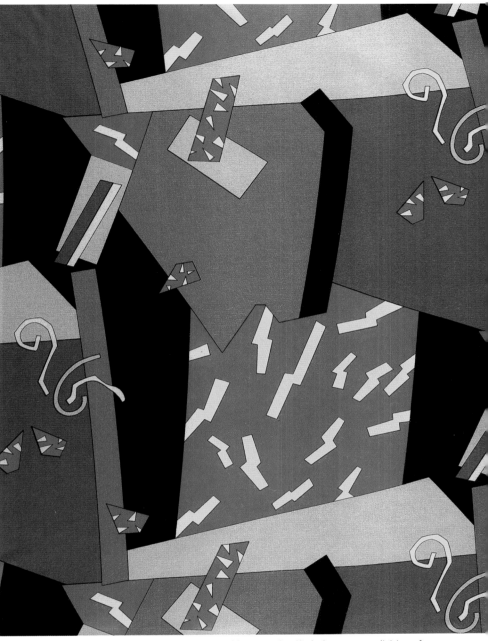

A contemporary apparel design, bold in color and layout. *The Cloth Company, a division of Cranston Print Works Co.*

BOTANICAL

A botanical is a very realistic, well-drawn design using botanical motifs such as those found in illustrated books on plants, flowers, and herbs. Drawing technique is very important for this type of design, which is detailed with a fine pen line and sometimes incorporates lettering, identifying the botanical species.

Color combinations for botanicals range from pastel to bright. The traditional large patterns are usually intended for home furnishing, although they can also be adapted for apparel.

"Botanica," a design that simulates antique botanical watercolors. *Clarence House Imports, Ltd.*

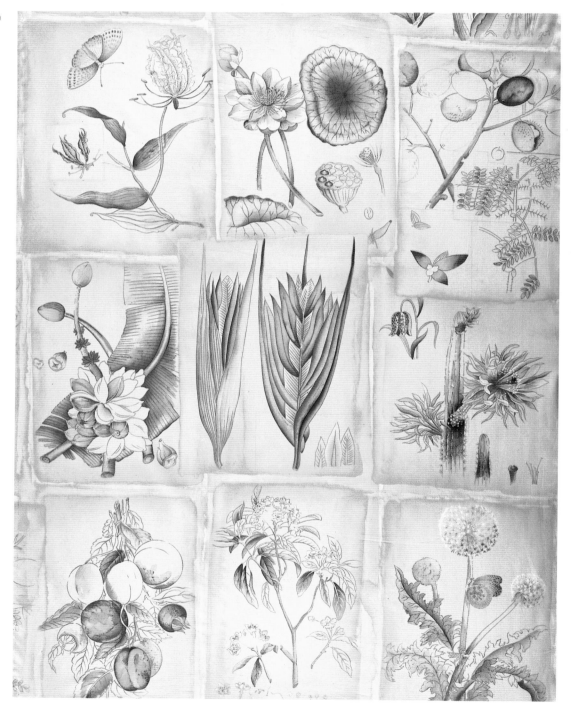

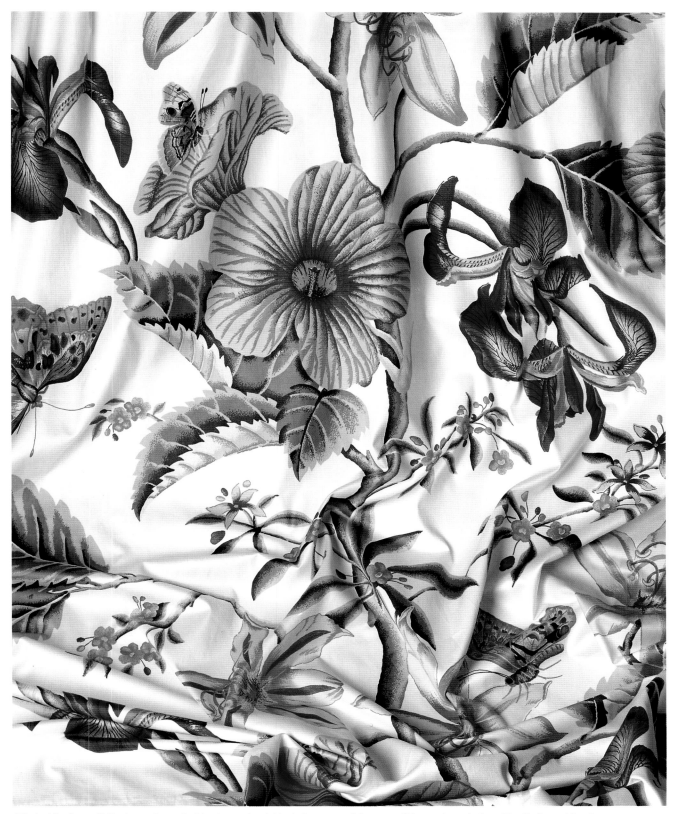

"Umbel," a beautifully drawn botanical for home furnishing. Courtesy of *Boussac of France, Inc.; designed by Sheila and Lee Stewart, Lee Stewart Associates Incorporated*

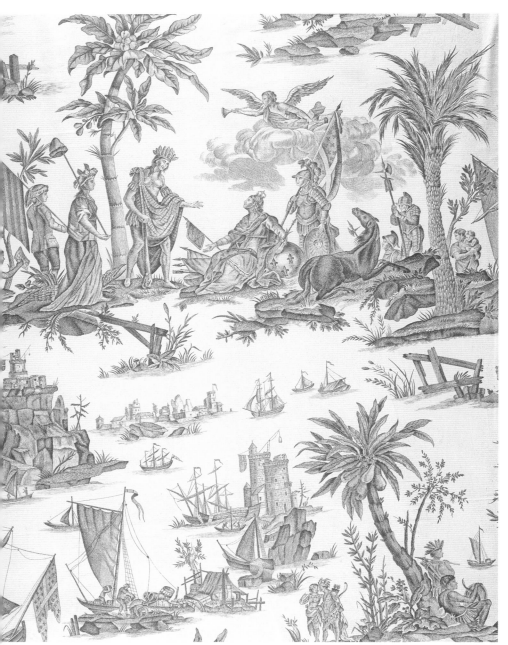

"Lafayette," a finely drawn historical toile. *Pierre Deux*

TOILE (DE JOUY)

Toile de Jouy means "cloth from Jouy." Jouy is a French town whose world famous print works were founded in 1760. The textiles originally produced there depicted finely illustrated stories of current events as well as romanticized landscapes and figures. Many museums and book collections have useful reference materials on the old toiles.

Contemporary toile designs are composed of pictorial or scenic motifs rendered in dark, fineline outlines on neutral backgrounds, and are traditionally used for classic home furnishing patterns. Layouts are predominantly all-overs or stripes.

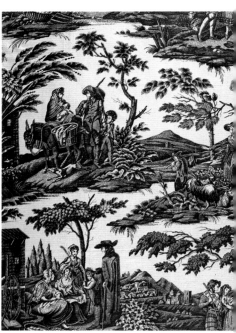

"Les Miserables," a toile depicting a French rural scene. *Clarence House Imports, Ltd.*

SCENIC OR LANDSCAPE

Scenics or landscapes are designs in which the motifs are placed in a horizontal layout and, when combined with the subject matter, suggest a scene.

Rural subjects such as trees, birds, animals, water, and clouds, as well as cityscapes are illustrated. The style of drawing tends to be realistic, and a three-dimensional look can be created through the use of airbrush, stipple, or other special techniques. Colors range from pastel to bright. Scenic patterns can be either small (for apparel) or large (for drapery, sheets, pillowcases, and other domestics).

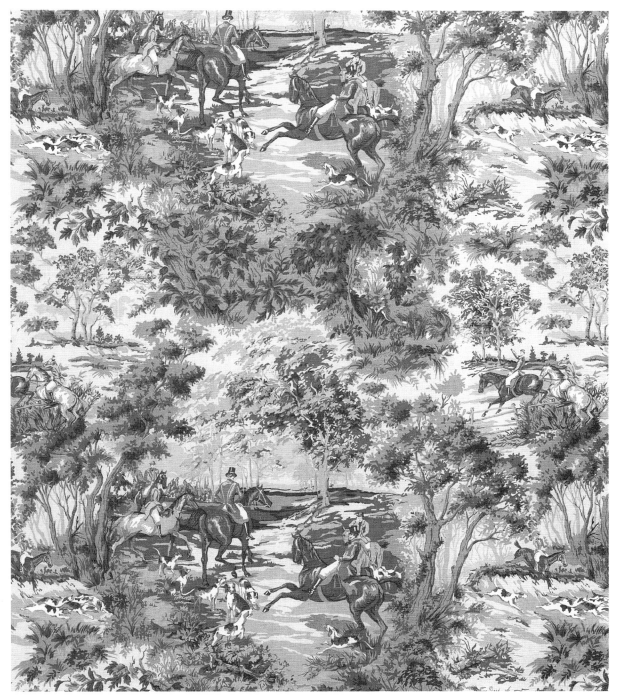

"Tally Ho," a traditional scenic pattern with a sporting theme for home furnishing. *Schumacher*

COUNTRY FRENCH

Printed from woodblocks carved by artisans, country French designs originated in eighteenth-century Provence. Although they retained a basic rustic look, Indian and Asian motifs and influences were gradually incorporated into the traditional Provence designs. Country French designs are often bright in color, but more subtle combinations can also be used.

Contemporary country French designs, both small set patterns and large chintz florals (sometimes with separate elaborate borders), are designed and colored to coordinate with each other. They are greatly favored for home decorating as well as for apparel.

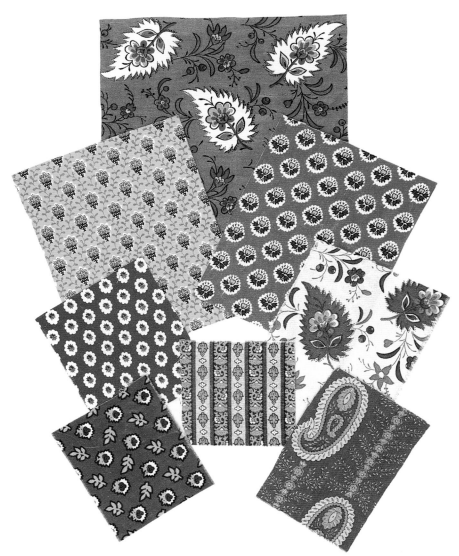

A group of pillows using small country French designs with coordinated borders. *Souleiado for Pierre Deux*

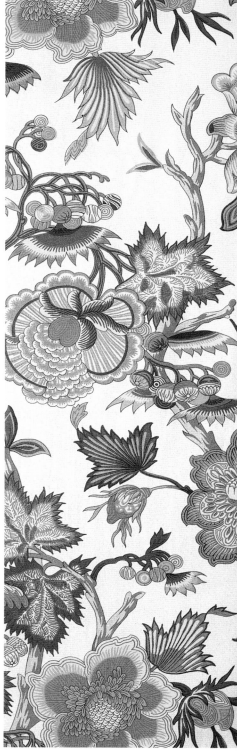

The same country French designs shown separately, in bright colors on light and dark grounds. *Souleiado for Pierre Deux*

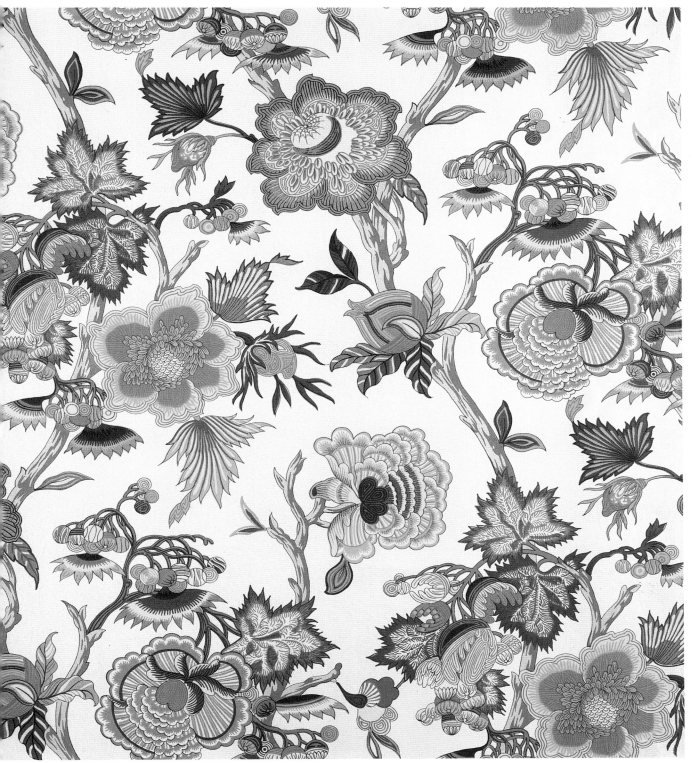

"Favenay," a classic country French chintz pattern. *Pierre Deux*

TROPICAL

Tropical designs use motifs and colors inspired by the lush and sunny tropical regions of the world. Landscapes of flowers, leaves, trees, animals, birds, insects, and fish as well as figures and geometrics can be used, mostly in primary colors. Layouts are most often a profusion of tossed, all-over motifs.

When used for apparel, tropical designs are often referred to as resort or cruise wear; a good example is the classic Hawaiian shirt. They are also used for home furnishing and sheeting.

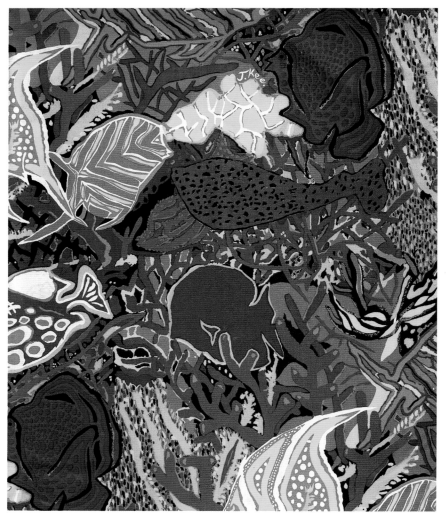

"Tropakee," a brillant tropical sheet pattern using aquatic motifs. *Jenny Kee Australia*

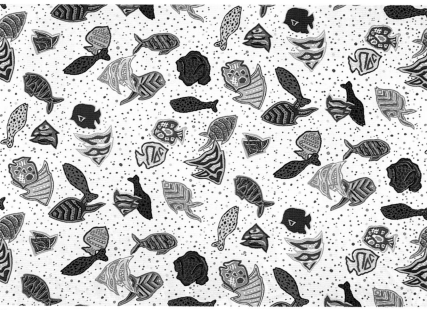

The coordinate, with smaller spaced fish motifs. *Jenny Kee Australia*

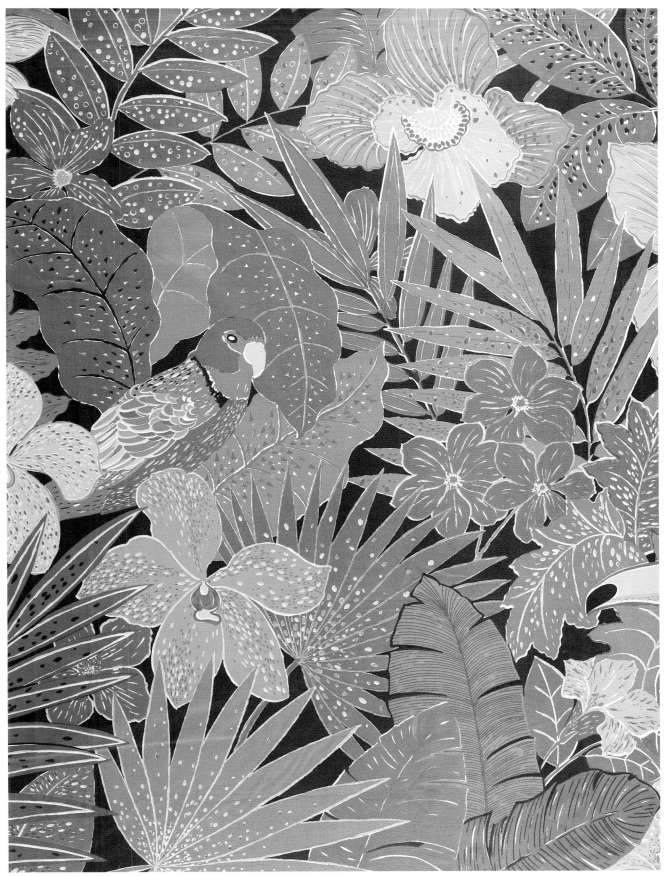

"Capricorn," a bright tropical jungle pattern for sheets. *A Sheridan Design*

TAPESTRY OR WARP

Tapestry or warp designs imitate the look of elaborate embroideries or woven jacquard fabrics. This effect can be achieved in various ways to emphasize the vertical *(warp)* or horizontal *(weft)* threads that appear in woven fabrics.

To imitate the warp look, you can use either paint or pen and ink to render the vertical lines in and around the edges of the motifs in the design. The result is a slightly blurred or stitched effect. Another method is to use graph paper as a guide to paint each little square area of color, producing a woven jacquard look.

The subject matter for tapestry designs can range from romantic florals for apparel to ornate antique tapestries for home furnishing.

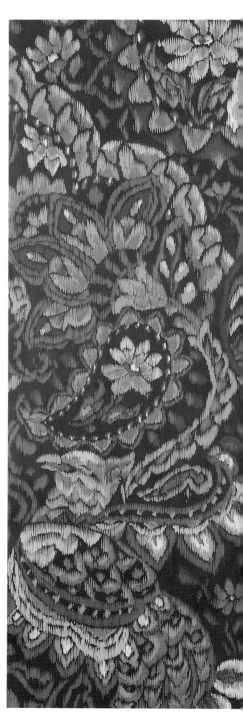

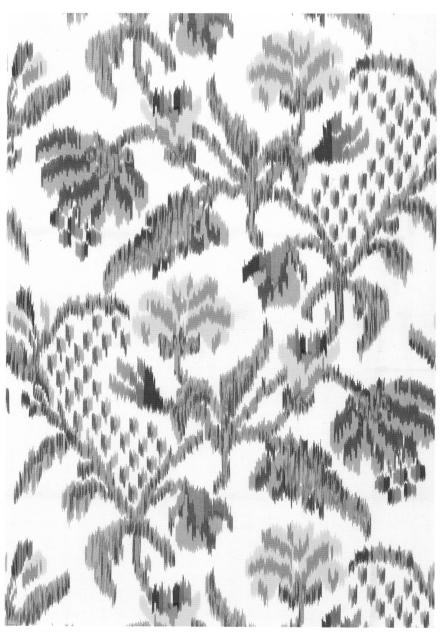

"Marly," a floral warp chintz for home furnishing. *Courtesy Brunschwig & Fils, Inc.*

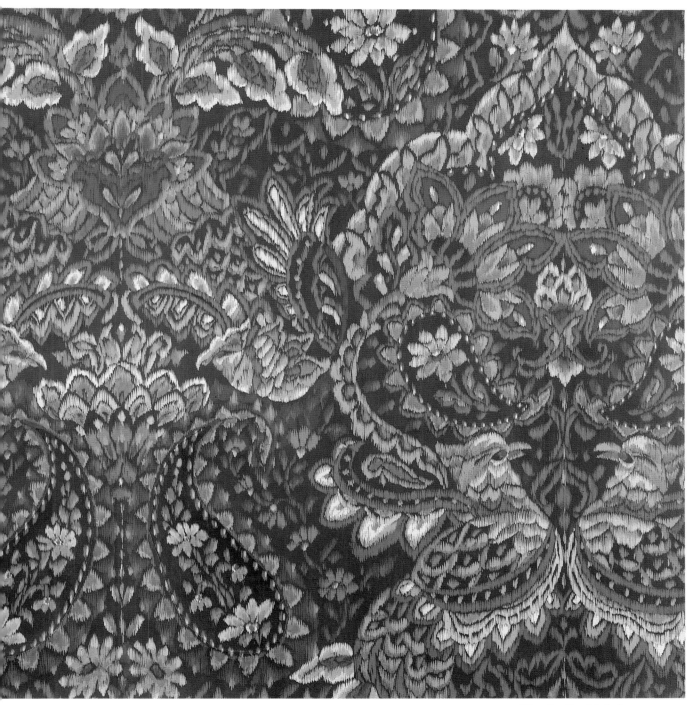

"Paradiso," a detailed warp design inspired by paisley and Persian motifs. *Copyright © Lynn Johnson, designer*

NEOCLASSICAL

The term "neoclassical" refers to any style that uses ancient Greek and Roman forms as a starting point and then embellishes them. Motifs such as acanthus leaves, plaques, floral urns, griffins, swans, horses, lions, and the human form are common. Other neoclassical forms are the ornamental flowing curves of baroque, American Empire, and English Regency styles. Layouts and motifs are formal, balanced, and harmonious, and are intended to make a decorative statement of power, solidity, and tradition. Neoclassical designs are most suitable for home furnishing fabrics and wallpapers.

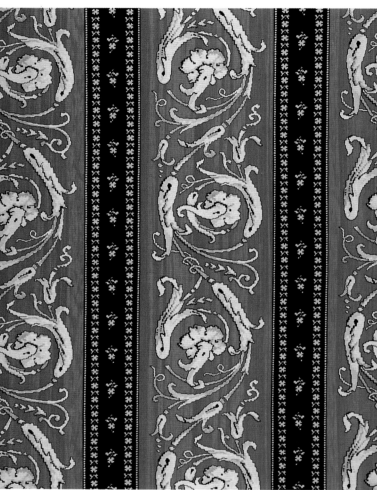

"Roman Stripe," a neoclassical home furnishing pattern. *Clarence House Imports, Ltd.*

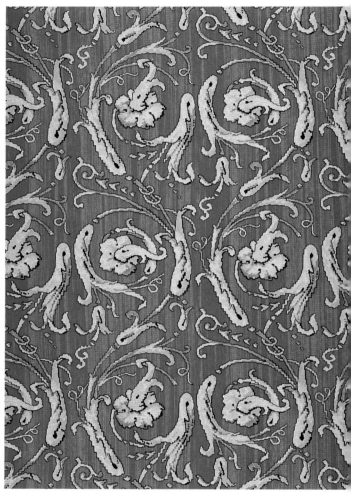

The coordinate for "Roman Stripe," in an all-over layout. *Clarence House Imports, Ltd.*

DAMASK

Damasks were first produced in the city of Damascus, Syria, in the thirteenth century. They are elaborately patterned woven fabrics that are produced on jacquard looms. Printed damask designs seek to imitate this woven look.

Damasks are usually done in all-over or stripe layouts. They have a traditional look and often incorporate formal designs and dark-to-light combinations of the same color. They are primarily used for a variety of home furnishings, including drapery, upholstery, and table linens. Brocade is another fabric of this type.

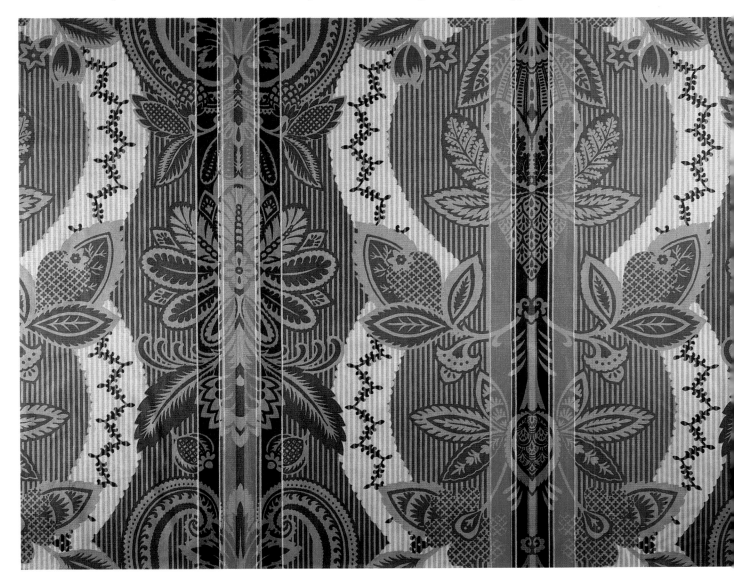

"Allegro," a modern printed version of a damask. *Designed by Jay Yang*

DOCUMENTARY

A documentary design is inspired by or adapted from a decorative historical document or fabric. The source for a documentary design may be supplied by any culture, and the designer's job is to adapt the historical reference material to today's market, often by changing the colors or by modifying the layout and motifs. At times, however, the document is closely copied to satisfy traditional decorative tastes.

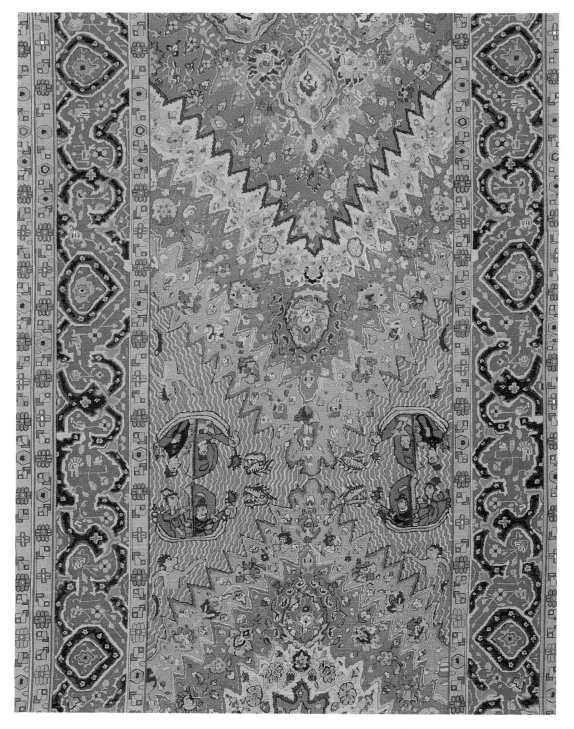

"Sultan of Gujarat," a documentary design based on a very rare carpet from Lahore, India, circa 1600–1650. *Courtesy Brunschwig & Fils, Inc.*

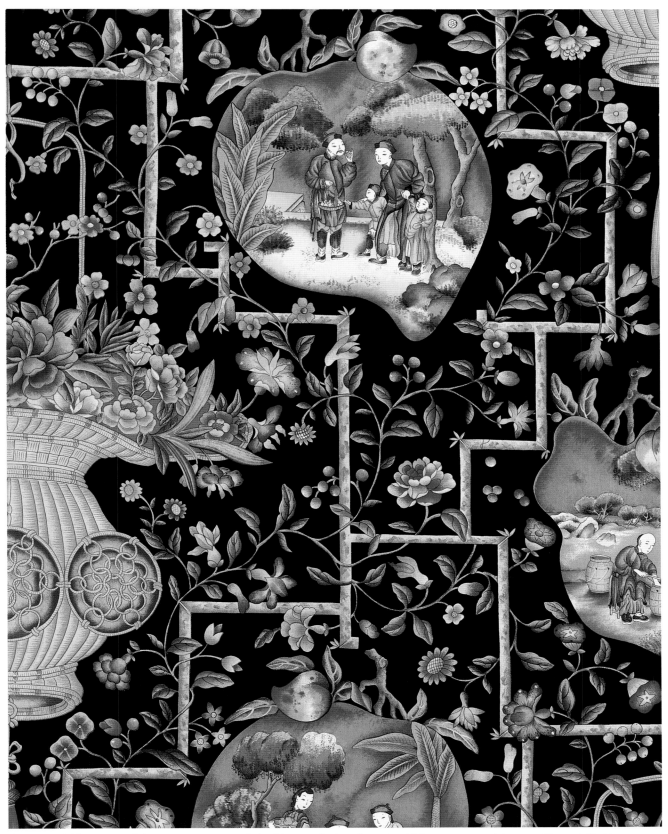

"Coromandel," an unusual documentary pattern derived from a nineteenth-century Chinese coromandel screen. *Clarence House Imports, Ltd.*

COORDINATE PATTERNS

A *coordinate pattern* (sometimes called a *twin, companion, extract,* or *pull-out*) is a design created with the same feeling, colors, or motifs as another pattern so that the two may be used together. Sometimes three or four coordinates are printed in a line of designs, for either apparel or home furnishings, making it possible to combine several for a coordinated look.

Coordinate patterns can be instrumental when furnishing and decorating interiors, and are used to relate a range

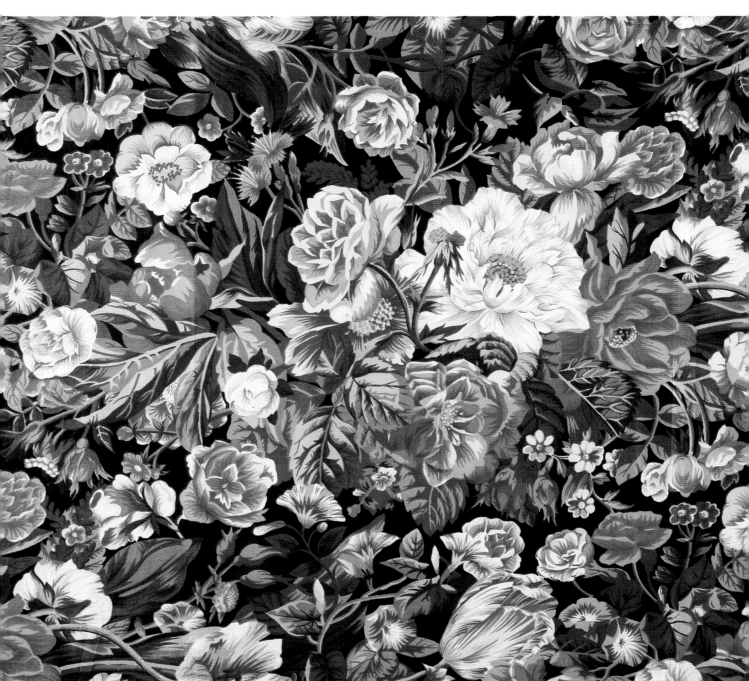

"Interieure Napoleon III," a beautifully drawn realistic chintz for home furnishing. *Clarence House Imports, Ltd.*

of domestics and decoratives, including bedding and towels, wallpaper and draperies, and pillows and upholstery.

Coordinates can be made in many different layouts—all-overs, stripes, borders—and also have coordinated colorways. Coordinates are often designed to contrast in layout and size, such as a small packed design with a bold, spaced border design. It is not necessary for a coordinate to include a motif extracted from its companion print. It can be an entirely different design, providing an interesting contrast through the use of similar color, technique, or theme.

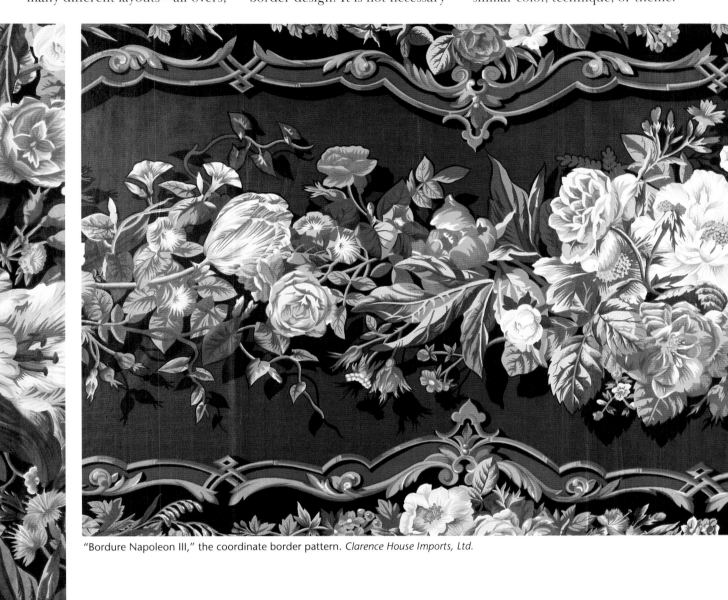

"Bordure Napoleon III," the coordinate border pattern. *Clarence House Imports, Ltd.*

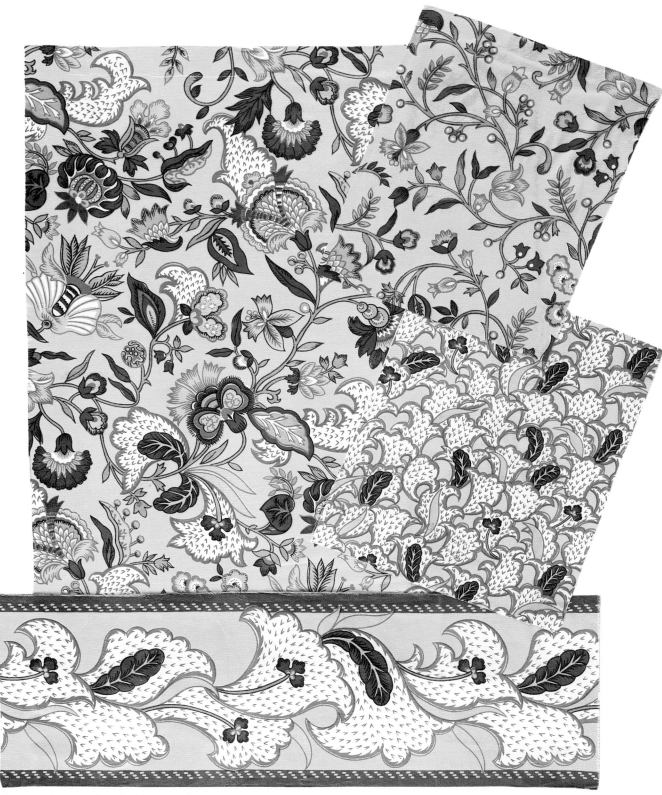

A group of country French chintz coordinate patterns with a separate border to match. *Pierre Deux*

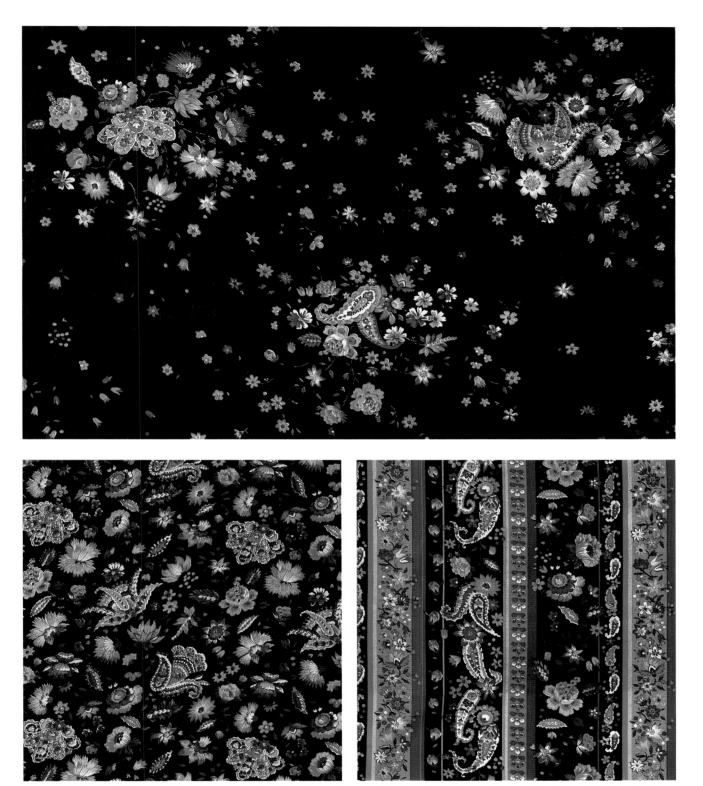

Three apparel coordinates using the same motifs in different layouts: spaced *(top)*, packed *(lower left)*, and stripe *(lower right)*. *The Cloth Company, a division of Crantson Print Works Co.*

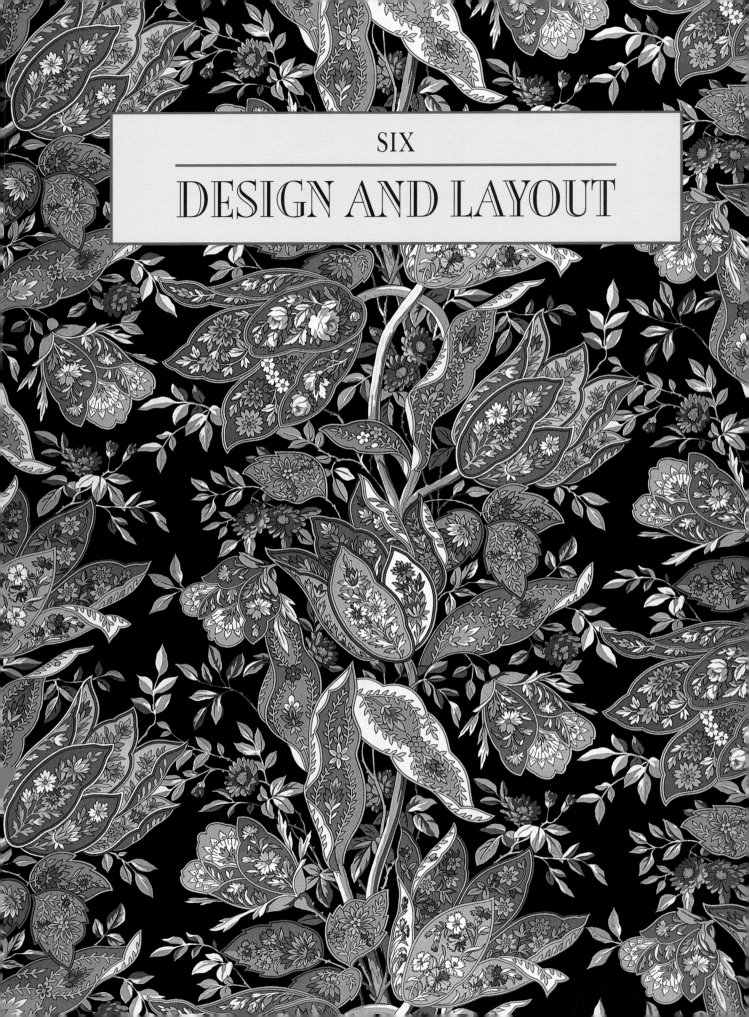

SIX
DESIGN AND LAYOUT

"Tulipes Russes," a beautifully detailed chintz in a loose stripe layout that is not confined within rigid outlines. Refer to page 84 for a discussion of stripe layouts. *Clarence House Imports, Ltd.*

Designing a textile requires a knowledge of layout, color, tracing, and painting techniques, as well as the proper use of materials, supplies, and reference material. The various types of layouts—all-over or tossed, free-flowing, stripe, border, set, scenic or landscape, handkerchief square, patchwork, and five-star—both one-way and two-way, give designers a wealth of options with which to create innovative and provocative looks. When developing a successful design, it is often best to progress from large to small, from the general to the particular, refining the layout and the motifs to achieve balance and flow. While there is no one way to begin a design, formulate a layout, or outline or rub down a clean tracing, the fundamental methods detailed in this chapter will prove helpful, particularly for the beginning designer.

An apparel design with a prominent irregular floral border flowing into a pale, monochromatic field. See page 86 for more information on border layouts.

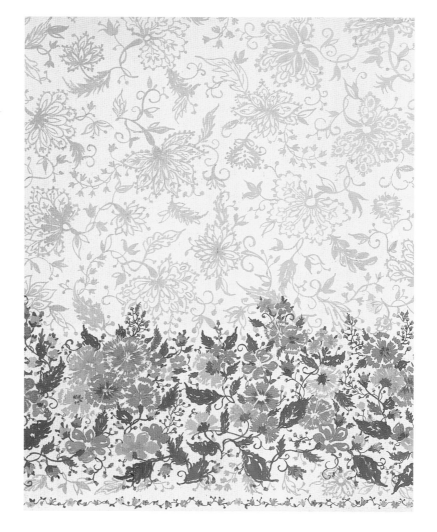

DESIGN

The following guide is for creating a design that is not in repeat. While it is possible to design in repeat, most beginners find that the technical aspects of repeats will inhibit their design approach. Therefore, the idea is to create a design that has the illusion of a repeat, which is done by distributing and duplicating the motifs in a balanced and flowing layout (shown later in this chapter) without worrying about the discipline of an actual repeat. The design can then be put into repeat later, in a separate procedure (see Chapter 8).

STEP-BY-STEP GUIDE TO CREATING A DESIGN

1. Gather the reference material you plan to use for ideas and inspiration.

2. Make a small pencil sketch of the proposed design, and list any color ideas.

3. Decide on the best paper, paints, and supplies to achieve the desired results in the easiest way.

4. Lay out the design on tracing paper. Double check the layout for balance. If it is necessary to design in repeat, lay out the design on tracing paper in exact repeat size. Then continue to the next step. (As an alternate method, some studios make multiple photocopies of the motifs and use them to lay out the design.)

5. Transfer the design from the tracing paper to the drawing paper using one of the methods described later in this chapter. If the design is painted on top of a ground color, paint the ground on the drawing paper first, before transferring the design.

6. Mix the colors; put dabs of them next to each other on scrap paper to see how they work together before making final choices.

7. Paint a small sample sketch, or *croquis,* of the design in color to determine which techniques will work best to achieve the final look you have in mind. When this look is satisfactory, proceed with the final painting.

LAYOUT

Probably no other art form requires as thorough a knowledge of layout as textile design. In textile patterns the design repeats itself on the fabric and must balance and flow smoothly in all directions. A poor layout will show up plainly on the final printed goods, whereas an interesting layout can transform an ordinary idea into a good design.

TIPS ON LAYING OUT A DESIGN

- There is no standard paper size required for a design that is not done in repeat. The size of your finished design depends entirely on the size of its motifs. For instance, an apparel design consisting of very small flowers and without an unusual color distribution could require a painted area of only 3 or 4 inches. However, a home furnishing design with a variety of large motifs in different colors might require up to 36 inches or more. Think about the color distribution in your design. A plain black-and-white design might require an average-sized layout, but the same design with an occasional red motif tossed on top would require a layout large enough to accommodate it.
- When you begin to lay out a design, try to envision the overall design as a broad canvas with all the motifs and elements moving and balancing together. Draw a small sketch of the design first.
- Look at your design from a distance to get a perspective on the layout. Hang it on a wall or

look at it in a mirror, which reverses the design and gives you a different view of it.
- Pay attention to small details. For instance, stems should be graceful and in proportion to the flowers, neither too long and thin nor too heavy.

TRACING

The use of proper tracing techniques is an important part of the design process. Sloppy and inaccurate tracings are not acceptable in textile design studios. The following tips on the use of tracing paper should be carefully observed.

USING TRACING PAPER

- Your tracings should always be clean and clear. To achieve a clean tracing line, always keep your pencil sharp. Draw single lines to outline the motifs. Do not use scratchy or double lines.
- When tracing, use a light touch. Do not dig the pencil into the tracing paper.
- Always start a design with a piece of tracing paper larger than the size of the design you are doing. Do not start tracing on the edge of the paper. Leave a few inches all around to accommodate changes or additions and to avoid tears along the edges of the tracing.
- When creating a design, you can place motifs or groups of motifs in different positions on the tracing paper by using smaller pieces of tracing paper. First trace the desired motif on the smaller piece; then place it under the larger tracing layout, tossing or turning it in any position the design requires. Always write the directional "top" on the upper edge of all tracings to avoid confusion.
- When painting your design with dyes on waxed rice paper, always work out the completed design

on tracing paper first. Pencil lines cannot be erased from waxed rice paper and will show through the dyes. When you are ready to paint, simply tape the waxed paper on top of the tracing paper and start painting. When painting your design in opaque colors (gouache or tempera), transfer the design onto the drawing paper by using the rubdown method described below, or by using the transfer paper method (see the section on "Saral Transfer Paper" in Chapter 3).

- Always save design tracings until a job is completed.

RUBBING DOWN A TRACING

A traditional method that textile designers use to transfer both single motifs and whole designs from tracing paper to drawing paper is called a *rubdown*.

1. Draw the motif or design cleanly on the tracing paper. Write "top" on the front to avoid confusion.

2. Turn the tracing paper over and *back* it, or retrace the pencil lines of the motifs exactly on the reverse side of the paper.

3. Turn the tracing over to the front and place it on the drawing paper in the position in which it will be rubbed down.

4. By using tape or by holding the paper tightly with your other hand, position the tracing so that it will not move. Then hold a spoon between your thumb and forefinger by its bowl, and use the edge of the bowl to rub down the penciled motifs from the back of the tracing to the drawing paper beneath. If the tracing appears too light on the drawing paper, you are either not rubbing hard enough or you are not using the edge of the spoon. Other implements that can be used to rub down a tracing are a blunt-edged knife or a rubbing bone, which can be purchased at an art store.

You can rub down the same tracing over and over again until the motifs on the drawing paper are difficult to see; then you can *back*, or retrace the motifs, on the tracing, or make a new one. When rubbing down a tracing on a dark ground, back it with white Conte crayon (keep the point sharp).

ONE-WAY AND TWO-WAY LAYOUTS

Most apparel and some home furnishing designs are done in what is known as a *two-way* or *nondirectional* layout. In a two-way layout the motifs are positioned in two or more directions, so that when the fabric is turned around or upside down there is no discernable difference in the pattern. This type of layout minimizes fabric waste, as the design can be used in any direction when garments or upholstery are cut. In a one-way layout the motifs on the fabric all move in the same direction, which makes it more difficult to piece together a garment without some fabric waste.

A two-way layout is usually less stiff than a one-way layout and, surprisingly, flows better. Beginning designers are often bewildered when asked to place a figure, house, tree, or animal upside down in a layout. After working on two-way layouts a few times, however, it seems perfectly normal to them, as well as aesthetically pleasing.

In home furnishing, nondirectional layouts are sometimes called "choppers" because the fabric can be cut or chopped in any direction to fit the upholstery pattern. However, for other home furnishing designs, such as wallpaper or drapery, a one-way layout is more suitable.

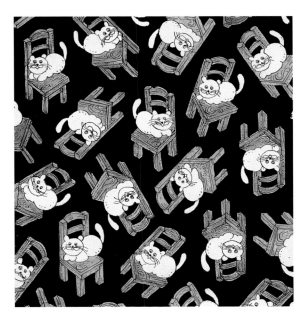
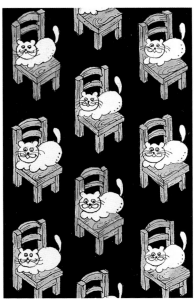

A conversational design in a two-way tossed layout *(far left)*, and the same design motif in a one-way set layout *(left)*.

TYPES OF LAYOUTS

The following layouts are the most frequently used in textile design.

ALL-OVER OR TOSSED

An *all-over* or *tossed* design is one in which the motifs are arranged in a variety of positions to achieve a varied but balanced effect. The amount of space that the motifs cover on the background (known as *coverage)* can range widely from *packed,* where the motifs are placed very close together, to *spaced,* which shows a good deal of background.

A good way to start an all-over design is to lay out, or *spot,* on tracing paper the largest or most important motif or unit of design. Next spot the second motif, and so on until the smallest motif has been laid out; the remaining background space can often be filled in with these. To save time you can substitute circles for the motifs, and rearrange them until you are satisfied with the overall layout. The circles can be filled in with their corresponding motifs and then erased.

If there are spaces in the background that form paths running through the design that are uninterrupted by motifs, break up the paths by rearranging the motifs. You should avoid motifs forming straight lines

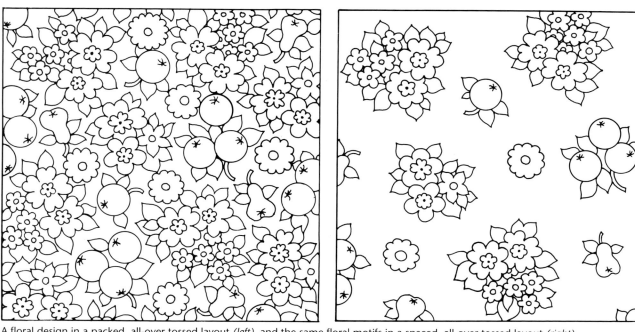

A floral design in a packed, all-over tossed layout *(left),* and the same floral motifs in a spaced, all-over tossed layout *(right).*

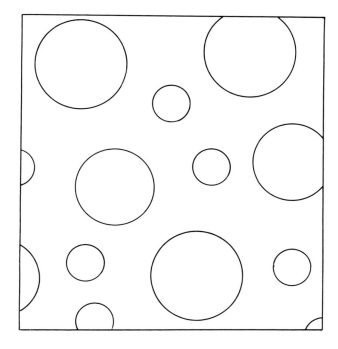

A tracing layout using circles to spot the motifs in the design above right. The motifs can be drawn in and the circles erased when the layout is perfected.

(known as *line-ups*) or placing motifs so close together that they cause clusters in one area and holes in others. An exception to this is when the spaces are deliberate, and are consistent within the layout. If line-ups occur, redistribute the motifs until the overall layout appears balanced. Moving one motif may necessitate moving others until the design flows properly, so as you make changes be aware of the design as a whole canvas, and of its overall flow and balance.

When the design calls for a packed all-over layout, do not be afraid, for example, to have motifs such as leaves or flowers touch each other, appearing to grow and wind under or over each other as in a garden. The opposite is true of a spaced layout, in which both the layout of the motifs and the background spaces must be carefully balanced.

Your design should always give the illusion of a repeat, which is easily achieved by having all its motifs, or as many as possible, appear more than once in the design. Remember to use a two-way layout unless a one-way layout is specifically requested. In either case, the more closely your finished design on paper resembles a printed piece of fabric, the more confidence the customer or stylist will have in it—and in you.

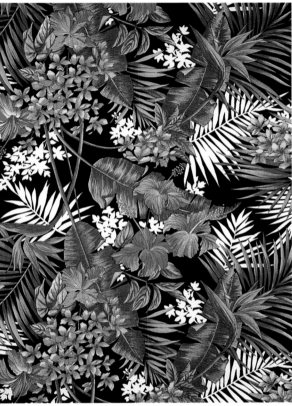

A tropical floral apparel design in a packed all-over layout in which the motifs overlap and intertwine. *The Cloth Company, a division of Cranston Print Works Co.*

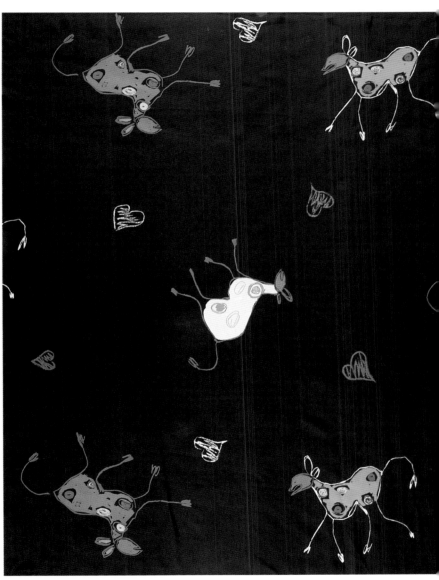

A fun apparel design in a spaced layout with a lot of background showing. The spotting of the motifs is carefully balanced. *Printmaker International, Ltd.*

FREE-FLOWING

All designs must have a sense of balance; while some are evenly spaced, others have unconventional or asymmetrical layouts with a lot of flow and movement. For the latter type of design (referred to as *free-flowing,* and sometimes called *pattern on pattern)*, you must learn to use your eye to *spot,* or space, the elements of the design.

A free-flowing design must be laid out on a large piece of tracing paper. Start by sketching in the first background motif, using outlines only. To create the desired flow and movement, don't be afraid to place motifs on top of or beneath one another wherever necessary. Next, sketch in the second motif, and finally toss the other motifs on top. Once you have finished the overall layout, take a fresh look at it and make any changes necessary to improve it. Then you can perfect the drawing and add details.

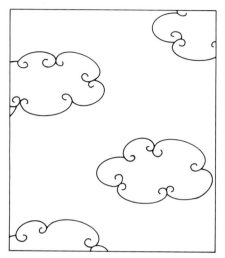 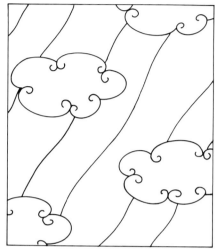 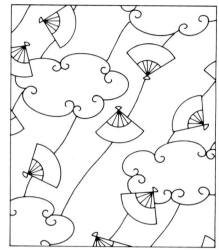

The first motif is sketched in a free-flowing design *(left).* The second motif is then added to the layout *(center).* Finally, the third motif is tossed on top to complete the design *(right).*

STRIPE

A design in a stripe layout must be carefully planned, measured, and laid out. Whether the design uses a tight ruling pen stripe or a free-flowing one, you must measure the stripes precisely or the design will be crooked. Always use a triangle to square off the design; the triangle gives you an exact right angle from which to measure the widths of the stripes with your ruler. Any combination or variety of stripe widths can be used and combined with florals, geometrics, or other design elements. Refer also to Chapter 8 for special instructions for stripe repeats.

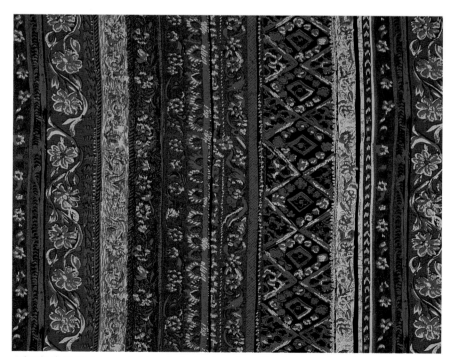

A freely designed apparel stripe, featuring loosely outlined stripes of varying widths. *The Cloth Company, a division of Cranston Print Works Co.*

"Chinoise," a beautifully detailed home furnishing stripe chintz, with the motifs confined within ruling pen outlines. *Copyright © Frank Delfino, designer*

BORDER

Borders provide an opportunity for some of the most versatile layouts. A border design can range in scale from a small blouse pattern to a huge drapery design. The border can be placed on one or both ends of a design, either the same border or two different ones. The remainder of the printed fabric above the border is called the *field*. Borders are often used in designs for sheets, pillowcases, and comforters.

The border can serve as the focus of the design, with the field much lighter in feeling. The reverse can be equally interesting: A very elaborate field can accompanied by a narrow, rigidly confined border. Of course, it is also possible to make the border and the field equally bold.

The motifs in a set border or field must be carefully planned and measured with a triangle and ruler. You must also begin a more freely drawn border by making a right angle with a triangle at the bottom of the tracing paper. This will give you guidelines from which to measure a grid for the motifs, as you must make sure the elements are not crooked. Draw a right angle a few inches above the bottom of the paper so that the motifs will not be cut off at the bottom and there is room for a hem, which is usually in a solid color. Refer also to the section on "Border Repeats" in Chapter 8.

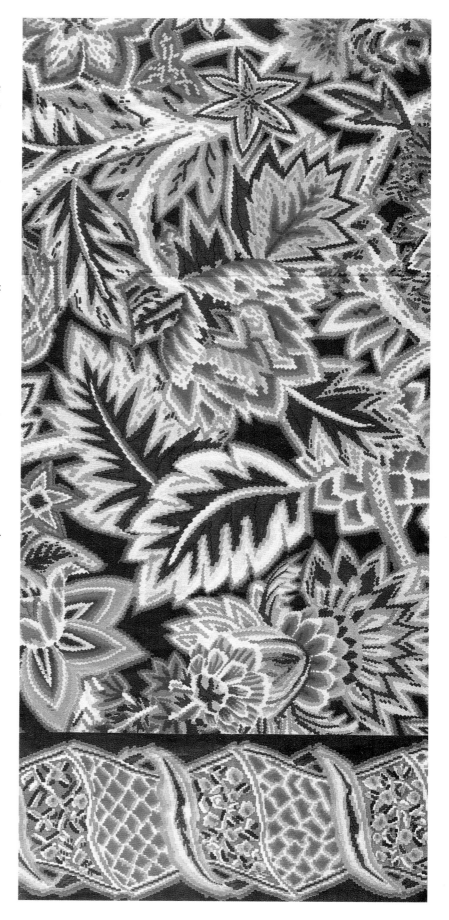

"Garden of Allah," a home furnishing design with an elaborate field that dominates a rigidly set border. *Clarence House Imports, Ltd.*

An apparel design utilizing the full width of the cloth. A different border on each selvage creates an unusual dramatic effect. *The Cloth Company, a division of Cranston Print Works Co.*

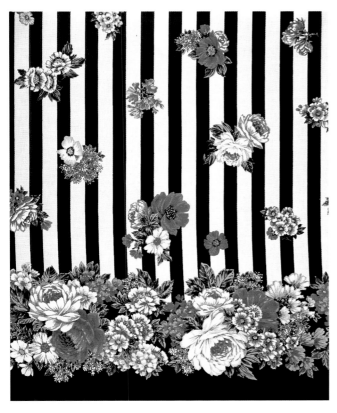

A brightly colored floral border with bold background stripes for apparel. *The Cloth Company, a division of Cranston Print Works Co.*

SET

A set layout is one in which the motifs are repeated in exact measured spaces, in either a square or half-drop repeat. Set designs can be easily laid out in a finished repeat size, as they must be measured exactly anyway.

To work out a set layout, place a piece of graph paper of the correct measurement under your tracing paper and use it to calculate the spaces between the motifs in the design. A light box can be helpful with this type of layout.

To save time and assure uniformity in drawing the motifs, only one or two neat renderings of the motifs can be drawn on a smaller piece of tracing paper that has register marks on it. These can then be aligned underneath the large tracing paper grid and traced as many times as necessary to complete the layout. When the layout is complete, use either the rubdown method or transfer paper to transfer the design to the drawing paper. Precise circles require an ink compass, which can be used with ink, paint, or dye.

Another way to draw a set layout is to measure your own grid or graph with a triangle and ruler, either on tracing paper or directly on your drawing paper. If a grid is drawn directly on the drawing paper, a simplified version consisting only of register marks can be lightly drawn. (Register marks work well on papers that do not erase easily, such as painted gouache grounds.) Then the motifs can be aligned on the register marks and rubbed down directly on your final paper.

On dark painted grounds, go over the register marks lightly with white paint or a white pencil so that they will be visible through the tracing paper.

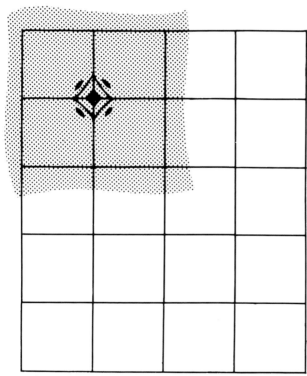

A motif drawn on tracing paper (dotted area) and aligned on a drawing paper grid, in position to either trace or rub down a set square repeat.

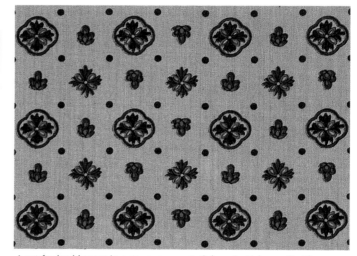

A set foulard layout in a square repeat. *Schwartz-Liebman Textiles*

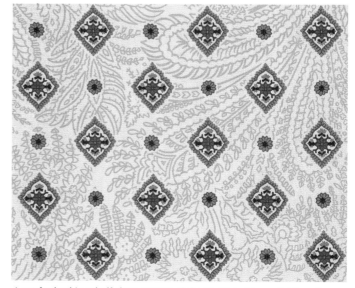

A set foulard in a half-drop repeat. *Cohama Riverdale, a division of Richloom Fabrics Group, Inc.*

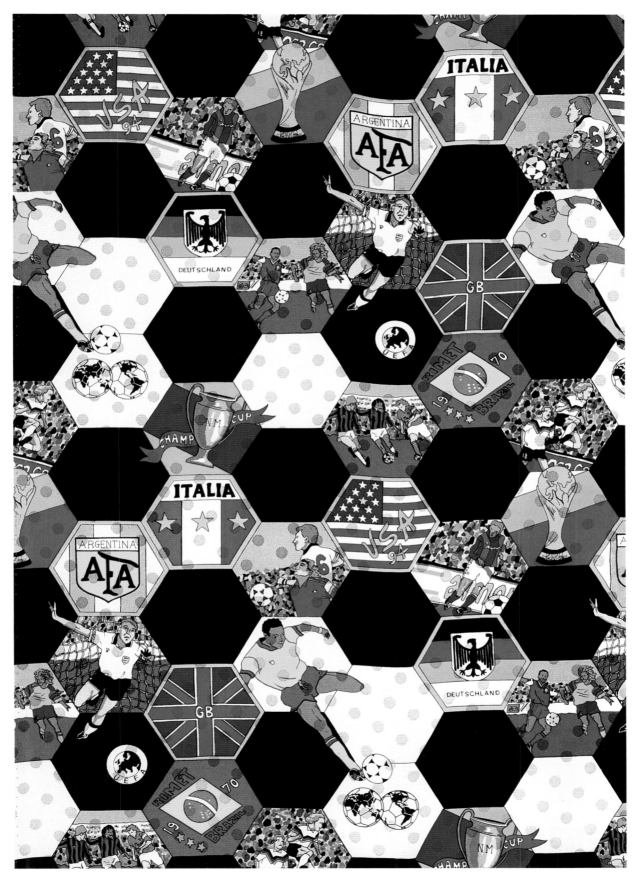

A sports conversational showing a set hexagonal background with the motifs tossed on top. *Copyright © Nicole Miller*

SCENIC OR LANDSCAPE

A scenic or landscape design is worked on a horizontal layout. These designs simulate a landscape of various outdoor themes, both rural and urban.

To lay out a scenic, first rough in the horizontal lines in the spacing required. Next, lay out the largest or most important motif or group of motifs, well balanced on the paper. Then add the second most important motif, and so on, until the layout is complete. Try to envision the overall look as you lay out the design (as on a large canvas), not just the individual motifs. Turn some of the motifs around if a two-way layout is necessary. Don't forget: To help with your layout, you can simply draw in circles where the motifs belong and then trace the details in when you are ready.

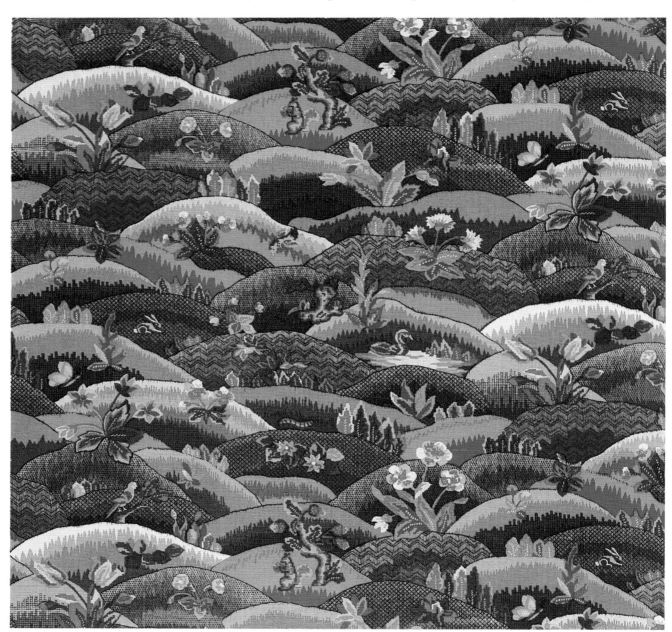

"Tudor Embroidery," a tapestry landscape pattern for home furnishing in a one-way layout. *Schumacher*

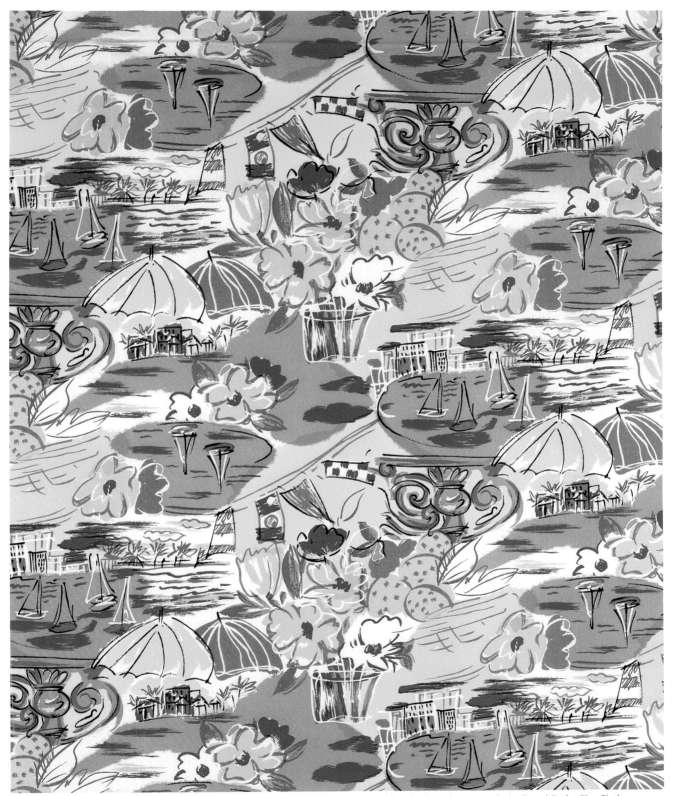

A scenic beach design in a two-way or nondirectional layout for apparel inspired by the French watercolorist Raoul Dufy. *The Cloth Company, a division of Cranston Print Works Co.*

HANDKERCHIEF SQUARE

A handkerchief layout, which can be either in a diamond or a square pattern, looks like a number of bandanas or handkerchiefs, each with its own border, attached in a continuous pattern. Draw the layout as you would for any set pattern, making a grid using a triangle and ruler.

A handkerchief square layout can be adapted to accommodate many design approaches, including Americana, floral, and a variety of ethnic themes.

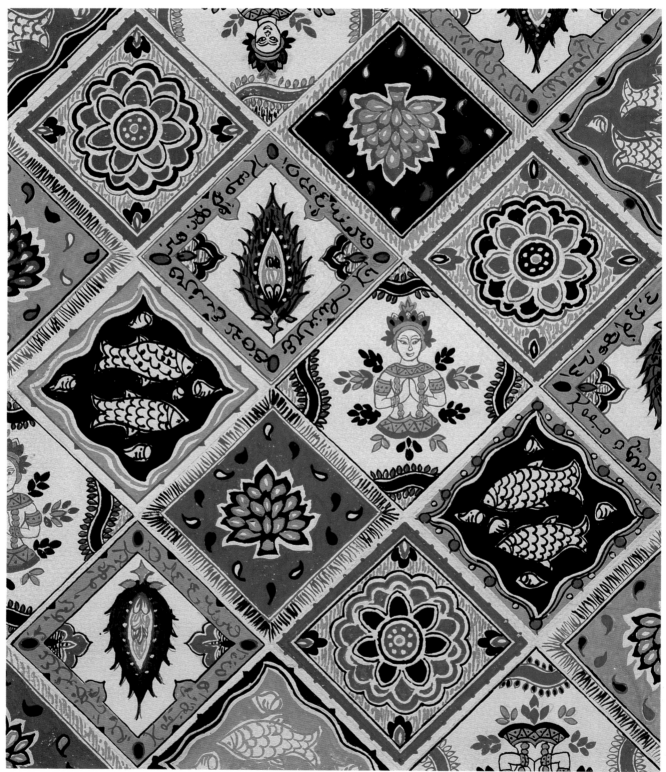

A handkerchief square design worked in a diamond layout, inspired by traditional Asian motifs.

PATCHWORK

When you are doing a design with a traditional set patchwork layout, follow the method for set layouts by making a graph of the required spacing for your design.

When you are creating a patchwork design with a free-flowing or tossed layout, the outlines of the large shapes should be laid out first on tracing paper. In both cases, the motifs can be created and laid out on separate pieces of tracing paper. These tracings can then be placed in position under the grid on the large tracing, and the patchwork designs retraced and filled in.

To achieve an authentic patchwork look, each section of the design should appear to be cut out of a larger piece of printed fabric. Therefore, the motifs must be traced and painted right up to the exact edges of each patch. If an appliqué look is desired, you can simulate stitching around the edges and on top of the motifs to make them appear as if they are cut out of a piece of cloth and then sewn onto the background.

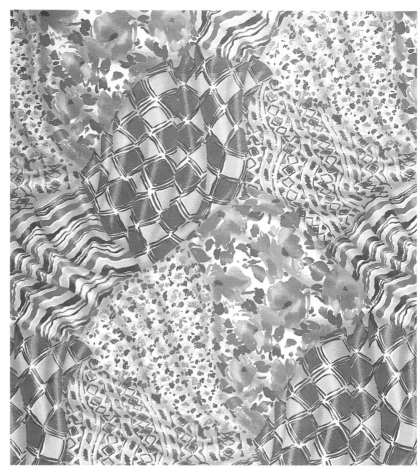

"København," a modern patchwork sheet design in a loose flowing layout. *Stylepoints Collection, Cameo Interiors*

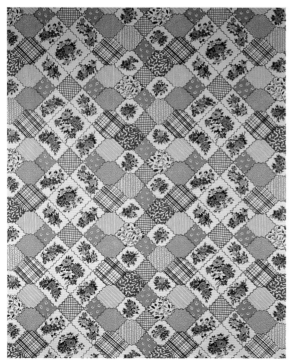

"Country Quilt," a bright patchwork in a set layout. *Bloomcraft, a division of P. Kaufman*

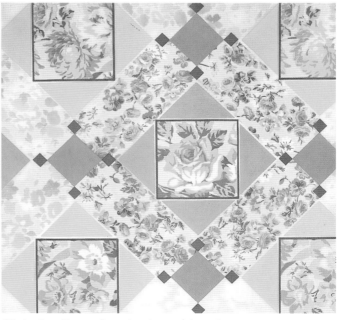

"Quiet Rose," a comforter in a large-scale set layout; a contemporary version of a traditional patchwork quilt pattern in pastel colors. *Copyright © Frank Delfino, designer*

FIVE-STAR

A five-star layout (also called a *center bouquet* layout) generally uses one central motif, often a large traditional bouquet, repeated in a one-way, half-drop layout. This type of layout is used mainly on upholstery, where the large motif can be centered on the cushions and back of a sofa or chair to accommodate the cutting needs of the customer. The five-star layout is also used on drapery and wallpaper where a one-way look is desirable.

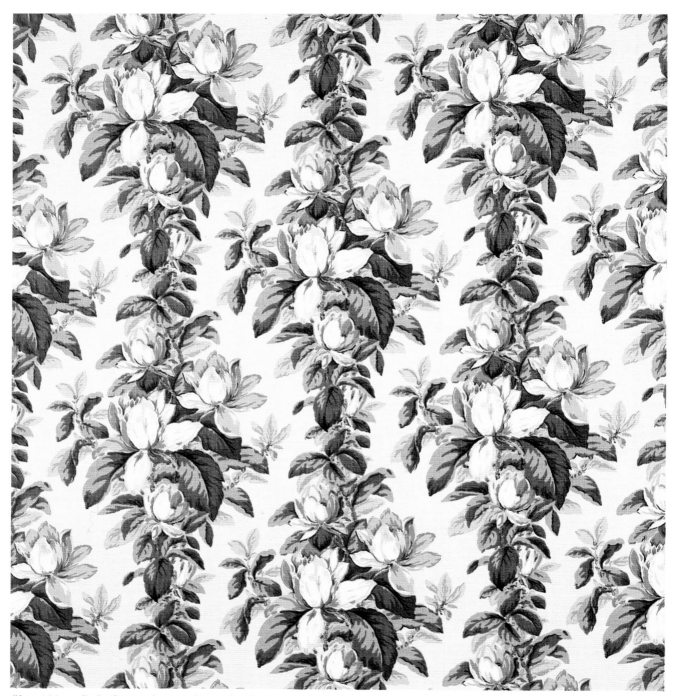

"Sweet Magnolia," a five-star bouquet layout that forms a stripe. *Bloomcraft, a division of P. Kaufman*

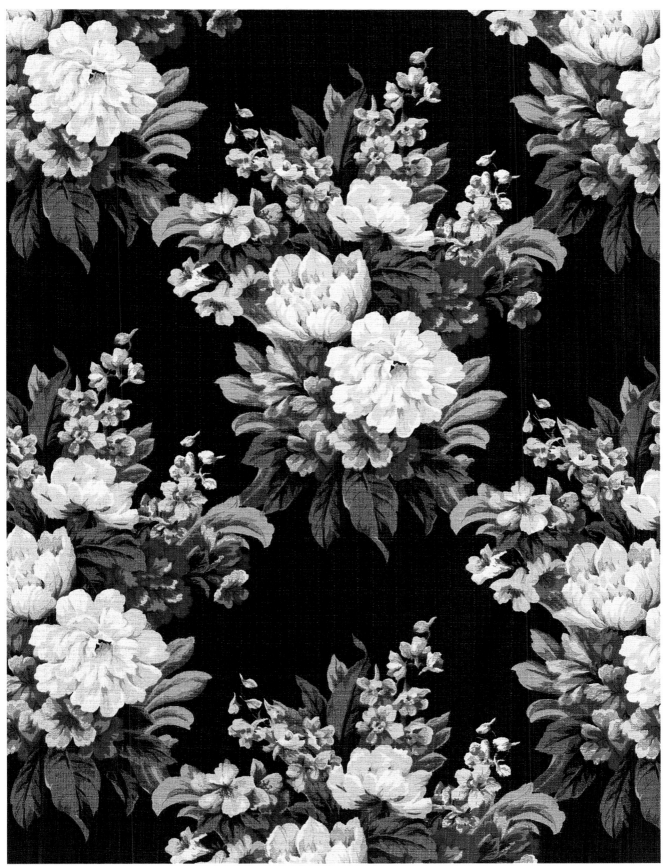

"Waldorf," a typical five-star bouquet layout for upholstery. *Bloomcraft, a division of P. Kaufman*

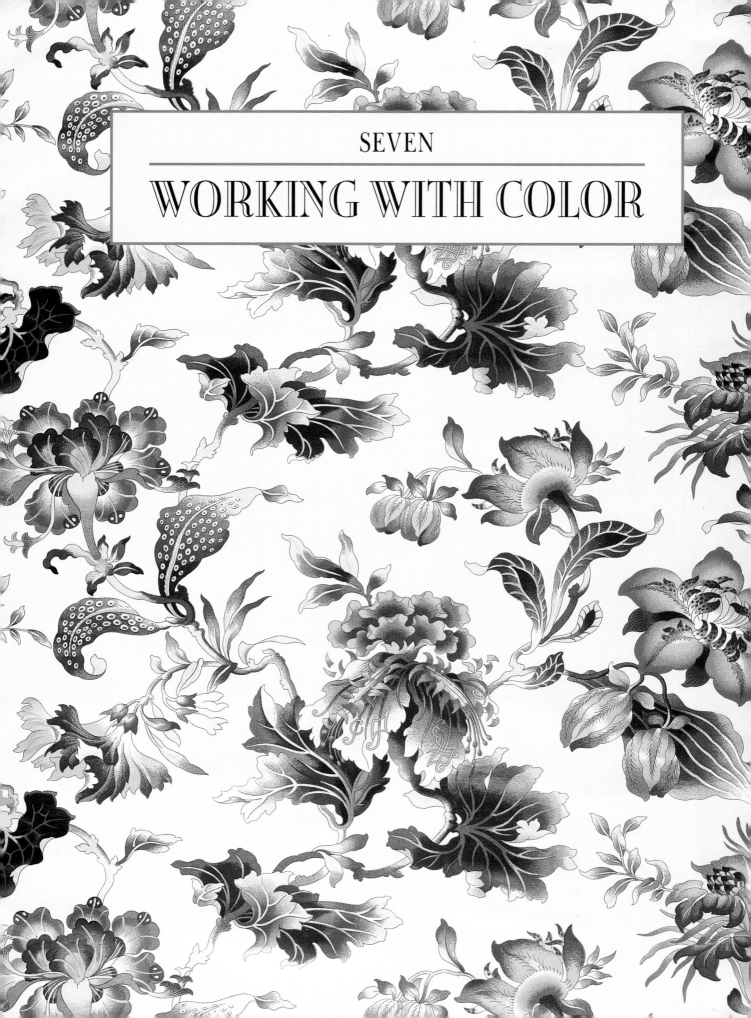

WORKING WITH COLOR

T he way that color is used in a design greatly influences its success. A mediocre design can be made into a good one with beautiful color, and an excellent design can be spoiled with poor color choices. Many converters employ colorists, who only work on colorways for the patterns. While some companies, particularly those in the apparel market, color their designs on the computer, this chapter deals exclusively with the traditional handpainted techniques of working with color: creating colorways, mixing and matching colors, making colored grounds, and painting blotches with gouache and dyes. The general principles discussed in this chapter apply to working with color on both designs and colorways.

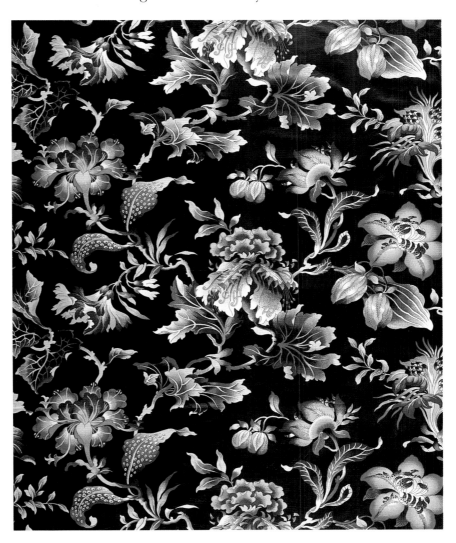

COLORWAYS

Every textile design is printed in several different *colorways,* which are also called *color combinations* and *colorings*. A colorway is a squared-off portion of a design that is large enough to contain all the colors in the design. The same section of the design is used for each colorway, and is usually painted with the same materials and paper that were used for the original design. A small square of each color, called a *color tab* (also known as a *chip* or a *gam),* usually accompanies each colorway. The number of colorways painted for each design varies from at least three to ten or more, depending on what the stylist requests. If a design has sold successfully, it is often recolored for presentation in a new season, or to add new color combinations to the line.

To save time, some studios prefer that you place acetate on top of the design and paint the colorways right on the acetate. Be aware, however, that colors tend to look different on acetate than they do on paper. When you are mixing and matching colors, paint small dabs of each color on a test sheet of paper to see how they work together. This is when you must make color changes (for example, by either darkening or lightening them) before using them in the final colorway.

A time saver for colorways with black outlines is to make photocopies of the outlines before any color is applied, thereby eliminating the tedious outlining process. Have the copies made on your own drawing paper, or request heavier-weight photocopy paper, which will take the paint better. Dyes are usually used with this technique, as they do not cover the outlines. Colorways can also be made by using color photocopies, particularly for monotone designs. However, this technique should be used sparingly when preparing your portfolio, as most stylists want to be able to evaluate your painting skills.

COLOR AND PRINTING

In preparation for printing, a screen or roller is made for each color in a design. While most apparel designs usually use up to six colors and home furnishing patterns usually use twelve or more, new developments in rotary screen printing now make it possible for designers to choose even more colors. When you are working out colorways on a pattern, the stylist will usually give you references, such as color tabs or a swatch of material to match (see "Mixing and Matching Colors," later in this chapter). At other times, you will only be given the *key,* or main, color in each new combination. Sometimes, after being advised of the general color look desired in a particular pattern—such as primary, pastel, or neutral—you will be responsible for selecting all the colors.

USING A COLOR CHART

Whether you are given complete or partial direction for completing a set of colorways, you must begin by studying the color relationships in the original design you are working from. These color relationships will furnish the clues to the new colorways. To assist you in working out colorways, study the floral design and chart on the opposite page, which shows a set

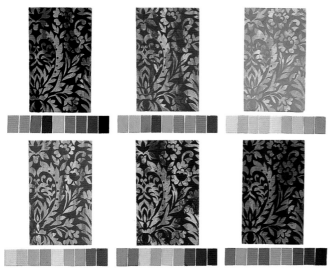

A set of six colorways with color tabs attached, for a home furnishing tapestry pattern, "Versailles." *Malden Mills Industries, Inc.* © 1991

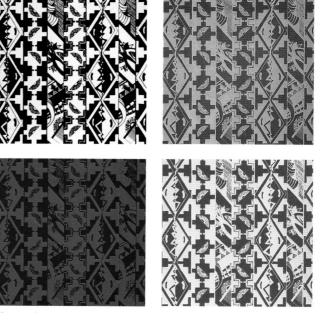

Three colorways made by laser photocopy; the original design *(top left)* is painted in black and white. *Copyright © Theresa Ruck, designer*

A group of colorways showing a design done in four different color treatments: *(top left)* primary, *(top right)* neutral, *(lower left)* bright pastel, and *(lower right)* monochromatic. *Copyright © Frank Delfino, designer*

of three new colorways that were worked out for it. Working out a color chart will help you to analyze the color relationships in your designs and to make decisions about new combinations.

WORKING OUT A COLOR CHART

1. Draw a chart as shown. In column 1, list all the colors in your design in the order of their importance. Make column 1 as long as needed to include all the colors in your design—don't forget to include outline and background colors. Try to list the colors that relate to each other (such as orange and yellow) together. This will instantly remind you to keep this same relationship when you choose substitute colors in the new colorways.

2. Head columns 2, 3, and so on with the key color for each of the new combinations. Using the original design and column 1 of the chart as guides, work out in column 2 the first new colorway. Then work out the second colorway in column 3, and so on.

3. The colors you list in the color chart only serve as a guide. After mixing a color you may find that it simply doesn't work well on the colorway. In that case, refer back to the chart and rethink that color choice. Note that when one color is changed, other colors may need to be adjusted.

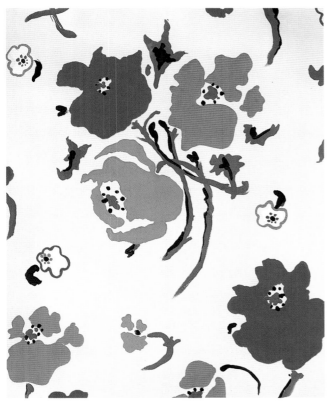

A floral pattern accompanied by a chart that shows a set of three colorways worked out for the design. The colors in the original design are listed in column 1. The corresponding new colorways are listed in columns 2, 3, and 4. *Copyright © Frank Delfino, designer*

TIPS ON USING AND CHOOSING COLORS

• Because you use a color for one colorway does not mean that you cannot use a different shade of that same color in another. If you use similar colors in the same set of colorways, however, make sure that each colorway is sufficiently distinct in feeling from the others. Sometimes, all the colors chosen for a set of colorways are the same value and intensity as those in the original design.

1	2	3	4
Red	Blue	Brown	Purple
Orange	Aqua	Rust	Fuscia
Gold	Mauve	Beige	Peach
Light Green	Ocher	Light Teal Blue	Light Olive Green
Dark Green	Brown	Dark Teal Blue	Dark Olive Green

At other times, one or two different looks are included.

- Once again, remember that a screen or roller is made for each color in the design. Therefore, make sure, for example, that if you substitute blue in the new colorway for orange in the original, that the blue always replaces the orange, and so on with all the colors selected for the new colorway.
- If you use different tones of one color—for example, a light blue and a dark blue—each tone counts as a separate color.

An exception is when a single color fades from dark to light (a technique known as *shading*).

- The color of the outline also counts as a color. The outline does not always have to be black; you can use navy, gray, sepia, and others.
- White does not usually count as a color, but it depends on the process used to print the textile. Make sure you confirm whether white is a color for each job with the stylist.
- If you feel that your colorway is either too bright or too muted, try combining two or three bright colors with two or three neutral colors in order to balance it.
- Try experimenting with unconventional ideas: Leaves do not always have to be green—they can be gold, rust, beige, blue, or any color that enhances the design. Also, keep in mind that there are many shades of green, and that using a bright primary green instead of a muted olive green for a leaf color can make a big difference. To create a new look, try combining colors that would not ordinarily go together.

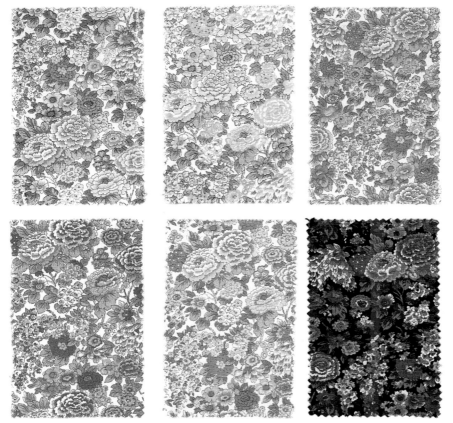

(Above) A set of six colorways for "Elysian," a Liberty floral design (see page 48): five bright pastels, and one with a black background. *Liberty of London Prints*

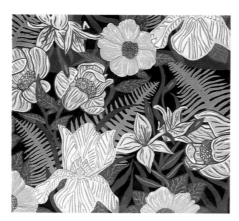

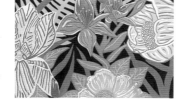 

(Right) A tropical floral in which unconventional pink and blue leaves are used in the colorways. *Copyright © Theresa Ruck, designer*

MIXING AND MATCHING COLORS

Each design presents its own color problems and should be approached on an individual basis, with the designer emphasizing an overall color feeling. The amount of coverage of each color, the amount of background color, the layout and spacing of the motifs, and many other subtleties all make a difference in how the colors in each design relate to one another.

If the distribution of the colors in your design looks unbalanced—for instance, if there is too much of one color concentrated in one area—the following procedure will help you see at a glance how to redistribute the colors: Make a separate tracing overlay for each color by simply making circles or markings with different color crayons or by using the letter R for red, B for blue, and so on, on each overlay to indicate that particular color. Study the overlays and, if necessary, respot the colors in the layout so that the final layout is well balanced.

TIPS ON MIXING AND MATCHING COLORS WITH GOUACHE AND DYES

Mixing and matching colors in opaque gouache and transparent dyes are two of the most important skills in producing successful color combinations for your designs and colorways. When painting colorways, you will be called on to match colors from color tabs or chips, from swatches of fabric and other painted designs, and from assorted scraps and clippings of all kinds. Many stylists are very picky about matching colors; others are more casual. It is best to assume that the stylist will be particular, and to develop high standards yourself.

Although there are rules for using and combining primary and secondary colors, these rules do not always work when applied to textile design. The best way to learn how to mix color is to experiment with colors on your own designs. As a start, the following are some basic rules for mixing colors with gouache and dyes:

- Use a vessel large enough to mix and hold the amount of paint you will require to finish your work, as well as a small amount for possible touch-ups.
- When mixing a shade of dye, imagine a scale from 1 to 10, 10 being the strongest color, straight from the bottle. As a general rule, if the strength of the tone you are matching is 5 or below on the scale (medium to light), start with water, and slowly add the dye to it. If you start with the dye, which is extremely concentrated, you will have to add water endlessly

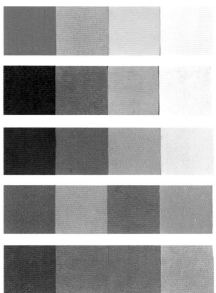

A chart of dyes (concentrated water colors). The first three sets of color tabs *(from top)* show a progression of shades, from the bright undiluted dye *(left)* to progressively lighter tints *(right)* as more water is added. *(Second row from bottom, from left to right)* Grass green and orange (undiluted), grass green mixed with small amount of orange, and orange mixed with a small amount of grass green. *(Bottom row)* Various shades of purple and blue made by mixing hot pink and turquoise. All shades have been lightened with water.

to arrive at the desired color. This is not only frustrating but also wasteful, as you will probably end up with much more color than you need. If the tone you are mixing is above 5 on the scale (medium to dark), start with dye, then add water a small amount at a time, until you get the desired shade.

- When mixing dyes, start with the color that is closest to what you are trying to get, then add the secondary colors needed to arrive at the exact shade. If necessary, use water to lighten. Remember that concentrated dye colors are very powerful, and that even a drop of dye added to another color will immediately change the shade. For example, if you want to tone down hot pink, just a touch of yellow will do it; too much yellow will make the pink

turn orangey. It is best to err on the side of discretion by adding too little rather than too much, as you can always add more if needed.

- Matching a color is a trial-and-error process. Use the following method to test a color for a match: After mixing a color, dab it on the edge of a scrap of the same kind of paper that the colorway is on. Let the color dry thoroughly (wet color is very different from dry color). Then place your color chip directly on top, overlapping the color you are matching. You will immediately be able to see whether the color you are mixing is too light or too dark, and so on. If the paint mixture needs to be adjusted, add the colors necessary to correct the shade. Make another test dab, let it dry, and repeat the comparison process. You may have to do this many times before you are satisfied that you have matched the color.
- When matching a color with opaque gouache or tempera, use white to lighten the color. Mix the paint with just enough water to obtain a creamy, smooth consistency that covers flat and opaque when applied to the paper. If light streaks appear when applying gouache, the paper is showing through because the mixture is too watery. If it appears thick and grainy, too much paint has been applied.

MAKING COLORED GROUNDS

A designer must be able to produce a ground of any color or size, whether he or she works at home or in a studio. While there are many colored papers available to use as backgrounds, a specific shade may not be when needed for a design or colorway. There is no substitute for knowing how to make your own colored grounds.

TIPS FOR MAKING GROUNDS

- The vessel you use to mix your ground color should be large enough to mix paint for two grounds, which will give you a backup ground in case of mistakes. Save any leftover paint for touch-ups.

- Purchase an inexpensive 3- or 4-inch natural bristle ground brush; a 1- or 2-inch brush is good for smaller grounds. If this is not possible, select a good-quality natural or nylon bristle brush of this size at a hardware store. While I prefer to use a brush, other tools can also be used to paint grounds, including small rollers and flat polyfoam brushes of various sizes.

- Do not paint to the edges of the ground paper unless it is taped or tacked down. Leave about 2 inches of unpainted edge on all sides of the paper or it will curl up, making it difficult to handle. Work on scrap paper to avoid mess, and have a large water container on hand for cleaning your brushes.

APPLYING GROUND COLOR WITH OPAQUE PAINTS

There are two methods for applying ground color with opaque paints. Dip a slightly moist ground brush into the paint and apply it with even strokes, back and forth and then up and down across the paper, moistening the brush as needed. An alternative method is to first brush the paper lightly with a very thin coat of water, which helps to spread the paint over the paper. In either case, the trick is to brush quickly and evenly until the ground looks smooth. Always work from top to bottom and then from side to side.

During the process, add more paint or water as needed and brush it on evenly. When you've finished painting the ground you can smooth it out by feathering it lightly with the tip of the brush before it dries. Put the completed ground aside to dry and paint the second one. If a ground does not dry smoothly, do not waste time doing a design on it; either use the second ground or make a new one. Once again, not enough paint has been applied if light streaks show through the ground color, and too much paint has been applied if the ground appears thick and grainy.

APPLYING GROUND COLOR WITH DYES

When painting a ground with dyes, apply the same general rules as when using opaque paints. Note, however, that transparent dyes deepen in tone as each additional coat is brushed on. Therefore, test a small area first, brushing back and forth. If the test ground dries too dark, add water to the mixture and test it again. Proceed when the test area dries to the desired shade.

While you are painting the ground, do not let the dye dry; work quickly, brushing back and forth with even strokes, first vertically and then horizontally.

PAINTING A BLOTCH

The term *blotch* refers to a background color that is painted around the motifs in a design. Although blotching can be done in both gouache and dye colors, it is easier to paint around motifs with flat opaque paints than with dyes. Dyes may show overlaps and create an uneven ground, particularly when blotching a large area with a lot of ins and outs around the motifs; small areas are generally not as problematic. It is necessary at times to blotch large areas with dyes, so practice this technique. I often paint the motifs in dyes and then use gouache for the blotch background. If a dye blotch is unsatisfactory, correct it by matching the same color (or mix an entirely new color) with gouache and simply apply a coat on top of the dye. A tight blotch is painted right up to the edges of the motifs; a blotch that is painted loosely around the motifs creates a more casual effect by leaving white ground showing randomly around them.

The blotch technique can also be used to enhance a design by creating white motifs in the background spaces. Consider the possibility of leaving white areas unblotched to form motifs, such as small flowers and leaves. This can be done by eye, or by sketching the new motifs in the white background in a balanced fashion and then proceeding to blotch around them. Touches of color can then be added to these motifs, or they can be left all white.

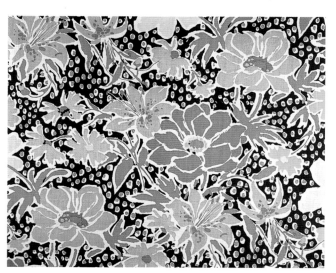

Another floral, loosely blotched. The random dot is left white as the paint is applied in the background. *Bloomcraft, a division of P. Kaufman*

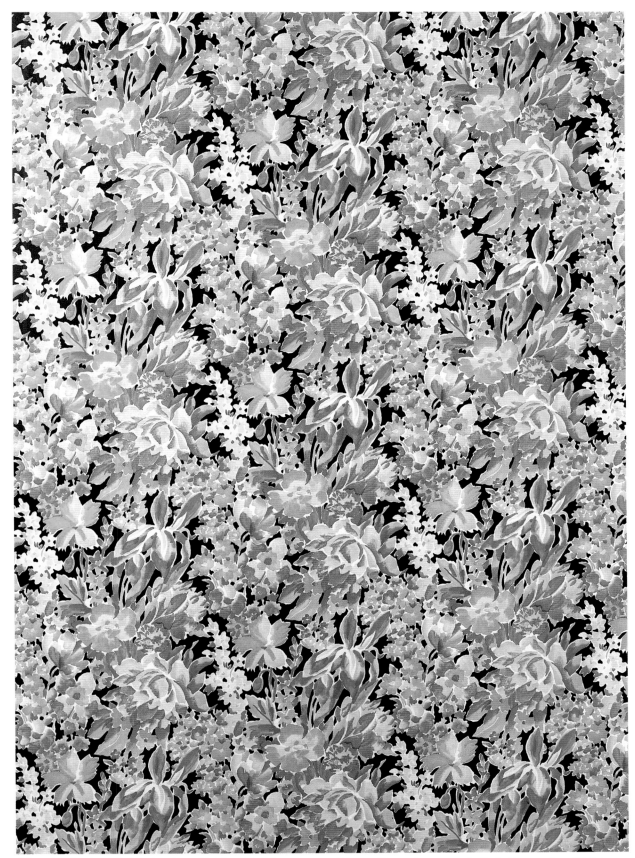

"Blooming," a floral design showing a blotch painted loosely around the motifs creating a casual effect. *Bloomcraft, a division of P. Kaufman*

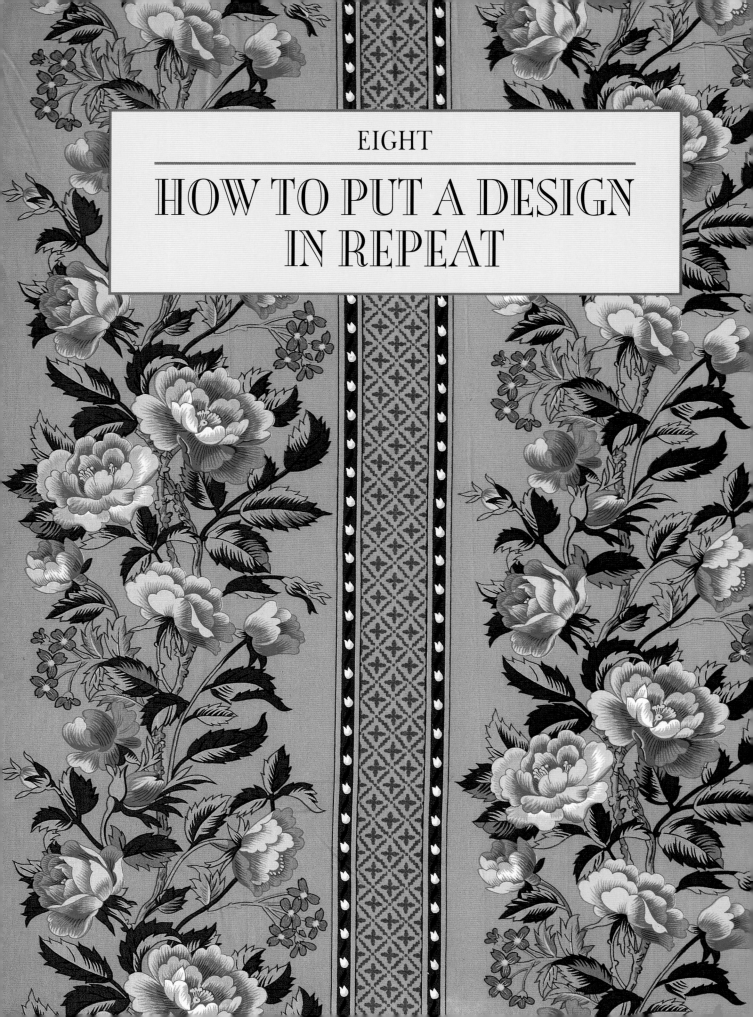

EIGHT

HOW TO PUT A DESIGN IN REPEAT

"La Roseraie Bordure," a realistic floral stripe in a one-way, half-drop repeat for home furnishing. See page 21 for this design's coordinate. *Clarence House Imports, Ltd.*

The unique characteristic of designing textiles is that, unlike other commercial art forms, a design must be prepared to be printed over and over again in a continuous flow, without apparent interruption in the pattern. The rendering of this artwork in a predetermined measurement is called a *repeat*. Understanding what a repeat is and its relationship to the printing process will prepare you to use the step-by-step guide for working out a repeat in the traditional method, described later in this chapter. Once you understand this basic formula, you can put any design into repeat no matter how odd or asymmetrical the layout. You will also be able to follow and learn other repeat methods, such as multiple photocopies and computer software, which some studios use. As you gain experience, you may discover shortcuts or learn other ways to do repeats. Until then, however, you should carefully follow the steps outlined in this chapter.

A stylized floral stripe in a two-way square repeat for apparel. Refer to pages 115 to 116 for a discussion of stripe repeats.

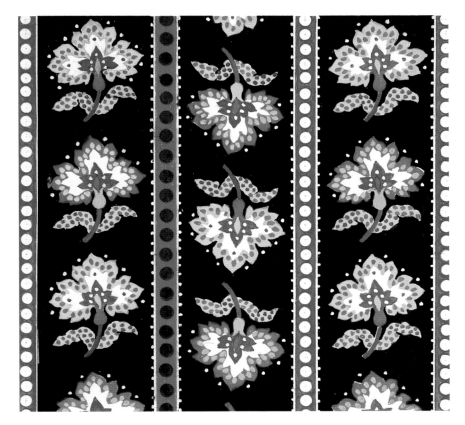

Every design must be put into repeat before it can be printed. This means that the motifs in the design must be organized in a balanced layout that fits into an exact measurement so that repetition of the design will not overlap in the printing process. When the repeat is finished it is sent to the textile printing plant, where a separate screen or roller is prepared for each color, and the design is then printed on fabric. When a repeat is done properly, the pattern is smooth and flowing, with no discernible trace of a *repeat line*, which is where the repetition of the pattern occurs in printing. Rotary screen printing accounts for 90 percent of all apparel and home furnishing printing, with a small amount done by flat-bed screen or copper roller printing. Regardless of the printing method used, the preparation of the repeat is the same (see Chapter 11, "The Printing Process," for more details).

Since every design must be put into repeat eventually, why not simply put every design in repeat to start with? The main reason is that it is faster and easier to concentrate on creating a beautiful design when unencumbered by the technical demands of the repeat. Moreover, a stylist will often make changes on an original design, and these changes must then be incorporated into the repeat. When you work as a freelance designer, you obviously cannot always know the exact repeat size that the purchaser requires. You may spend a great deal of time creating the original design in repeat, only to find that a different size is required, or that some motifs or colors must be changed.

Therefore, a design is usually created to give the illusion of a repeat. When successful, this results in a repetition of motifs in a balanced layout that are not actually measured out in repeat, but appear to be. It is only after all the decisions have been made about how the design will be printed that the actual repeat is worked out. Sometimes a slightly revised version of the design must be created in order to incorporate all of the desired changes in the repeat. However, the changes usually do not appreciably alter the original design, so if you are the originator do not be upset about having to make them. The design is still basically yours, and occasionally the changes may improve it. Sometimes the repeat on a pattern is done by its designer and at other times by a repeat artist.

This does not mean, however, that you never design in repeat. There are times when designing directly in repeat is required or makes sense. For example, you may hold a salaried position and all the pertinent repeat information is supplied to you by the stylist. If you are freelancing, the repeat size may be supplied to you when you are assigned to the job. The stylist also might approve a sketch for a design that is laid out in a predetermined repeat size; your job would then be to simply continue it and paint it to completion. It also makes sense to design in repeat when you are creating a pattern in a set layout such as a stripe, border, or other pattern that must be laid out in exact measurement anyway.

It may surprise you to learn that every design, even one that looks odd or very complicated, can be put into repeat with the proper manipulation of the motifs. Always remember to keep as much of the original design as possible in the repeat, and to try to keep to the spirit of the original whenever you make a change. Few people will be able to discern the differences between the original design and the repeat if the changes are done artistically. Usually a design will look even better in repeat than it did originally because more thought and organization have been put into the finished work.

Some of the changes on an original design that may be required for a repeat are adding or eliminating motifs, making a motif larger or smaller, moving motifs closer together or farther apart, or combining two motifs at the repeat line. By making these changes, the repeat artist is attempting to create a smooth, flowing effect at the repeat line.

REPEATS AND THE PRINTING PROCESS

The circumference of a rotary screen usually ranges from $25 \frac{1}{4}$ to 36 inches, which can accommodate both apparel and home furnishing designs. The measurement of the repeat's length, or the vertical repeat, must fit within the overall length of the rotary screen, but any measurement that multiplies exactly into the repeat size may be used. This means, for instance, that if you are asked to put a design into a 36-inch repeat and the motifs do not require 36 inches for a good layout, you can put the design into an 18-inch repeat, which will fit twice on the screen. A 9-inch repeat will fit four times on the screen; if the design is even smaller, it might require only a 6-inch repeat, and so on. The printed fabric will show the same design repeated over and over down the length of the cloth, with a unit reappearing every 6, 9, or 18 inches, or whatever other repeat size is used. Of course, on a plain striped design the fabric will only show a continuous stripe running the length of the cloth.

The design must also fit within the width of the rotary screen, which is the width of the cloth from selvage to selvage, and can range from 36 to 60 inches, and may be wider for bedding and some upholstery. This measurement is called the *side, horizontal,* or *width repeat.* When you are given a repeat you will always be told the vertical repeat size. For home furnishing designs sometimes the side repeat size is also given, in which case the side repeat is divided equally, based on the width of the fabric. When no side repeat size is specified, as for most apparel designs, you can make the side repeat narrower or wider to fit the demands of the design. This flexibility is sometimes an advantage, as a wider side repeat allows more space, if needed, for a balanced arrangement of motifs.

The vertical repeat must always multiply equally within the given repeat size. Since you only need to paint one full unit of the design in repeat, do not try to save time by compressing the motifs into a repeat size that is too small; make sure that the repeat size you choose allows enough space to include everything. Deciding on the correct repeat size requires careful examination of the design for the variety of motifs, distribution of colors, and so on.

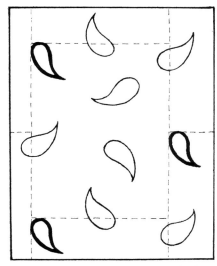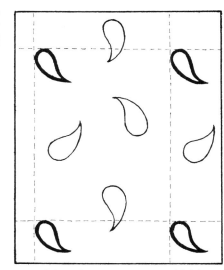

The same paisley motif laid out in a half-drop repeat *(left)* and in a square repeat *(right).* The dotted lines and dark motifs in each indicate the two different repeats.

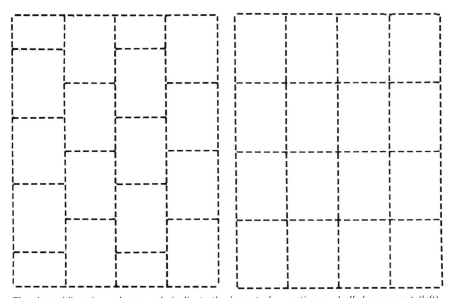

The dotted lines in each example indicate the layout of a continuous half-drop repeat *(left)* and a continuous square repeat *(right).*

HALF-DROP AND SQUARE REPEATS

There are two basic kinds of repeats: half-drop and square. The half-drop is often preferred, as it flows better and appears less stiff. A *square repeat* is laid out in the same arrangement as squares of tile on a floor: Each side of "tile," or unit of design, matches up with the side of the next one, to create a continuous pattern both vertically and horizontally. This is fairly easy to visualize, but the term "square repeat" is somewhat misleading. A square repeat is not necessarily equal in length and width: Any rectangular or box-shaped side repeat is considered a square repeat.

A *half-drop repeat* is laid out on the same basic principle as a square repeat, except that you simply drop the side repeat at exactly half the vertical repeat size. On a 36-inch repeat, for example, the half-drop is at 18 inches; on an 18-inch repeat, the half-drop is at 9 inches; on a 9-inch repeat, the half-drop is at 4 1/2 inches; and so on. The term "brick layout" is sometimes used to refer to the half-drop repeat because it resembles the way that bricks are laid out.

Occasionally, a one-third drop repeat is requested by the stylist, which means that you would drop the side repeat at exactly one-third the vertical repeat size. In this case, follow the instructions for the half-drop repeat and substitute a one-third drop.

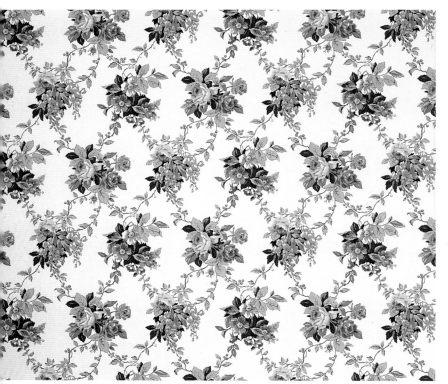

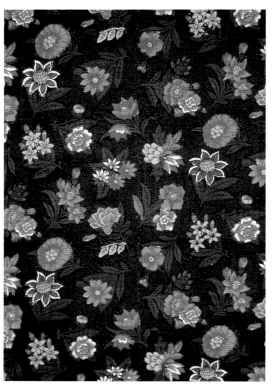

"Dianna," a home furnishing floral in a set layout in a half-drop repeat. *Bloomcraft, a division of P. Kaufman*

"Indienne," a country French provincial design in a half-drop repeat. *Souleiado for Pierre Deux*

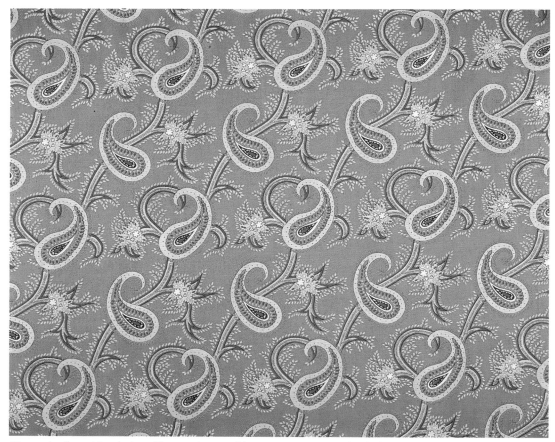

"Beaucaire," a paisley designed in a set layout with a square repeat. *Souleiado for Pierre Deux*

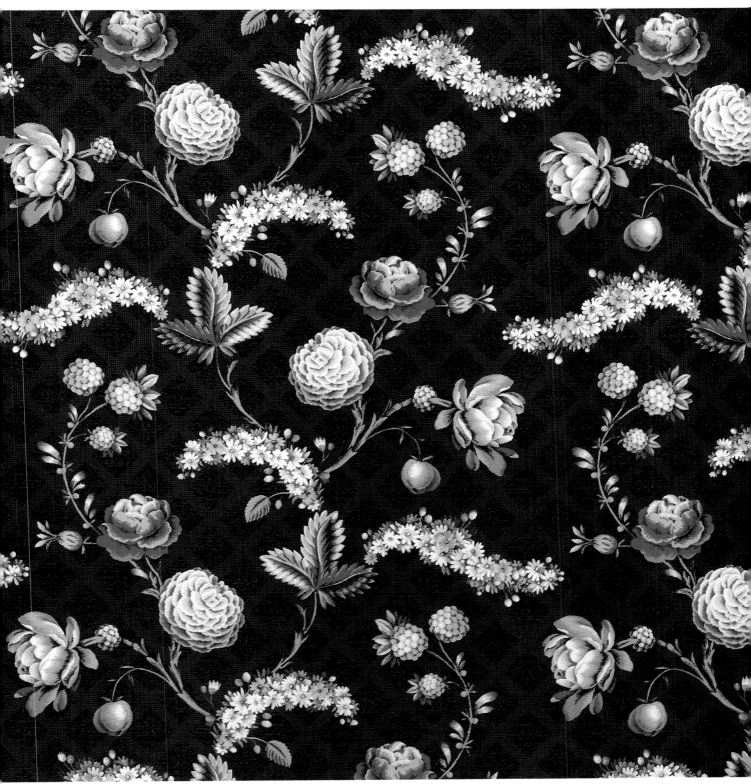

"Orangerie," a home furnishing floral design in a one-way square repeat. The position of the bouquet is reversed in alternating rows. *Designed by Jay Yang*

STEP-BY-STEP GUIDE TO HALF-DROP REPEATS

This formula can be applied to all types of designs and on all sizes of repeats. I have based the description below on the design shown at right, on an 18-inch half-drop repeat (which multiplies twice into a 36-inch rotary screen), a repeat size suitable for both apparel and home furnishing.

The vertical repeat line is worked out first. Remember, any measurement that can be divided equally into the given repeat size can be used.

STEP 1. STUDY THE DESIGN TO DECIDE WHICH VERTICAL REPEAT SIZE WILL FIT BEST

To do this, pick out a motif in the upper left-hand corner of the design. Place your ruler at the top of this motif and glance down to 18 inches. Envision that same motif starting again at that point. Now study the other motifs in the design. Does the design need the full 18 inches to fit in all the motifs and color variations? Glance down to 9 inches on the ruler: Would that work?

Here is where careful judgment must be used. A small repeat size will obviously save you some work, but don't be too stingy or you will be squeezing the design into a repeat size that is too small—one that does not allow enough space for a good layout. (Also consider the possibility of making a wider repeat to provide more space.) When you have determined the proper repeat size for the design, you are ready for Step 2.

STEP 2. RULE OUT TWO PIECES OF TRACING PAPER WITH THE VERTICAL REPEAT MEASUREMENT

Square off two pieces of tracing paper with your triangle, measure both of them to the exact size of the repeat, and number them 1 and 2. Put in the half-drop line on the right side of both tracings, at exactly half of the vertical repeat

The tossed floral design on which the step-by-step guide is based.

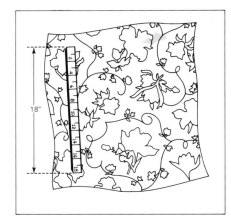

Step 1. Measuring the design to determine the repeat.

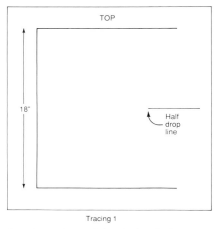
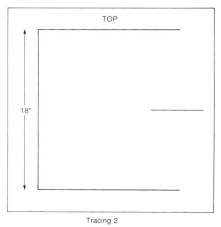

Step 2. Tracing 1 *(left)* ruled with the exact vertical repeat measurement and the half-drop line. Tracing 2 *(right)* is a duplicate of Tracing 1.

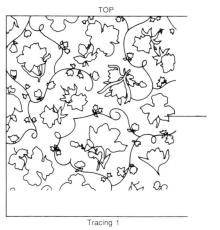

Step 3. Tracing 1 with the complete design traced on it.

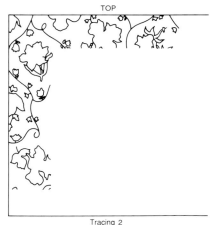

Step 4. Tracing 2 with only the top and left side of the design traced on it.

size (at 9 inches for an 18-inch repeat, at 4 1/2 inches for a 9-inch repeat, at 3 inches for a 6-inch repeat, and so on). Immediately write "top" at the top of all tracings. As your work progresses the tracings will be turned over and around many times, and it is very easy to confuse the top and bottom. Clearly written, "top" will eliminate the confusion.

For most home furnishing designs, the side repeat size will also be supplied. In these cases, measure and draw in the side repeat line when you reach this point in the step-by-step guide; when you come to Step 6, you may disregard the step given to determine the side measure, since the side repeat line is already drawn.

STEP 3. TRACE THE COMPLETE DESIGN ON TRACING 1

If possible, position the upper left-hand corner of the tracing paper on top of the design so that a full motif is included. This will provide an instant visual marker as you make changes in the repeat. Tape the tracing down on the drawing paper and trace neatly using a sharp pencil.

STEP 4. TRACE ONLY THE TOP AND LEFT SIDE OF THE DESIGN ON TRACING 2

The key to doing a successful repeat is working with two tracings, matching them back and forth and making changes at the repeat lines. Make sure that the tracings are always in alignment, and that any change made on one tracing is also made on the other.

STEP 5. BUTT THE TOP REPEAT LINE OF TRACING 2 AGAINST THE BOTTOM REPEAT LINE OF TRACING 1

With the two tracings in position as seen below at left, you can easily see how the design looks at the repeat line. You now make the necessary changes and adjustments by adding, eliminating, moving, or combining motifs to make a smooth flow at the repeat line.

Once again, any changes or additions made on one tracing must be made on the other tracing. Here are some problems you may encounter in making these adjustments:

- *The original design is smaller in overall size than the size of the repeat.* For example, only 15 inches of the original design has been painted, but it requires an 18 inch repeat. This means that 3 inches of the design must be filled in on the tracing paper to complete the repeat. Make sure that when you fill in the 3 inches the flow of all the motifs in the design is balanced. Do not try to cram a lot of little motifs together to fill in the space, or to squeeze in a motif that's too large for the space. In order to achieve an overall balance as you fill out the extra amount of design, you may have to change the position of some or even all of the motifs.

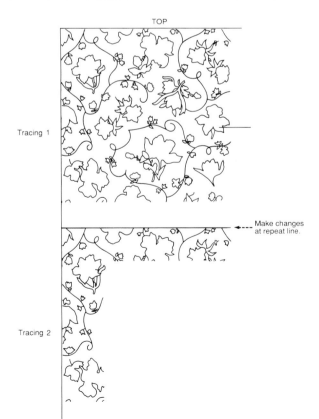

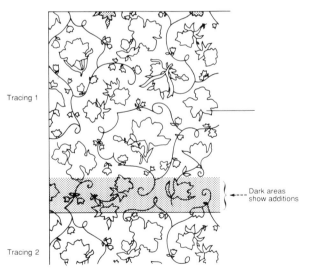

Step 5. Tracing 2 butted against the bottom repeat line of Tracing 1 *(left)*. Dotted lines show additional designs filled in to complete the repeat *(above right)*. All additions and changes must be made at all corresponding repeat lines (as shown by the shaded motifs at the top repeat line).

When a design needs to be extended by only a very small amount, it is possible to do the repeat without adding new motifs simply by slightly enlarging all the motifs in the design. (A photostat or photocopy is convenient when the design is too complicated to enlarge by eye.) However, do not do this if the enlargement of the motifs significantly changes the scale of the design.

- *The original design is larger than the repeat size.* For example, the original design is 24 inches and the repeat is 18 inches. In this case, you must eliminate and/or combine motifs at the repeat line. When these changes are made, be sure that the area does not look either too crowded or too sparse. This can be checked by looking at the layout from a distance, or in a mirror in order to see it in a different perspective. Another way of checking the layout is to make a separate tracing of one particular motif, eliminating all the other elements in the design. This tracing will tell you at a glance whether the distribution of that motif balances in the layout. Separate tracings can then be made of other motifs to ensure that they are also distributed evenly.

- *The spaces formed by the background are not balanced.* If there is a conspicuous hole in the background, fill it either by moving the surrounding motifs or by adding other motifs. This may create new spaces in the background and require changing the position of some of the other motifs to obtain a balanced layout.

If a vertical, horizontal, or diagonal channel is being formed in the background that does not appear elsewhere in the design, a correction must be made. Always keep an eye on the overall layout. Moving

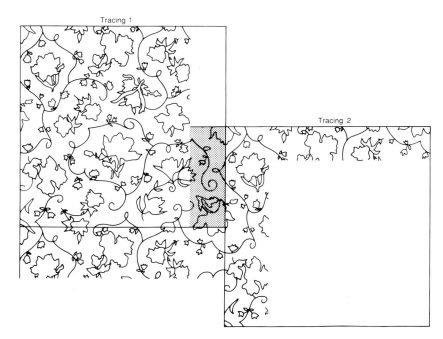

Step 6. The top of Tracing 2 placed at the lower half-drop line of Tracing 1 *(above)*. Tracing 2 moved to the upper part of the half-drop line *(below)*. The shaded areas in each illustration indicate additions that had to be made to complete the repeat.

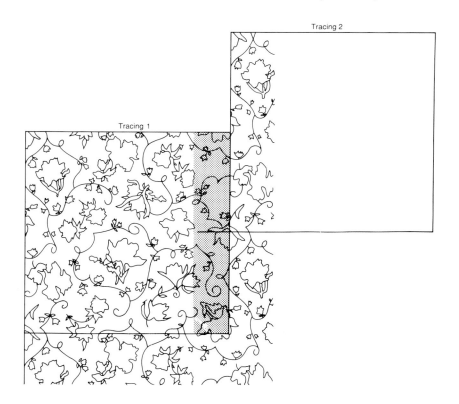

one motif can sometimes mean having to move many others in order to balance the spaces. Sometimes it is possible simply to take elements of motifs that already appear in the design, such as a leaf or small flower, and fill in an open spot. Make sure, however, that any additions are compatible with the surrounding area and the overall design. Also check to see whether the motifs are forming a line that does not appear elsewhere in the design. If they are, break up the line by redistributing some of the motifs. Also remember to distribute the motifs in two directions if the design requires it.

Again, let me emphasize that when you make a change or addition on one tracing you must make the same change on the other tracing so that the tracings will always match as you work back and forth between them.

STEP 6. YOU ARE NOW READY TO WORK OUT THE SIDE MEASUREMENT OF THE HALF-DROP REPEAT

Repeats for home furnishing designs, such as wallpaper, sheets, pillowcases, and most draperies, require a specific side measurement that divides equally into the side repeat size. On most apparel designs, however, the repeat artist can decide the width of the repeat; in this case, the number of times the pattern is repeated across the width of the fabric (from selvage to selvage) does not matter. This gives the artist the option of making the repeat wider or narrower, as is required to accommodate the motifs. If the design can be worked into a narrow repeat, it has the advantage of being a smaller area to paint.

In a repeat where the side measure is left to the discretion of the repeat artist, use the following procedure:

- Butt the top of Tracing 2 at the lower part of the half-drop line of Tracing 1. Decide within what measurement (narrower or wider) the lower part of the half-drop fits.
- Move the bottom of Tracing 2 to the upper part of the half-drop line of Tracing 1 and decide at what point the upper part of the half-drop fits. There is a possibility that one of the halves will require more space to fit the motifs, in which case the other half must be adjusted and moved to fit within that measurement. When you have determined the measurement that will accommodate both the upper and lower parts of the half-drop, draw in the side repeat line.

In a repeat where a specific side measurement is required, simply draw the side measurement on both tracings and begin at the following step:

- You are now ready to rearrange the motifs at the half-drop side repeat lines. Return Tracing 2 to the lower half-drop line on Tracing 1, and add, eliminate, or move motifs to make the design flow smoothly. (Again, any changes or additions that are made on one tracing must be made on the other tracing so that the two always match.)

- Return Tracing 2 to the upper part of the half-drop line on Tracing 1. Rearrange the motifs as you did on the bottom half-drop line, making sure that the motifs flow smoothly at the line where the two halves meet.
- Do not be afraid to place a motif on top of the repeat line that is drawn on the tracing paper because you think that all the motifs have to be enclosed within its rigid outline. On the contrary, placing the motifs in a tossed layout on the repeat line prevents the creation of an obvious space that frames the repeat and thus helps to create a layout with a continuous flow. If a motif is on the repeat line on the tracing paper, half of it will appear in one unit of repeat on the fabric and the other half of it will appear in the next unit.
- When you have completed the vertical and horizontal repeats, drawn neatly on Tracing 1 (if this is too messy, redraw the finished repeat on clean tracing paper), square off the repeat with a triangle; it is now ready to be prepared for painting. The artist is responsible for painting one full unit of the repeat plus small overlaps on the bottom and right sides, as shown below.

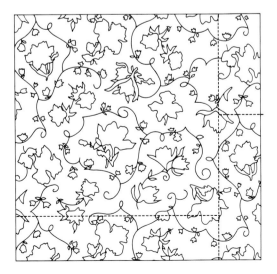

The completed tracing of the half-drop repeat, with small overlaps on the bottom and right sides, ready to prepare for painting. This illustrates the area of the repeat that must be painted.

STEP-BY-STEP GUIDE TO SQUARE REPEATS

Follow Steps 1 through 5 in the section on half-drop repeats, delete all half-drop lines, and proceed as follows:

1. Butt Tracing 2 next to Tracing 1 so that the top lines of both tracings align. Decide within what width measurement (narrower or wider) the motifs at the side repeat line will fit best. (If an exact side repeat size is given, any measurement that multiplies equally into that figure may be used.) Now draw in the side repeat line on both tracings.

2. You are now ready to rearrange the motifs at the side repeat line by eliminating, adding, moving, or combining motifs to make the design flow smoothly.

3. Tracing 2 can now be moved down to complete the square repeat, which is shown below, in the lower right-hand section.

4. When you have completed the square repeat, drawn neatly on Tracing 1 (if it is too messy, redraw it on clean tracing paper), square it off with a triangle; it is now ready to be prepared for painting. As with half-drop repeats, the artist is responsible for painting one full unit of the repeat plus small overlaps on the bottom and right sides.

Tracing 2 positioned next to Tracing 1, ready for the side repeat line to be determined. (For home furnishings, the side repeat usually divides equally into the width of the fabric.)

Tracing 1   Tracing 2

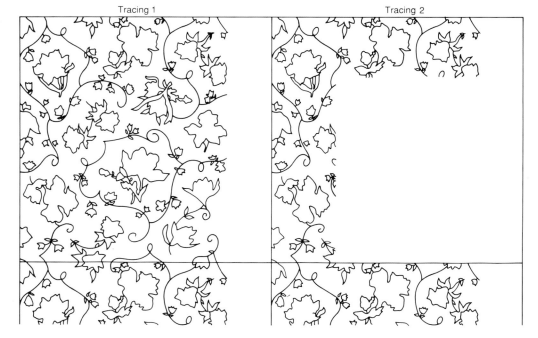

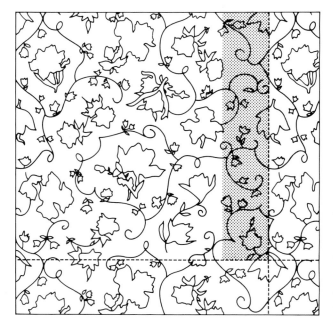

The completed square repeat. The shaded areas indicate additions or changes that had to be made at the side repeat line. This also illustrates the area of the repeat that must be painted.

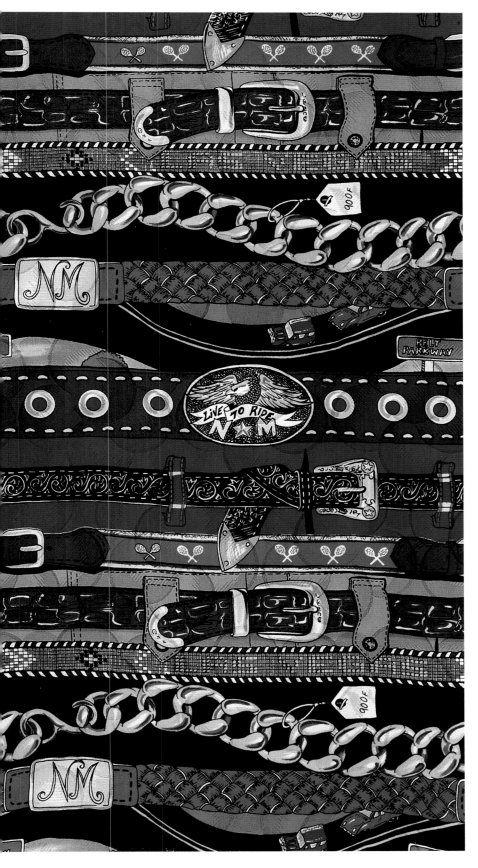

STRIPE REPEATS

As mentioned earlier in this chapter, a plain stripe pattern appears as a continuous stripe running the length of the fabric when printed. This kind of simple stripe requires only a side repeat, though most stripes are designed with other motifs and thus require both vertical and side repeats. When doing a stripe repeat, follow the step-by-step guide for half-drop and square repeats and the special instructions listed on the following page. Although a tossed design was used to illustrate the guide, the formula was devised to work for all types of designs.

A conversational designed in a horizontal stripe layout for apparel. *Copyright © Nicole Miller*

SPECIAL INSTRUCTIONS FOR STRIPE REPEATS

- A stripe repeat has a vertical and a side repeat that must be worked out for the design, as for any other repeat (follow Steps 1 through 5 for half-drop repeats). Note that the side repeat on a stripe design can be either a half-drop or a square.
- Always square off the paper with a triangle when you start a stripe layout. This gives you a horizontal line and a vertical line, from which you will measure the width of each stripe. A stripe can also be designed in a horizontal layout.
- Always measure the width of each stripe, even if the design calls for the motifs to be loosely laid out; that is, not entirely confined within the rigid outlines of the stripe. This is done so that the stripes will never be crooked.
- Measure the position of the motifs in each stripe so that they divide equally into the repeat size.
- Measure the spaces between the motifs in each stripe to be certain that they also divide equally into the repeat size.
- Remember that all the motifs in each stripe in the design, even minor ones, must be put into repeat, so that the design can be printed in a continuous flow.

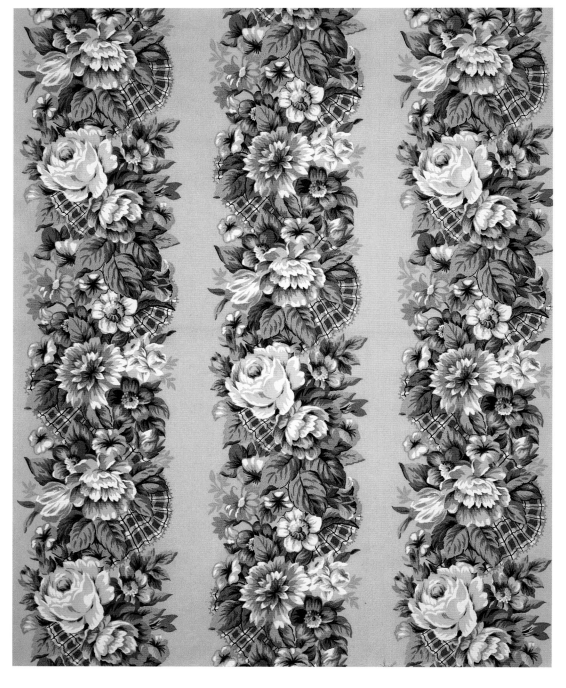

"Garden Walk," a pastel floral stripe for sheeting in a one-way half-drop repeat. *Cameo Interiors*

BORDER REPEATS

The unique characteristic of a border repeat is that it is turned so that the selvages are at the top and bottom of the design, instead of on either side. This ensures that the border will be printed down the entire length of the fabric.

A repeat of this type is sometimes called a *railroad repeat* and is done to accommodate the cutting needs of the customer, for instance, for some sheeting and upholstery designs. Another example is swimwear, where the direction in which the lycra fabric stretches determines the cut of the garment, and requires that the repeat be turned in this manner.

SPECIAL INSTRUCTIONS FOR BORDER REPEATS

- The pattern that appears above the border is called the *field*.
- Because the border on a design is printed along the selvage, the design is turned on its side when the repeat is made.
- A border is put into a vertical repeat the same way as for a stripe.
- The field is put into either a half-drop or a square repeat, with both a vertical and a side repeat.
- One full unit of the field painted in repeat is enough to indicate to the printer that the remainder of the field continues in the same way across the width of the fabric.

The correct position for a border design when working on the repeat. The dotted lines show the border and field repeat lines.

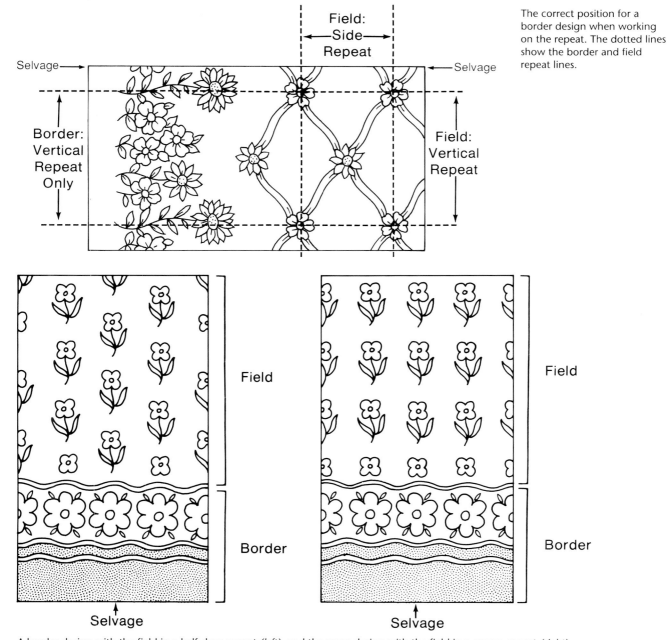

A border design with the field in a half-drop repeat *(left),* and the same design with the field in a square repeat *(right).*

BORDER DESIGNS WITH A FLIP REPEAT

Another variation on the border design shows a pattern with a border along both selvages. When folded in half, the design creates an exact mirror image of itself. This is called a *flip* or *flop repeat:* Half of the design is painted in repeat, then it is flipped (or flopped) during the printing process to complete the design across the width of the fabric.

Sometimes a pattern requires that only a quarter of the repeat be painted, because all four quarters are exactly the same. Flip repeats are usually found on designs for handkerchiefs, scarves, and towels as well as for some piece goods.

If you have a flip repeat in which the center motif is not a mirror image, paint half (or one quarter) of the design in repeat, plus the entire center motif. The rest of the design will be flipped during the printing process.

COLOR DISTRIBUTION

You will usually need to create a color distribution layout before you can begin to paint the completed repeat. Unless a color change has been requested by the stylist, the distribution of the colors in the repeat should closely resemble that of the original design; however, as is the case with motifs, colors can be moved around wherever necessary to balance them.

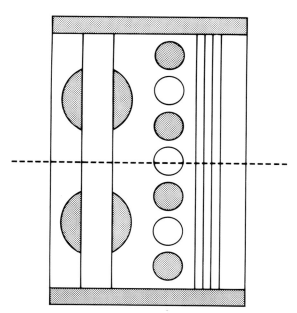

A design for a towel that creates a mirror image when folded in half. Only half of the design has to be painted for the repeat, as indicated by the dotted line; the other half is flipped in the printing process. This is called a *flip* or *flop repeat.*

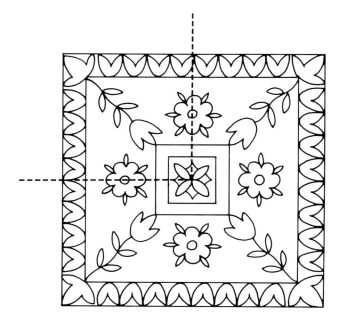

(Above) A scarf design in which all four quarters are the same. Only one quarter has to be painted for this flip repeat.

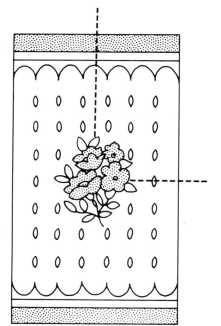

(Left) A flip repeat on a towel in which only the center motif is not a mirror image. One quarter of this design plus the full center motif must be painted for the repeat.

To create a color distribution layout, place a clean sheet of tracing paper on top of the repeat. Use colored pencils, crayons, or just letters—for example, Y for yellow, B for blue, and R for red—to indicate the different colors. Separate tracings can be made of each color to double check that the color distribution balances in the overall layout, and especially at the repeat lines. Often one color will be overrepresented at the repeat line as a result of the redistribution of the motifs. To correct this, rework the distribution of that color; the surrounding colors often have to be changed as well.

When you are satisfied that the color distribution is correct, you are then ready to mix your paints. Make sure to mix enough of all the colors to finish painting the repeat and have some left over for touch-ups.

PAINTING REPEATS ON OPAQUE PAPER

When painting a repeat on opaque paper, use one of the following two methods to transfer the repeat from the tracing paper to the drawing paper:

1. Back one full unit of the tracing in pencil before rubbing it down (see "Rubbing Down a Tracing," in Chapter 6). Always rub down the same unit when you move the tracing to the half-drop or square repeat lines. This is a good way to check on the correctness of the repeat. If the rubdown does not match up at all the repeat lines, you can identify the error and make the correction on the tracing before you start painting.

2. Trace the repeat onto the drawing paper with Saral transfer paper (see Chapter 3). Of course, if a ground is required it must be painted before the repeat is transferred.

The next step is to measure out the repeat lines on the drawing paper. Do not make heavy pencil marks on the drawing paper, unless the drawing paper permits easy erasures or you will eventually cover them with opaque paint. Register marks are usually sufficient.

Position the tracing on the drawing paper, matching the repeat lines or register marks exactly. Tape the tracing down and either rub down or trace (using transfer paper) the repeat on the drawing paper. Next, move the tracing to the vertical repeat line, match up the repeat lines, and rub down a small overlap of the repeat. Move the tracing to the right, to the lower part of the half-drop or the square, and match up the repeat lines. Rub down the overlap. Finally, move the tracing to the upper part of the half-drop and rub down that section. Square off the completed repeat with a triangle and you are ready to start painting.

Keep the original design in clear view as you paint. The tracing tells you where to paint but doesn't show the technique or the subtleties of painting the motifs. Only the original design, whether it was created by you or someone else, can indicate this. Look at the original design frequently as you paint to make sure, for example, that the flowers are not becoming too large or the leaves too heavy. Remember, the customer has bought a design and expects the repeat to look as much like it as possible, even though layout changes have been made.

If the repeat does not require too many changes from the original design, and a large portion of the original matches the repeat exactly in layout and color spotting, it may be possible to use part of the original in the repeat. Carefully cut out the usable section with an X-Acto knife or scissor and paste or tape

it on a fresh piece of drawing paper. Use the same procedure as above: Draw register marks on the drawing paper and rub down or trace the remainder of the repeat. You can save time in doing the repeat by pasting up a portion of the design in this fashion.

PAINTING REPEATS ON WAXED RICE PAPER

When painting a repeat on waxed rice paper, there are a few special instructions to follow. Because it is hard to make erasures on waxed rice paper, you should not use a pencil to rub down or trace. Work out the complete repeat on tracing paper with the overlaps on the bottom and right. The tracing should be clear and accurate. Double check the repeat lines before starting to paint.

Next, place a sheet of waxed rice paper (which is transparent) on top of the tracing, and proceed to paint the repeat. Be sure that the waxed rice paper is taped or tacked down so it does not slip while you are painting. Finish the repeat, following the same procedure as described for painting on opaque paper.

When painting repeats, some designers prefer to fill in one color wherever it appears on the repeat before going on to the next color. Others prefer to complete all the colors in one section of the design, and then go on to paint the next area. Each person should work in the manner most comfortable for him or her. It is sometimes helpful to use one brush for each color.

When you have finished painting the repeat and erased all of the pencil lines, square the repeat off with a triangle, trim it, and mount it if necessary. It will then be used at the mill to prepare the next step in printing the fabric.

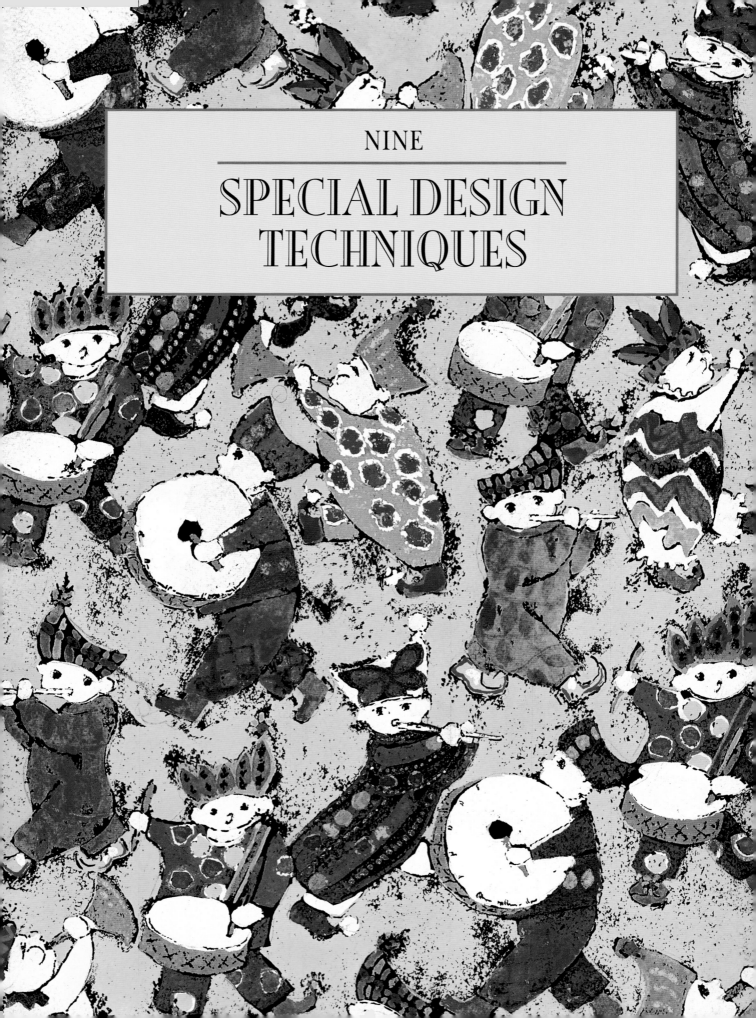

NINE

SPECIAL DESIGN
TECHNIQUES

A whimsical children's design done in the India ink–woodblock technique, which is discussed on page 136. *Copyright © Un Soo Lee, designer*

Designers must master a repertoire of special techniques to accommodate changing fashion trends and to create new looks. A portfolio with a variety of designs rendered in different surface textures is most desirable. A beginning designer's value to a studio often depends on his or her ability to imitate designs that contain special effects. This chapter describes some of these techniques, which can be used to create new designs or to enhance existing ones: batik, bleach effects, flower shading, stippling, sponge, spatter, warp, drybrush, India ink–woodblock, and photocopy. Various methods for touch-ups and corrections are also covered.

In this design, done with bleach on a dye background, the dark green ground was painted first; next, the black outlines were drawn in waterproof ink; bleach was then applied to all the motifs to make them white. Finally, red, blue, and yellow dyes were added to the bleached white motifs. Some motifs were left all white. Background vines were then added in pen and black India ink. Refer to page 125 for detailed instructions for the bleach technique.

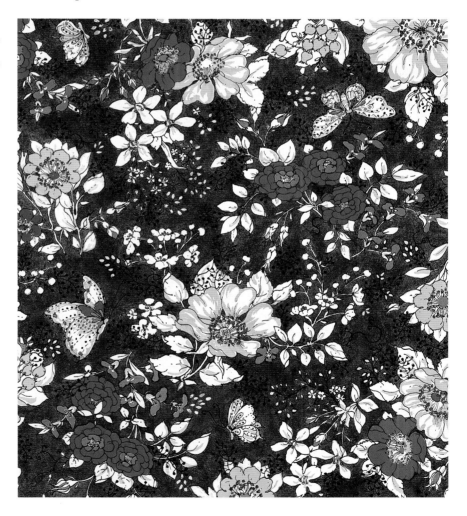

BATIK TECHNIQUE

Batik is an ancient wax resist method of printing designs on fabric. A design is applied in wax to the surface of the fabric, the fabric is then dipped into dye, and the areas that have been waxed resist penetration by that color. The wax for the first color is then removed, and additional designs can then be applied in wax to obtain different patterns and colors. A unique characteristic of batik is the crackle effect that is caused when the wax cracks and dye penetrates through the cracks to the fabric. However, we are not concerned here with batiking on fabric. The textile designer must imitate this crackle effect on paper so that when the design is printed commercially, the fabric will have a batik look.

BATIKING SUPPLIES

- A completed design painted in dyes, preferably on Tweed-weave, Bristol, or other watercolor paper, although designs on waxed rice paper can also be batiked. The design should be of the type that lends itself to the batik look, such as exotic florals, tropicals, and Asian, African, or similar ethnic motifs.
- A piece of waxed rice paper (this can be imperfect; refer to Step 1, below).
- Dyes. Sepia is a good neutral batik color that works well on most designs. Deep colors, such as red, blue, or grey, might also be suitable. A monotone design can be batiked with the same color.
- A No. 7 or 8 brush, or a small ground brush.
- A roll of paper towels.
- Wax Grip, Non Crawl, and/or liquid soap.
- Test paper. This can be the same kind that will be used for the batik. An old design or a piece of scrap paper will do.
- Scrap paper, to spread under the work to avoid mess.

(Do not use newspaper for this purpose as the print may stain your design.)

STEP-BY-STEP GUIDE TO BATIKING

There are several ways to create a batik effect on paper. The advantage of the following method is that you can apply the batik on top of any design painted in dye colors, often greatly enhancing it.

1. Take a piece of waxed rice paper, about 5 or 6 inches square. Crush it slowly in your hand, working firmly but gently, inch by inch, starting at the edges. Finish by crumpling the paper into a ball in the palm of your hand. Try not to tear it, but don't worry if you make a small rip. The crushed wax on the rice paper creates the cracks through which the dye will penetrate onto the design. After you have crushed the paper, flatten and smooth it out. Hold it up to the light and to see the cracks that will form the batik pattern when the dye is pressed through it.

2. Mix a few drops of Wax Grip or liquid soap in the dye to be used for the batik color. (Some designers prefer to apply Wax Grip or soap directly on the crackle paper.) Using either of these mediums helps to push the dye through the cracks; try both and decide which works better for you.

3. Next, apply a few strokes of dye on the crackle paper with your brush, leaving the edges unpainted so that the paper can be handled. Lay the crackle paper on the test paper, *dye side up*, and with a crushed paper towel press down, stroke, and push the dye through the cracks to the test paper underneath.

4. Lift the crackle paper to see how the batik effect has transferred onto the test paper. If the crackle is not coming through, press down again with the paper towel. Then try adding a little more Wax Grip to the dye or test paper. If the design still does not transfer, it probably means that the crackle paper is not cracked enough. Start over and crush another piece of waxed rice paper, this time more vigorously. If too much color is being transferred through the crackle paper, you have used either too much dye or too much Wax Grip.

5. When the batik effect looks right on the test paper, immediately place the crackle paper on top of the design to be batiked, dye side up, and press the batik through with the paper towel. Move the crackle paper to a new area on the design; after pressing it down, lift it again to check the batik effect. Add more color on the crackle paper as needed. When adding more color, test the crackle effect again on scrap paper before transferring it to the design. If the crackle paper is worn, throw it away and crush a new piece. Repeat this procedure until the design is covered with batik.

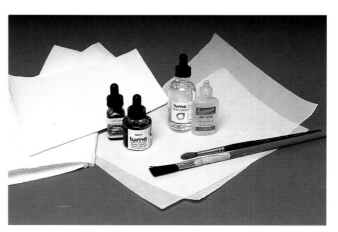

The supplies needed for batiking.

Step 1. Crush the waxed rice paper starting at the edges.

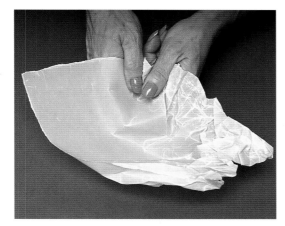

Step 2. Flatten the crushed paper.

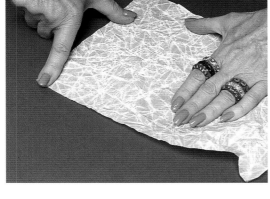

Step 3. Apply the dye (with Wax Grip) to the crackle paper.

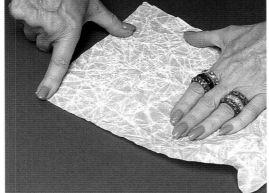

Step 4. On a piece of test paper, push the dye through the crackle paper with paper towels. Then lift up the crackle paper to check the batik effect. Repeat until the batik looks satisfactory.

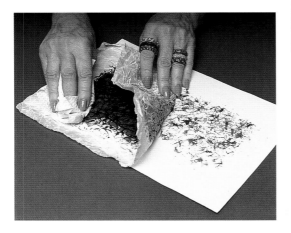

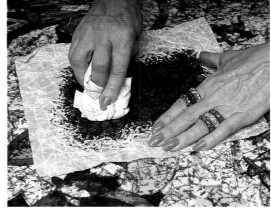

Step 5. Transfer the final batik onto the design.

The design fully covered with batik. *Copyright © Frank Delfino, designer*

By using a small piece of crackle paper, you get maximum control over the batiking process. You are able to move the crackle paper easily from area to area, checking the results as you work. You can add more batik, if needed, by pressing the crackle paper on an area two or three times.

It is also possible to use a large piece of crushed wax rice paper that is then placed over the entire design. Flatten out the crushed paper, place it on a test paper, and apply the Wax Grip and dye with a large ground brush. Press the batik through to the test paper with paper towels. When you determine that the large crackle pattern on the test paper looks right, place the crackle paper over your design and transfer the batik effect by pressing down with long strokes with the paper towels. Lift the crackle paper occasionally to check the batik effect. Add more color, if needed, and press down harder on areas where the batik is too light.

Incidentally, it is possible to reverse the process by starting with a batik background and painting the design on top of it. To do this, apply the crushed wax rice paper directly to a fresh piece of drawing paper and press the dye through it to create a batik background, ready for design.

BLEACH BATIK EFFECT

By substituting bleach for dye, the same method of batiking may be used to create a white or light batik on a design. This is especially helpful in areas where the design looks too heavy and dark. The combination of dark and light batik effects works very well on some designs. Wax Grip must be used with the bleach.

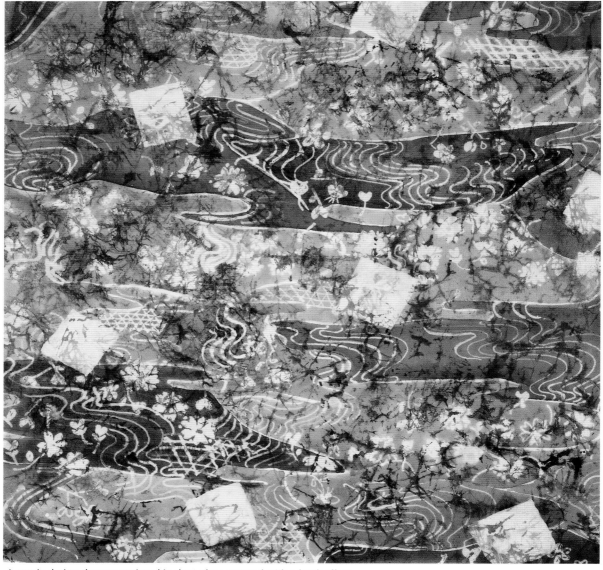

A scenic design that was painted in dyes, then covered with a batik effect.

BLEACH TECHNIQUE

The bleach technique is used on designs with a dye background, and is an alternative to painting the background around the motifs (called *blotching;* see Chapter 7). The bleach removes areas of color from a dye ground, making it possible to apply a new color to these areas, or to leave them white. This technique is particularly effective when light or bright colors will be used on darker grounds.

STEP-BY-STEP GUIDE TO DESIGNING WITH BLEACH ON A DYE BACKGROUND

1. Mix the dye and paint the ground (see "Making Colored Grounds," in Chapter 7). Save any leftover dye for touch-ups.

2. If the ground is painted on opaque paper, transfer the design to it by using either the rubdown method (see Chapter 6) or the transfer paper method (see Chapter 3). If the ground is painted on waxed rice paper, the design should be clearly drawn on tracing paper first. The waxed rice paper ground is then taped on top of the tracing and ready for painting. Dark grounds may require the use of a light box.

3. If there are fineline outlines in the design, draw them on the ground with waterproof ink or waterproof Magic Marker.

4. Decide on the color distribution so you can determine which motifs to bleach out. On motifs where the dye colors can be painted on top of the background color, it is not necessary to bleach them out. For example, orange, red, or green can usually be painted over a yellow ground without changing them in any significant way. Most colors painted on a beige ground, however, will be slightly muted but still will look fine. If you are uncertain about whether to bleach an area or not, test colors first. You may also want to bleach out all the motifs first and decide on the colors later.

5. A toothpick is best for applying bleach to small areas; use a cotton swab or something similar for larger areas. You may also apply bleach with an old brush. (Never use a good brush, as the bleach will eat away the bristles.) If using a toothpick, start by applying several drops of bleach in the center of the area you are working on, then push the drops toward the edges of the area, trying not to touch or go beyond the outlines of the motif with the bleach. However, if the bleach does go over the outline, the affected area can be touched up with matching color later. Waterproof ink lines should not bleach out. If this happens, change to fresh waterproof ink and touch up the bleached-out lines by carefully inking them over.

6. Leave the bleach on the motif for about a minute, then carefully

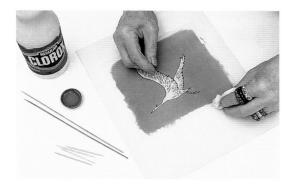

blot it up with a tissue. Do not leave the bleach on the paper too long and do not cover large areas with bleach or the surface of the paper will be eaten away. If the area does not look white enough after one application, apply the bleach again. The lighter the ground color, the faster the bleach will work. Dark grounds may retain a slight residue of color on bleached areas. This should not present a problem, as the color you apply over it will cover them. If you want the area to remain pure white, try another coat of bleach, or paint over it with Pro White.

7. Let the bleached areas dry well before reapplying color, or the new color will be eaten away by the residue of bleach on the paper.

Bleach can be used on designs painted in dyes to obtain different special effects. Use your imagination to create other effects with bleach.

Applying the bleach with a toothpick to make the feather treatment on the motif.

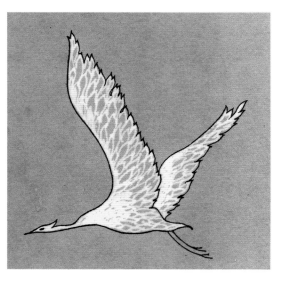

In this illustration, the dye background was painted first; then the outlines of the bird were drawn with waterproof ink. Finally, the white feather effect was achieved by drawing with a toothpick dipped in bleach.

THREE-DIMENSIONAL FLOWER-SHADING TECHNIQUES

Because flowers are the most frequently used motifs in textile design, a designer's ability to draw and shade them is very important. There are three simple ways to shade flowers to achieve a three-dimensional look. Dye, gouache, or tempera can be used in all of these techniques.

1. To create a three-dimensional look using three related colors, use the following technique:

- Mix three related colors (home furnishing designs sometimes use four or more related colors) in either gouache or dye: one light, one medium, and one dark. These can be either three tones of the same color—for instance, dark blue, medium blue, and light blue—or they can be colors that are related but not the same, such as red, orange, and yellow.
- Paint each petal separately. Start by applying paint to the petal near the center of the flower. The petal can either be entirely covered, or the ground color can be allowed to show

through. When applying paint, always be certain to follow the contour of the petal, as will provide the natural flow of the shading effect. Another method would be to apply the lightest color over the whole petal, then paint the medium color on top, and finally the darkest.

- Start with the lightest shade, applying each color separately, shaping the petal as you paint. Follow with the medium color, and apply the darkest color last. Small highlights of color or white can be added to enhance the three-dimensional effect. Ink or paint outlines or stipple effects can now be applied as finishing touches.

2. To achieve a three-dimensional look using one color, shading from dark to light (creating an *ombré effect*), use the following technique:

- Work on each petal separately. Paint a shape with the color, starting at the inside of the petal. As you apply the paint, always follow the contour of the petal.
- Quickly clean the brush (or use a second clean one), then

moisten it slightly. Begin shading the color, dark to light, toward the outer edge of the petal. Smooth out the shading to your liking.

- To make the flower look more realistic, one side can be shaded more heavily than the other. Highlights of the full-strength color or white can be added for emphasis. Once you have mastered this simple shading technique, you can create your own variations of it on leaves and other motifs. A good way to practice is to copy flowers from printed fabrics. Trace the motifs, and, using the techniques described above, paint them. This will help you develop an important skill. A good copy, along with the printed fabric, can be included in your portfolio.

3. Another very simple way to make a flower look three-dimensional is by using one flat color to shape the flower, without shading from dark to light. Once again, always follow the contour of the petal when you apply the paint.

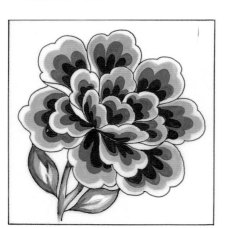

A flower in which three separate but related colors were used to create a three-dimensional look.

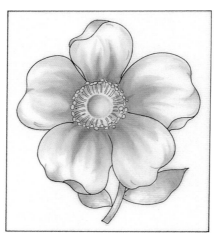

A flower shaded from dark to light using one color to achieve a three-dimensional effect.

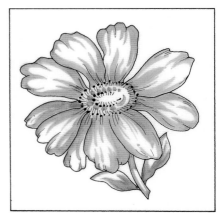

A three-dimensional look achieved by painting the contours of the flower with just one flat color.

STIPPLING

Stippling is a method of using small dots instead of lines or solid areas for shading motifs and backgrounds. Tools that can be used to create stipple effects are pen and ink, brush and paint, Magic Marker, technical pen, and a special dotting pen (see Chapter 3). Depending on the design, gouache, dye, colored pencil, and crayon can also be used to make the stipple dots.

Darker shading is achieved by placing the dots closer together. By gradually dispersing the dots, or by using gradations of color, from dark to light, a dark-to-light shaded effect is attained.

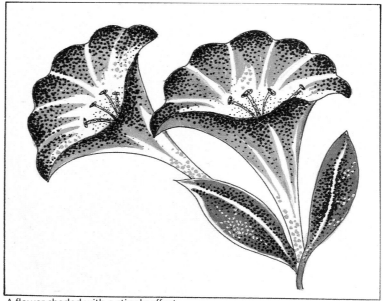

A flower shaded with a stipple effect.

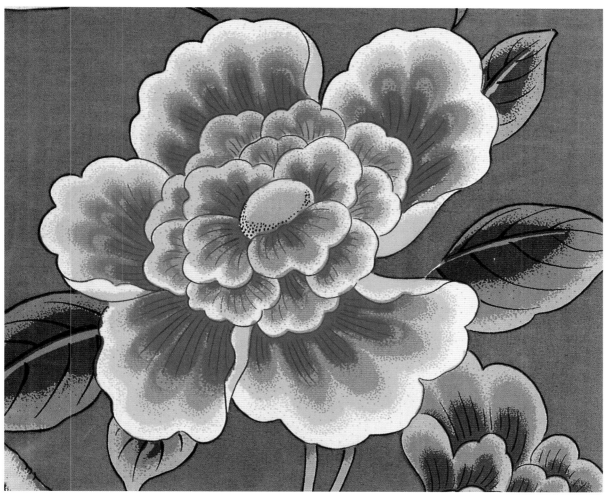

This flower uses several shades of the same color, enhanced by stipple work flowing into each color.

SPATTERING

The spatter technique uses a toothbrush and spoon to create shaded color effects that resemble those made by an airbrush. Spattering is similar to stippling, but can produce finer shading more quickly.

STEP-BY-STEP GUIDE TO SPATTERING

1. Mask off any areas on the design not to be spattered. This can be done with frisket sheets, masking tape, or liquid frisket, or by cutting a stencil and weighting down the edges with coins or positioning it with a touch of double-faced tape. Masking materials are lifted off when the spatter is finished. Other areas can then be masked off if a second color is needed, and the process repeated. Clear your work surface and cover the table before you begin, as spatter has a way of covering everything nearby.

2. Using either gouache or dyes, mix the color to be used for the spatter in a small container.

3. Hold the toothbrush—*bristle side up*—in your left hand between your thumb and index finger (use your right hand if you are left-handed). Hold the handle firmly, close to the bristles.

4. For maximum leverage, stand up over the design. Apply a brushful of paint to the toothbrush. Hold the toothbrush, *bristle side up*, and point it downward over the design. Hold the spoon in the other hand between your thumb and index finger. The inside edge of the bowl of the spoon should be tilted toward you, *facing down* over the bristles, at about a 45-degree angle.

5. Begin the spatter by making quick, short strokes with the lower edge of the spoon, *starting at the tip of the toothbrush,* moving up the length of the bristles, *always toward you.* Do not stroke away from

yourself, as the paint will spatter on you instead of the design.

6. Spattering steadily, move the brush and spoon at an even pace over each area to be covered. To make a heavier spatter, go over the area as many times as are necessary. To lighten an area that has been spattered too heavily, respatter with either white or the ground color. Bleach can also be

spattered on a dye design for a light textured effect that will be the same color as the original paper.

7. Always test the spatter first on scrap paper to make certain the density of the color is appropriate. The heaviest spray will occur when you first begin the spatter. As you continue, the spray will become finer. Add more paint to the toothbrush as needed.

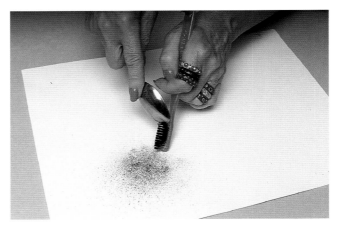

The proper way to hold the toothbrush and the spoon. Always start spattering at the front tip of the bristles, moving the spoon toward you.

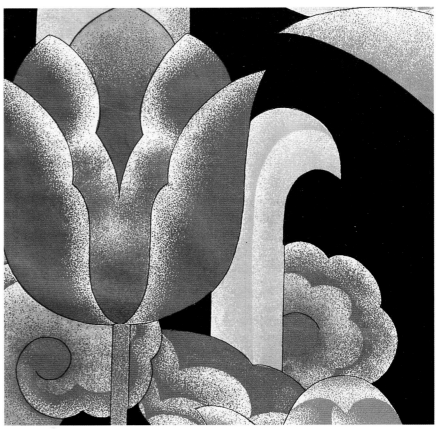

A detail of the spatter technique clearly showing the shaded effect. The complete design is shown opposite.

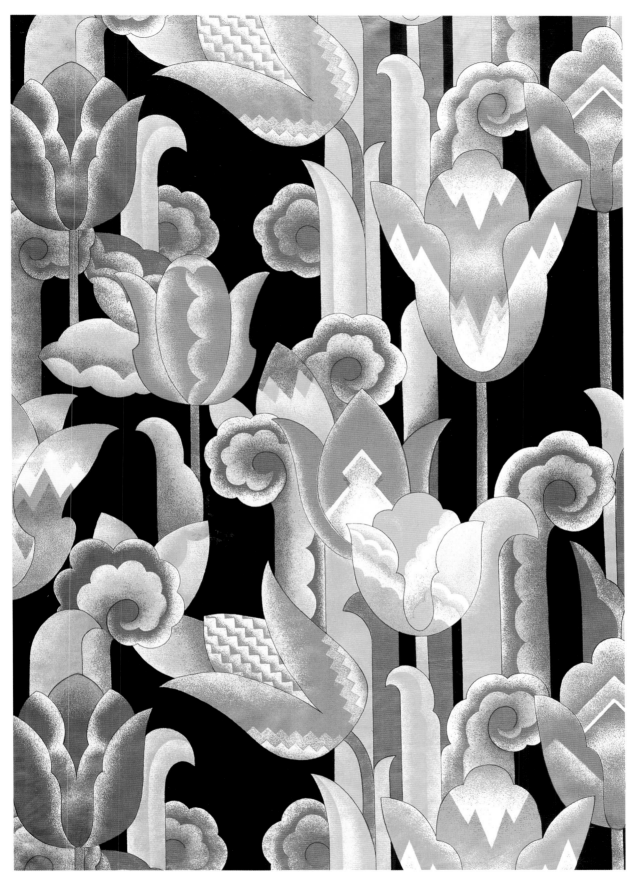

"Hollandaise," a stylized floral rendered with the spatter technique. *Clarence House Imports, Ltd.*

Spatter can be used to shade flowers and other motifs, or to create textured background effects, and to create plaids and stripes when a woven look is desired. Spatter does not produce shading as fine as an airbrush, but its advantages are that it is easier to reproduce, it is ecologically less toxic, and it is done with very inexpensive equipment, eliminating the need for an airbrush and compressor.

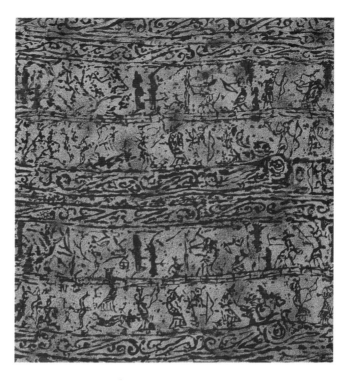

A design taken from Egyptian motifs in which spatter is used to create a textured background.

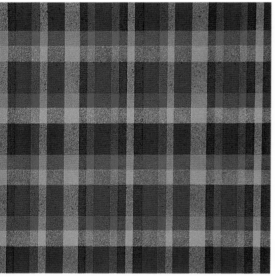

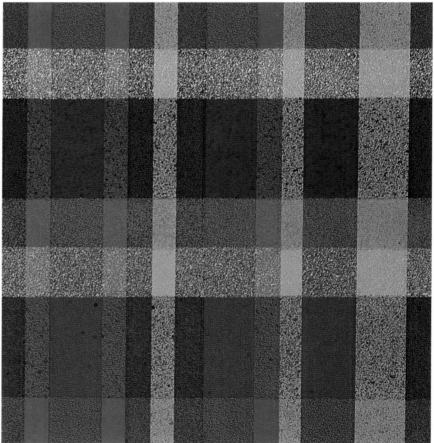

A plaid in which areas were masked off and spatter applied to create a woven effect *(above)*. A detail of the same pattern is shown at right. *Designed by Sheila and Lee Stewart, Lee Stewart Associates Incorporated*

SPONGE TECHNIQUE

The sponge technique is used to create textured effects on flowers or other motifs by using a sponge to daub paint on the design. Different sponges can be used according to the needs of the design. Fine-textured sponges can be purchased at cosmetic counters. Household sponges will create a coarser effect. The sponge itself can be cut into a shape and applied directly to the design. The sponge technique can also be used to form textured background effects.

Apply the paint to the sponge with a brush or dip the bottom of the sponge directly into the paint. Test the sponge on scrap paper to make certain the paint does not blob. The final test on the scrap paper should result in a suitable texture for your design. The textured effect can be heavy or light, depending on the pressure you put on the sponge.

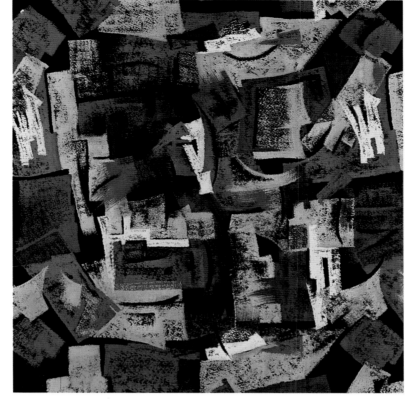

The textured effect on this abstract design *(above)* was made by using a sponge cut into wide strips to apply gouache paints directly to the black ground (see detail, *below*). Copyright © Frank Delfino, designer

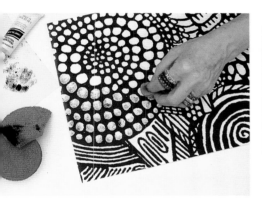

Applying a textured effect with a sponge. *Copyright © by Jason L. Peterson*

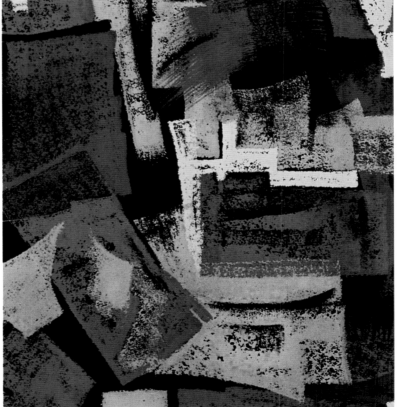

WARP TECHNIQUE

A warp effect on a design emphasizes the vertical or horizontal threads that can be seen on a woven fabric. The vertical threads are called the *warp* and the horizontal threads are called the *weft*. A warp look may be simulated by either painting or using pen and ink on top of and around the edges of the motifs. The warp effect can also be used in the background to give the whole design a woven look.

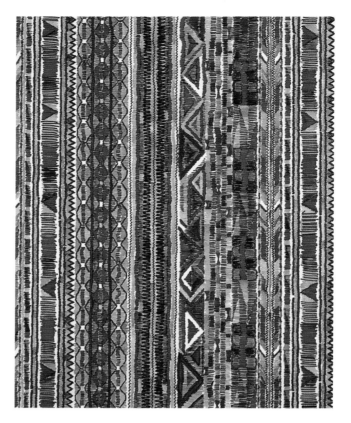

A warp stripe in which the woven effect is painted horizontally. *Copyright © Glenda Heffer, designer*

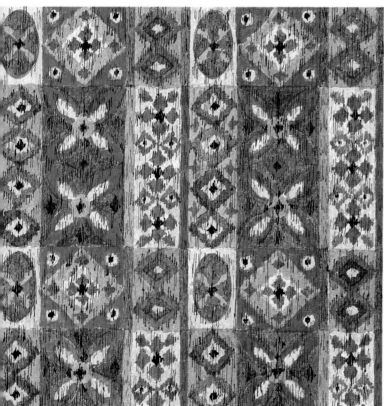

The warp effect on this geometric apparel pattern is drawn with vertical pen and ink lines on top of the painted design.

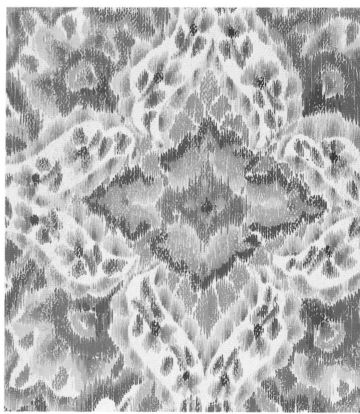

A detail of the tapestry warp pattern *(opposite),* enlarged to show the fine warp effect.

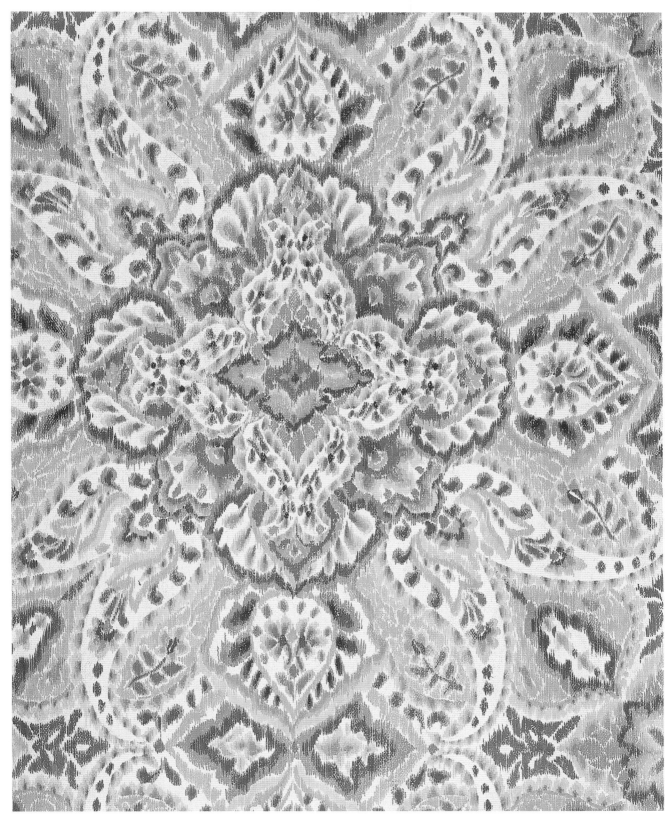

A home furnishing tapestry pattern in which paints were used to create the effect. *Copyright © Lynn Johnson, designer*

EMBROIDERY TECHNIQUE

A design can be painted entirely of embroidery stitches, or stitches can be used on top of and around the edges of the motifs so that they appear to be sewn onto the background, creating an appliqué look. Such effects, done in gouache or dye with a small brush, felt-tip pens, or pen and ink, are very effective in achieving a patchwork, folk art, or ethnic look for apparel and home furnishing.

Embroidery and appliqué techniques can be used with a variety of layouts, including all-overs, borders, and stripes. Color combinations can range from bright or dark grounds to subtle pastel tones.

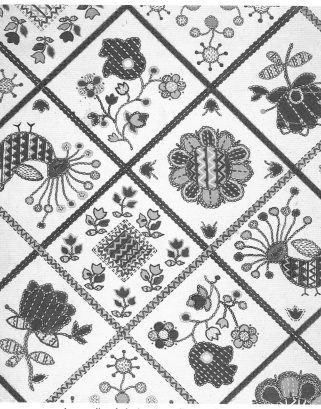

An appliqué design in a diamond layout. Stitching is used in and around all the motifs.

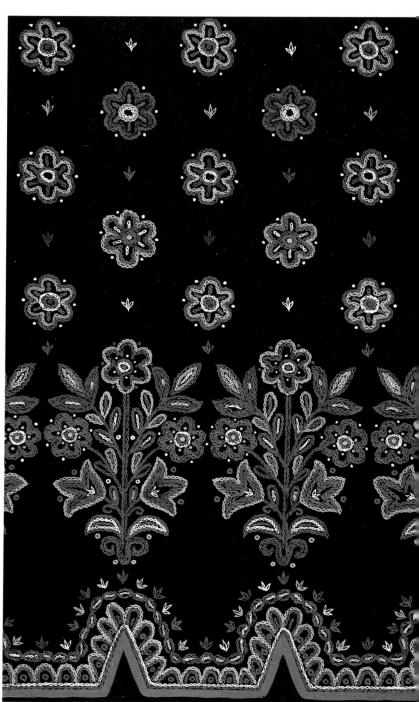

A folk art border design painted entirely with brightly colored "stitches" on a black background.

DRYBRUSH TECHNIQUE

The drybrush technique is used to paint a shaded effect with a brush stroke. Dip the brush into the paint (which should have a thick, creamy consistency) and stroke it back and forth on scrap paper, removing enough paint so that the paper shows through when a stroke is made. When the brush stroke is satisfactory, start painting your design, repeating the procedure as needed. Drybrush can be used for both motifs and backgrounds.

"Applause," a sheet design of splashy flowers done in the drybrush technique. *Cameo Interiors*

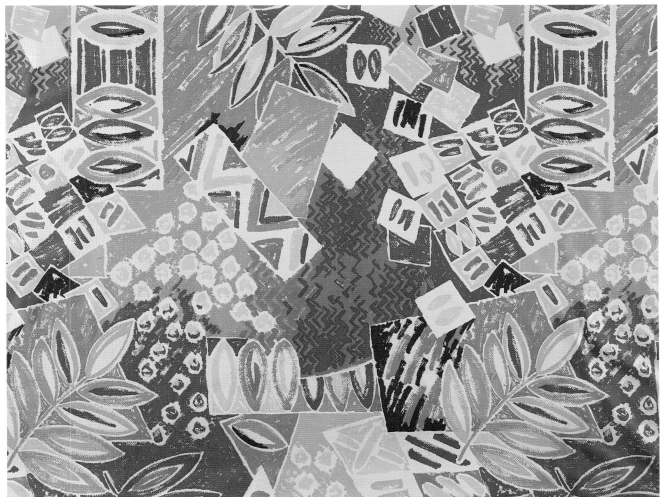

"Calypso," a modern home furnishing design of geometrics and leaves done in the drybrush technique. *Designed by Marilyn Schroeder for Bruck Textiles*

INDIA INK–WOODBLOCK TECHNIQUE

This technique simulates a woodblock or handblocked look. It is most effective on tropical florals, jungle, and animal patterns, as well as on African, Native American, Asian, and other ethnic geometric designs.

STEP-BY-STEP GUIDE TO THE INDIA INK–WOODBLOCK TECHNIQUE

Before trying it on a finished design, get the feel of this technique by working on a small sample design first, carefully following all of the steps.

1. Draw, rub down, or trace the design on three- or four-ply watercolor paper (use no lighter weight than Georgian).

2. Paint thick white gouache over all the areas that will be white in the final design. Use two coats if necessary.

3. Paint in all the other gouache colors. Always apply paint thickly, as it will act as a resist to the ink. It is best to mix your original colors a little stronger or darker to make up for any pigment that washes off.

4. Let dry for four or five hours, or overnight if possible.

5. Paint over the entire design with Pelikan Black Opaque Ink. Use a cheap ground brush, as the ink will ruin it. For colors other than black, use "Special Opaque" ink; other types are too thin and will streak.

6. Let the ink dry for four or five hours, or overnight if possible.

7. Hold the design under a water faucet or sprayer, using light to medium water pressure to control the flow. The ink will wash off all of the painted areas, revealing the color or white underneath, but will adhere to the parts left unpainted, which will remain black. Small bits and textured effects of ink will stick to colors throughout the design, enhancing the woodblock effect.

8. You may now touch up the design by adding to or strengthening any of the colors or by evening out the black textured effect. Use the drybrush technique or a finely textured cosmetic sponge dipped into thick gouache (wipe the excess from the sponge on scrap paper first). Remember that more color can be applied because some may have washed off; more of the textured effect can then be applied to balance the look.

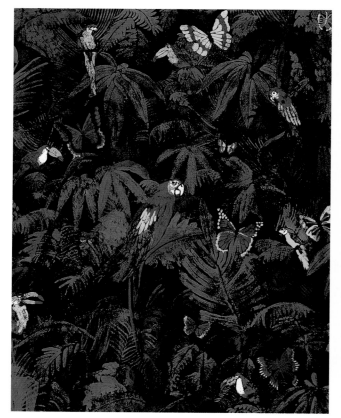

A tropical jungle pattern rendered in the India ink–woodblock technique. *Copyright © Joan Gampert, designer*

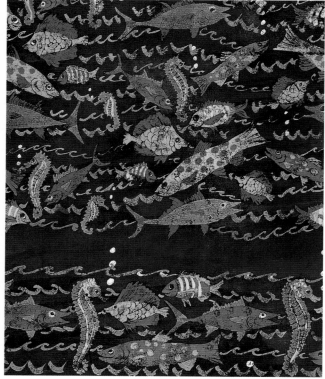

An India ink–woodblock tropical fish pattern. *Copyright © Joan Gampert, designer*

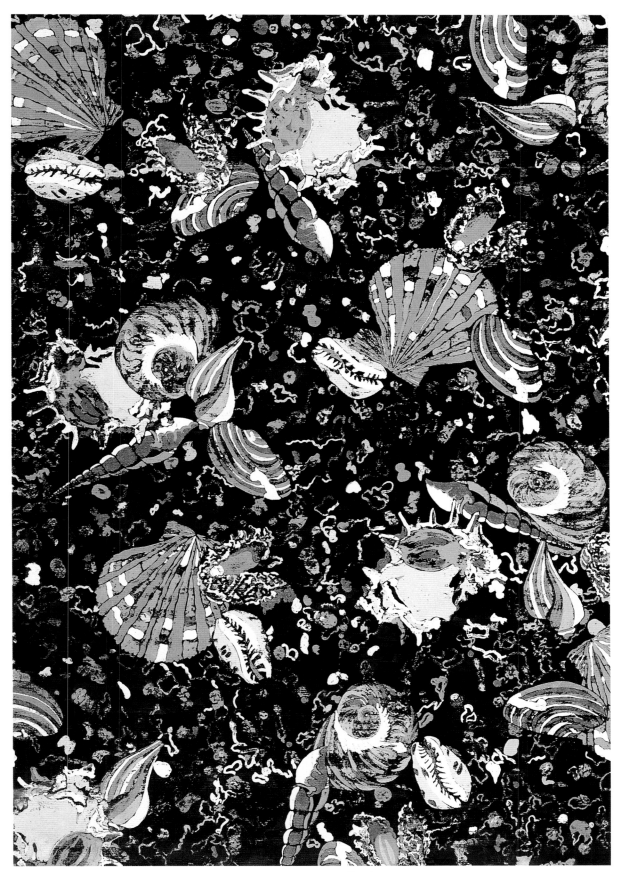

An India ink–woodblock seashell theme pattern. *Copyright © Glenda Heffer, designer*

QUICK PHOTOCOPY TECHNIQUES

A quick way to create a design is to use multiple photocopies of motifs, then paste them together in a layout to form a pattern. This technique can save much time and labor. It is used mostly for apparel designs, and only then when the subtle differences of handpainting are not required. It is often most effective when combined with painted areas. The following sample designs were all created with photocopy techniques.

SAMPLE DESIGN: PHOTOCOPIED BUTTERFLIES

1. The bright geometric pattern in the background was painted first with gouache or transparent dyes.

2. Next, a stencil of the butterfly form was drawn on a piece of heavy paper and cut out with a scissor or an X-Acto knife.

3. The black-and-white patterns of the butterflies were taken from pages in a book of Japanese stencil designs. Each page was photocopied several times.

4. The butterfly stencil shape was then placed on top of several copies of the black-and-white patterns and cut out with a scissor or an X-Acto knife. This was repeated until enough butterflies were cut out to complete the design.

5. The butterflies were then arranged in a balanced tossed layout directly on top of the painted background. The butterflies were held in place temporarily with a small piece of double-faced tape so that they could be lifted and moved around easily to achieve the most desirable layout. The butterflies were then pasted down in place (rubber cement, a glue stick, or other paste was used).

6. For the final step, a color photocopy was made of the finished design to avoid a messy look, as the pasted-down edges of the black-and-white photocopies tend to peel up. Two 11 × 14 inch color copies can be pasted together to accommodate larger designs. When overlapping the edges to paste two copies together, sometimes the motifs will not line up exactly. In this case, trim the motifs on the edge of the overlapping copy so that they will join the corresponding motifs and background spaces on the second copy. When cutting the overlapping motifs, keep them complete whenever possible to get a nice fit. Occasionally, the second copy must also be trimmed, with the two overlapping back and forth. When you are satisfied with the look, paste them down.

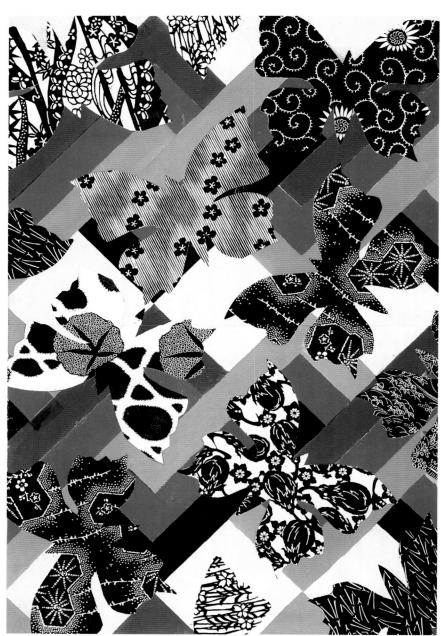

Sample Design: Photocopied Butterflies. The butterflies in this design were photocopied, cut out, and pasted on a painted background.

SAMPLE DESIGN: PHOTOCOPIED TEXTURED EFFECT

1. The background textured effect was photocopied from a book of decorative surfaces. At the copy shop, ask to have your photocopies printed on heavier paper, or bring your own. This will prevent the wet paint from warping the thin photocopy paper.

2. The outlines of the leaves were painted with waterproof India ink on top of the texture.

3. The leaves and background colors were painted in with transparent dyes.

4. Bleach was applied with a toothpick to bleach out the white details on the leaves and in the background.

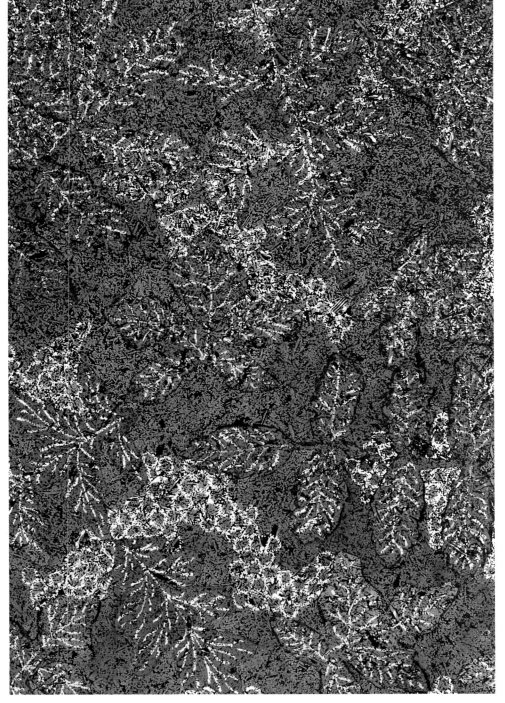

Sample Design: Photocopied Textured Effect. An apparel leaf pattern painted on top of a photocopied textured background. *Copyright © Susan Toplitz, designer*

SAMPLE DESIGN: PHOTOCOPIED AFRICAN MOTIF

1. Taken from an African costume, the black-and-white geometric designs were sketched loosely on one page with Magic Marker to imitate a handblocked look. The sketches were in the shape of five or six different rectangles, each containing a variety of motifs.

2. The page of sketches was then photocopied several times.

The rectangles were cut out, arranged in a balanced layout, and pasted together.

3. A photocopy was then made of the pasted-up design to obtain a flat surface. Again, use a paper that is heavier than standard photocopy paper.

4. The multicolored plaid was measured out, drawn in pencil on the photocopy, and painted with transparent dyes. (Gouache or

tempera paints could also have been used.)

5. To make the coordinate design, the same black-and-white sketches were photocopied and reduced in size. The rectangular motifs were then cut out and pasted together in a slightly different layout. The completed paste-up was photocopied, and splashes of color were painted over the copy with bright transparent dyes.

Sample Design: Photocopied African Motif. A painted plaid on top of a photocopied background. The black-and-white design is adapted from an African bark cloth costume; its coordinate appears on the opposite page.

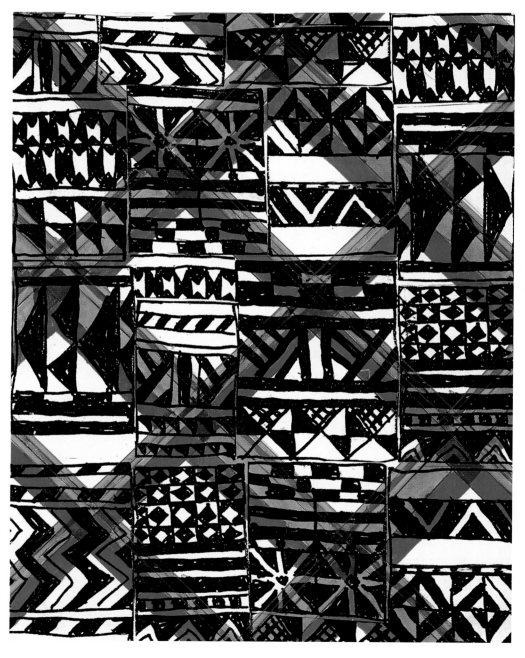

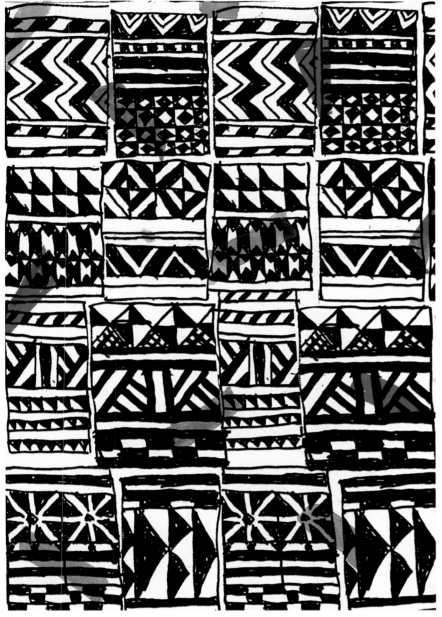

The coordinate to the photocopied African motif *(opposite)*.

TOUCH-UP METHODS

If a correction needs to be made on a gouache or tempera design you may paint right over it, as these colors are opaque. On designs painted with dyes try bleaching out mistakes. Use a toothpick, an old brush, or any other suitable applicator, and keep the bleach within the correction area (see "Bleach Technique," earlier in this chapter). If the bleach or gouache correction looks sloppy, or if the corrected area is not clean enough to paint over, follow these instructions:

1. Using an X-Acto knife or a single-edged razor blade, carefully cut out the area to be corrected.

2. Take a fresh piece of the same kind of paper that was used for the design you are working on. Make sure it is a little larger than the area that has been cut out.

Turn the design over, and apply rubber cement or other glue on the back around the edges of the hole. (Rubber cement can be used on all opaque drawing papers. On waxed rice paper, use double-faced transparent tape or a touch of any glue that will not show through, such as Elmer's, to paste down the edges of the insert.) Place the new piece of paper over the cutout area and paste it down.

3. Turn the design face up and peel off any excess rubber cement with a rubber cement pick-up. If the two papers seem thick along the glued seam, turn the design to the back again and use the edge of a spoon or knife to rub down the edges of the pasted area. This will flatten out and tightly adhere the two edges together, allowing you to paint smoothly over the area.

When this touch-up job is done well, it will give you a fresh, clean area to make the correction on that will be virtually undetectable. Corrections should not be pasted on top of a design: This looks sloppy and distracting.

Another method of cutting out areas to be corrected is called *double-cutting* or *splicing*. Take a piece of the same kind of paper that the design was painted on and place it underneath the area to be cut out. With an X-Acto knife or single-edged razor blade, carefully cut out the area to be corrected, cutting through both papers at the same time. This will give you a new piece of paper with the exact dimensions of the area to be corrected. Turn the design to the back and fit the clean insert into the hole. Tape it in place around the edges (use transparent tape on waxed rice paper), turn the design over, and make your correction.

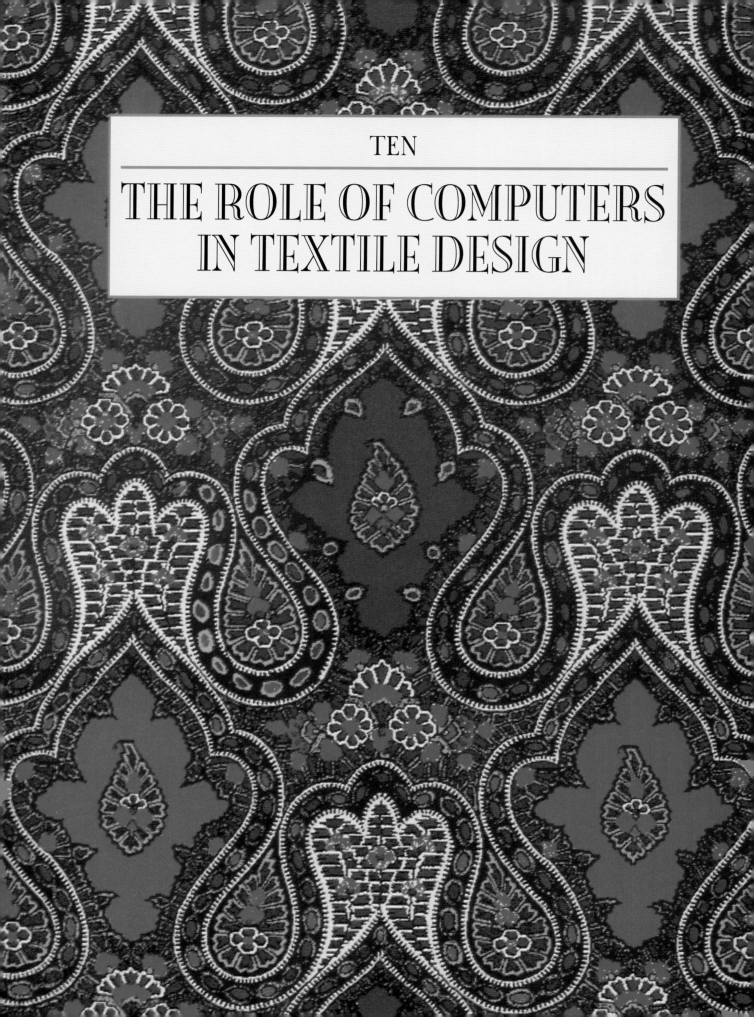

TEN

THE ROLE OF COMPUTERS IN TEXTILE DESIGN

A detailed paisley design, scanned into the computer and altered to accommodate the needs of the customer, by Deerwood Designs Inc.

Today, computers are accepted as one of the tools available to textile designers, and in some converters and design studios they have become an integral part of the design, color, and repeat process. The three interviews that follow explain the world of computer textile design in the experts' own words. Each professional expressed similar feelings about this relatively new technology, which has been available since the early 1980s. While welcoming the labor- and time-saving advantages provided by computer software, they also consider the computer's limitations, and emphasize that designers must have an understanding of traditional textile design aesthetics and handpainting methods.

An ethnic design by Deerwood Designs, scanned, rearranged, and recolored.

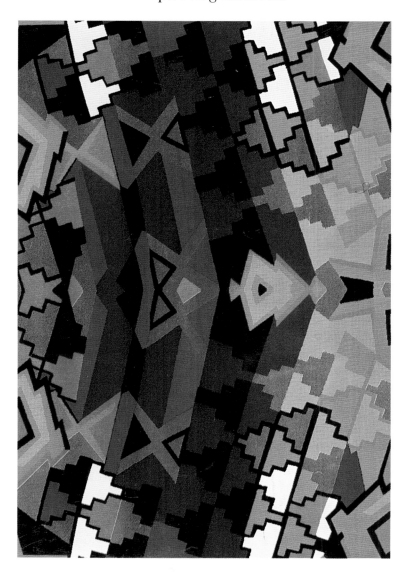

HOLLY HENDERSON

DESIGNER, DIRECTOR

DEERWOOD DESIGNS INC.

When I first studied fashion and textile design at the Fashion Institute of Technology in New York in 1978, there were no computers available at all. At one of my first jobs in the industry, I worked on the first small Apple computer that came out, to program knitting machines in black and white only. Then I graduated to an IBM computer with a six-color printer, and thought it was fabulous. By the mid-1980s, I was working on a system with 175 colors, and now, in the beginning of the 1990s, we have a selection of over 17 million colors to work with. Of course, there is always that one color the customer wants that you can't quite get, but we're talking about the most infinitesimal little differences in shades.

I worked for many companies in the garment industry, designing and coloring prints as well as knits. Finally, in 1988, we opened our doors as a fully computerized textile design studio. In the beginning even the apparel industry was reluctant to accept us. Now we do mostly apparel, and home furnishing is slowly coming around. We do custom work and service clients in different ways, including designing, coloring, and repeats. A customer may come to us and order a design line from soup to nuts, requiring a basic design concept or themes for a particular season. Sometimes we create the whole line ourselves or they give us a pattern that we change and recreate on the computer.

We get our design ideas and reference from library books and magazines; printed fabric ideas come from everywhere. You can take any reference, scan it into the computer, and recreate it by changing the layout, the size, or by adding or combining motifs, changing the colors, and so on. Many of our clients are afraid of getting sued over copyrights, so we assure them that we never directly copy anything on the computer. We change enough elements while keeping the spirit of the reference, so it constitutes a new design.

You arrive at a color on the computer the same way you would when mixing paint: by adding a

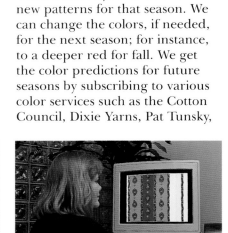

José Rusch of Deerwood Designs Inc. scanning a design into the computer.

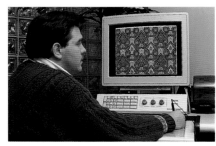

Another motif extracted from the design, and worked into a tossed all-over layout.

bit more red, a bit more blue, or whatever. Our customers usually want at least three colorways on each pattern. We like to establish a color story for the client, so once each color is mixed on the computer, we store it on a disk. Then it is always available to color new patterns for that season. We can change the colors, if needed, for the next season; for instance, to a deeper red for fall. We get the color predictions for future seasons by subscribing to various color services such as the Cotton Council, Dixie Yarns, Pat Tunsky,

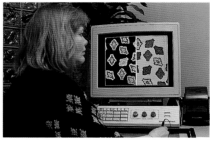

Holly Henderson of Deerwood Designs at the computer, extracting a motif from the original design and transforming it into a stripe layout.

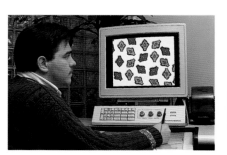

Two color combinations for the tossed pattern.

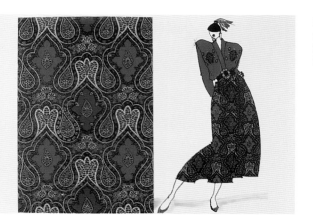

Finally, the design ready to be shown to the customer on the figure.

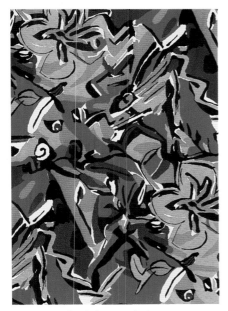

A computerized abstract design.

and Eleanor Douglas. This color information for the most part comes out twice a year, for spring-summer and fall-winter.

We have three different printers in the studio with various printout sizes that can accommodate repeats. On the Canon printer, we are limited to 8 × 10. Our photo-quality thermo printers are 11 × 17. We use several printouts put together to form a larger repeat. Occasionally, we have to do a repeat the traditional way, by using tracing paper. Computer designers should know all the basics and have a good foundation in traditional textile designing. At times, painting techniques are used on designs in conjunction with the computer.

Plaids, however, are something the computer can do better and faster than any artist. They look absolutely woven, and hundreds of plaid combinations and colorways can be experimented with on the system.

I definitely think that computers are the wave of the future in textile design. That is what I based my studio on, because I know that more and more companies will be using computer technology. I feel that any textile designer who is not at least knowledgeable about computers is going to be left behind. Designers must learn that technology is not going to take their jobs away and that their creative input is needed. The computer doesn't design for you; it's just like having another paint box with an unlimited palette, or brushes that you paint with in a different way.

A realistic floral, scanned and rearranged.

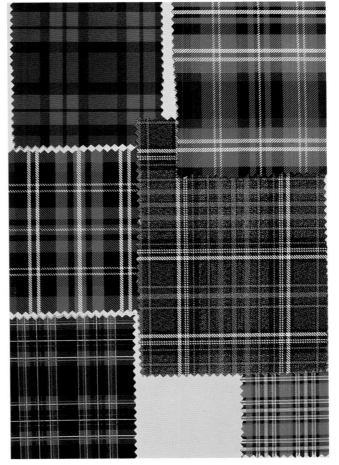

A group of computer plaids.

LINDA GREIFF

COMPUTER DESIGNER AND COLORIST

Computers are another tool in textile design. Companies use them in the most efficient way to get certain results. Computers do not replace people, and they do not replace the beautiful handpainting of an individual designer. However, computers are an integral part of the textile industry today.

I work for a very large company, that does everything from buying the gray goods, to designing, coloring and printing the fabric, to manufacturing the garments—for men, women, children, and infants—that are sold in our retail stores. We turn out lines for five seasons; summer, transition, fall, winter-holiday, and spring, and we use an established color palette for each season, with spring and fall being the biggest. We use the most advanced and costly computer system on the market. As of now, these upper-end systems are prohibitive for smaller companies, but larger ones may have many of these advanced computers, and find that they pay for themselves in a couple of years.

I have worked for both textile design studios and textile companies where I painted colorings by hand—tracing, mixing paints, and so on, all time-consuming. With the computer, I can supply instant gratification by making many, many color combinations very quickly. The final colorings are chosen out of many, and ultimately you get a better product if you don't have to send them back and forth to the artist for changes.

First you have to input or scan the design you are about to color into the computer system, which takes about 15 minutes to an hour, depending on the difficulty of the design. At this point, recoloring is very quick and efficient, providing you have an established color palette. In this case, it takes just about a minute to do a color combination.

However, if you do not have an established color palette and must match colors to a color chip or piece of fabric, you then have to feed the system the proper formula to arrive at each color. In this case it takes about an hour to do a coloring. By comparison, most artists who paint color combinations by hand can produce from two to six colorings a day, depending on the size and number of colors in each piece. The computer screen size is 12 × 14 inches. We use an Iris printer with a printout size of 24 × 24 inches, which allows many combinations to fit in the space of one printout, depending on the size of the colorings.

The computer is also an invaluable design tool. However, we still buy the original design, which is created and painted by a textile designer. We scan it into the computer, which has excellent software functions called Paint Box, Enhancer, and Fancy Load. These programs allow me to correct, rearrange, add, and change motifs on the design. They can also simulate brush strokes and other techniques.

Another function on the computer is called Half Drop, which allows me to shrink the size of the pattern, put it into a simple simulation of a half-drop repeat, and place it in the form of a garment (blouse, pants, and so on), showing what the printed fabric will look like on the finished product. These are called presentation boards. The presentation boards, if painted by hand, would take many days to do. But I can give my company a good idea of what the fabric will look like on the garment or product very quickly, thereby using the computer as a visual aid to help select the final looks and colors that will go into our retail stores.

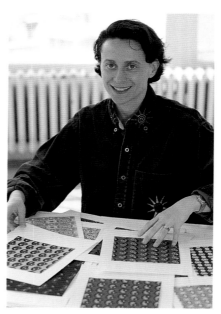

Linda Greiff choosing color combinations.

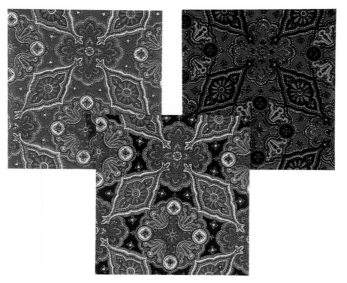

A group of computer colorways for a Persian design.

A set of computer colorways for a floral design.

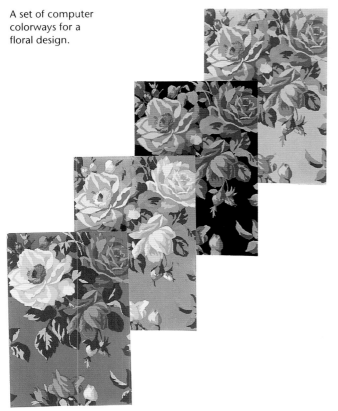

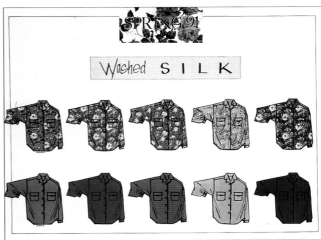

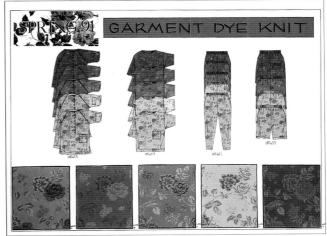

Two presentation boards showing colorways as they look on garments.

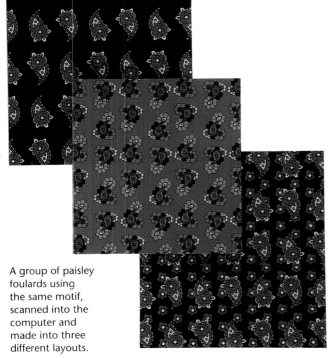

A group of paisley foulards using the same motif, scanned into the computer and made into three different layouts.

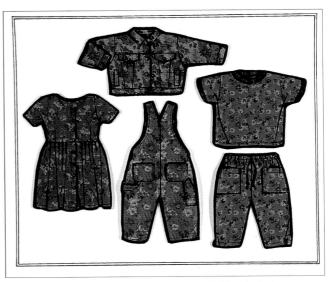

A presentation board showing designs on children's clothes.

Many plaids and stripes for both woven and printed designs are developed on the computer. I can create ten to twenty plaids per day, depending on their difficulty. Then, using a pre-fixed color palette, I can do as many as 100 colorways per day. By comparison, on a complicated plaid, about two or three colorways can be painted by hand in a day by using an airbrush or spatter technique, with tape and ruling pen—all very time-consuming.

However, there are limitations to the computer that designers should be aware of. It is not magic, as some people think. It takes a while to figure out how the computer is most useful and efficient for each situation. And as I mentioned before, the computer, for the most part, cannot produce the fine artistic quality and the individual variations and techniques that a creative designer can paint by hand. It also should be understood that sitting in front of the computer for an extended period of time without taking breaks can be exhausting. Wearing glasses with ultraviolet coating is suggested.

Computer textile design offers good career opportunities, especially for women, who are dominant in the field. However, one must first learn to paint designs and colorings and to do repeats in the traditional way before approaching the computer.

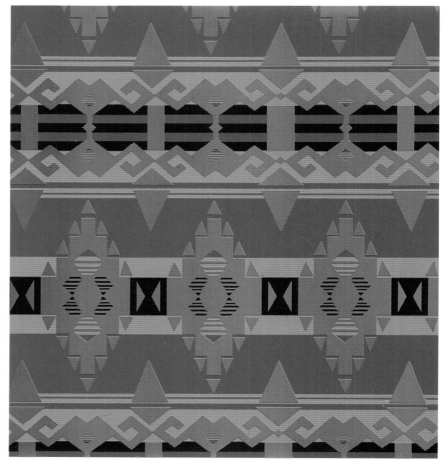

A bright ethnic computer design.

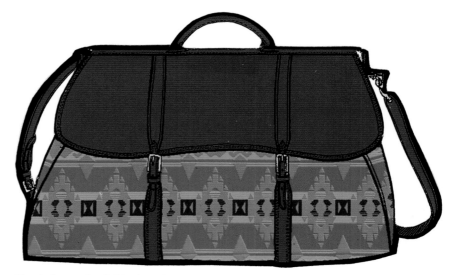

The design on the finished product.

KENJI TAKABAYASHI

COMPUTER GRAPHIC DESIGNER

SIMON POULTON

SALES MANAGER

COMPUTER DESIGNS, INC.

We are software developers for surface design, such as graphics and textiles. Our work is primarily based on an advanced computer known as a work station, which is more powerful than a personal computer. It allows the user to do many things at once because it is faster, with high resolution and top-quality programming and software. When you have a heavy workload this is very important. Our textile design programming is geared toward all aspects of surface design. However, the home furnishing market has been slower in adapting to the new technology. For the apparel market, it is now relatively commonplace.

This company has been in existence since 1983. In the last few years we have seen the attitude change from "What's a computer?" to total enthusiasm. In four or five years, high-tech computer systems will be used by most textile and surface designers. We do not advocate throwing away the brushes to make way for the machines. But this technology is industry-driven in that it all comes down to speed, production, and profit. The industry and designers must adopt all the available tools to achieve their goals. In the beginning the computer could execute plaids and some prints, but there was no "user friendliness." Today when you look at the software menu on the computer it is very straightforward: wovens, prints, jacquards, and so on.

Lingering in people's minds is the huge disparity between what you can do by hand and what you can do on a computer. We are in the middle of a computer revolution in textile design. We have just scratched the surface. We believe that within a few years there will be computers in every design studio in the country. This doesn't mean there will be no more artists and only computers; artists and computers will work together. There will always be tasks that are more appropriate for an artist, and others more appropriate for a computer. For instance, sometimes the feeling and attitude of a design can only be achieved by handpainting.

We now use a computer process called texture mapping, which allows a textile design to be draped on the figure in seconds and shows exactly what the finished product will look like on a model. For home furnishing, the design can immediately be seen on a couch or a window treatment. Before, they would have had to make the dress, drapes, or other item and have it photographed or drawn by an artist. We are now working on the software to make up a whole direct mail catalog on the computer.

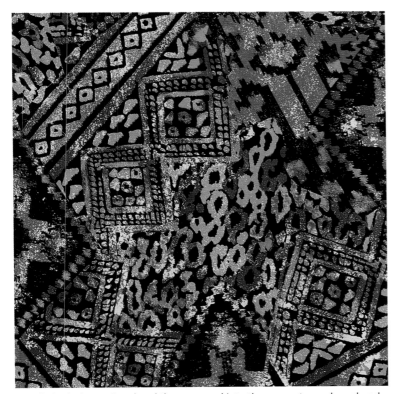

An ethnic design, painted and then scanned into the computer and recolored.

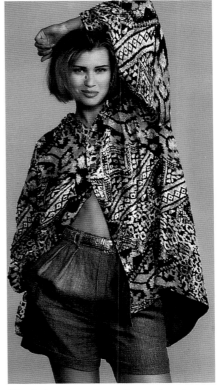

The design draped on a figure, done by a computer process called *texture mapping*.

The fear that another computer designer will create the same design is eliminated because each person selects from thousands of colors and weaves. No two people will make all the same selections. Also, the designer creates for the individual taste of the stylist that she or he works for.

As important as the speed of the new computers is the quality of the printout. A textile once looked beautiful on the screen but was unacceptable on the printout. Now the printout can simulate a painted textile design. The output of the highest-quality printer, called Iris, is up to 24 × 24 inches, which is great for large repeats. This printer costs about $90,000 now, which is, of course, very expensive. But large repeats can be achieved by using a cheaper and smaller printer and "tiling" them, which means printing the repeat in sections and then piecing them together.

The cost of the top-end computer system is about $200,000. There are lower-end systems starting at $50,000 that can be tailored to the quality requirements and budget of the user. Obviously the quality will be lower, and may not be acceptable to some stylists. However, these systems can do an adequate job, with speed compensating for quality.

Another reason that computers are going to be more prominent with manufacturers is that after the textile design is created on the computer, the system can then make the color separation and save it on a disk, which is then sent right to the mill for printing. The printers can then engrave the screens, going right from the disk to the mill. This eliminates any translation from the artist's design concept to the final printed fabric. As the artist conceives it, so it will end up on the fabric, and it is a huge time saver. The computer operator does an interface with a laser engraver at the mill, which will then print the fabric. The quality assurance built into this technology eliminates the time and expense that the stylist formerly spent at the mill supervising the printing of the strike-offs.

The more new products you get in the store, the more sales you can generate. The stores want new garments on the floor every month. That way they have the maximum newness so that the customer can go in one day and buy this and come back next month and buy that. They won't have to wait two months to buy something new. That's why we try to increase the speed of computers—to increase sales until people finally can't afford it. Until they just say, I don't want anymore—enough!—or until the stores get overstocked. Everything today is speed and price.

Most designing on computer now is taking what already exists, scanning it into the computer and adjusting, adding, and so on. To actually create a complicated design on the machine is not time efficient as of yet. Any painted or printed fabric design can be scanned onto the computer screen, then recolored and rearranged in multiple ways to suit the needs of the user. Some studios are doing repeats on the computer as well. In years to come there will be many more. Creating a coloring of a design takes seconds on the computer versus hours by hand, and that is the computer's greatest use to textile designers right now. About

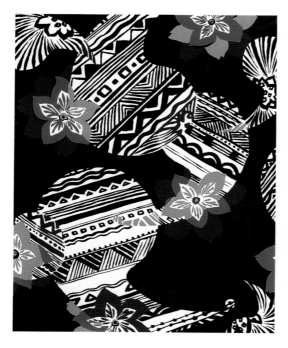

A printout of a paisley design.

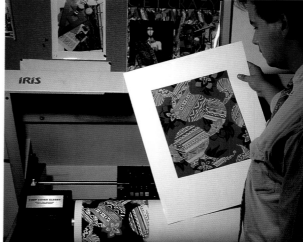

Kenji Takabayashi at the Iris printer holding a colorway of the paisley design.

70 percent of the work done on computers is coloring, and maybe 30 percent is actual designing.

You must "flatten" any design that you recolor in a computer. This means that when, for instance, you scan a three-color print into a computer, the computer views it in thousands of colors. So what is needed is to separate the print into only three colors. You do this by indicating to the computer that, for example, you want gold, black, and pink, and the computer works it down to those colors. From there on your next color combination is instantaneous; you can punch the new colors in very quickly. However, the time it takes can vary depending on the difficulty of the textile pattern. Prints like a dark-ground, elaborate paisley, or designs with a lot of gradations of colors take longer to flatten down than a simple design. Also, a design scanned in from fabric can be harder to recolor because the texture on the surface makes the image less sharp. Therefore, how it comes out on the computer depends on the clarity of the material you put in.

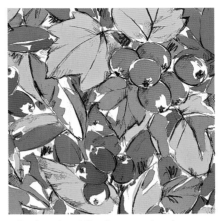

A freely painted floral, scanned and recolored.

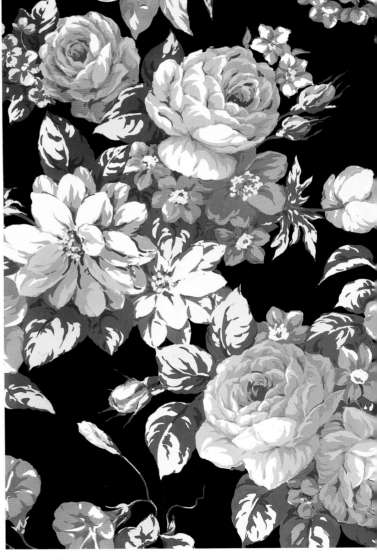

Two colorways on a cabbage rose chintz; the black blotch was added in a matter of minutes.

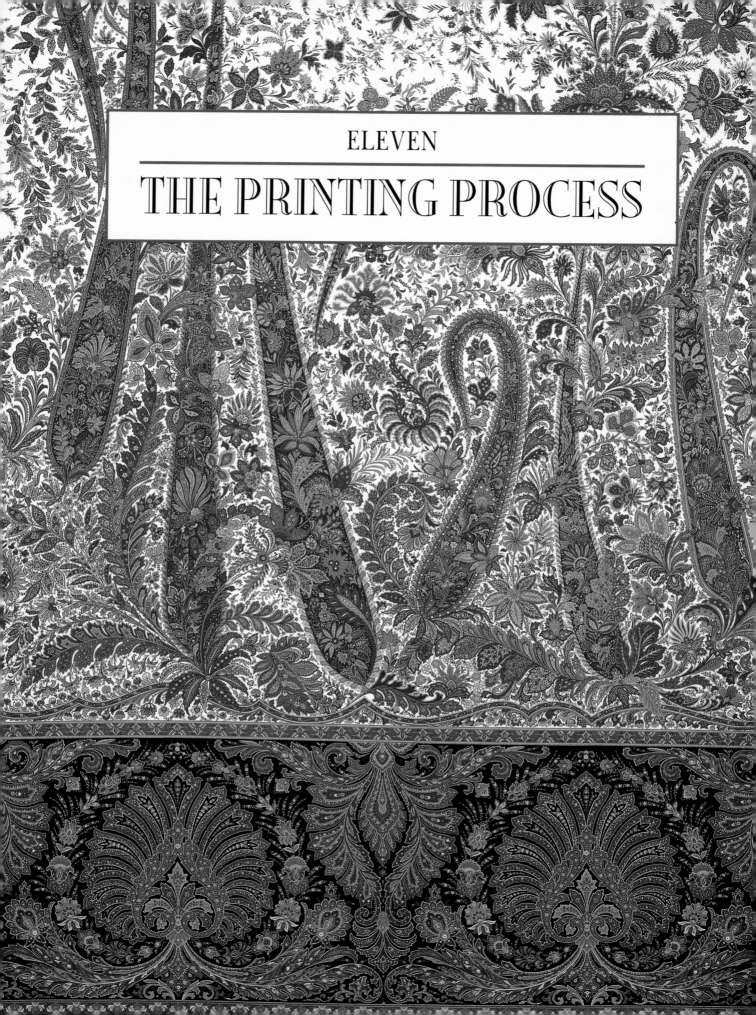

ELEVEN

THE PRINTING PROCESS

A detail of "Silver Jubilee," an extravagant panel measuring 54 × 112 1/2 inches, printed by the Italian firm of Ratti to commemorate the twenty-fifth anniversary of Clarence House. The design was inspired by an antique paisley shawl from the Ratti collection. The ten hand screens required to print the panel took two years to engrave. *Clarence House Imports, Ltd.*

ince the early 1970s, several important developments have occurred in the American textile industry. For example, in the apparel print market, the printing process has shifted from mainly copper roller to rotary screen printing, and much of the printing is now done in Japan, Korea, Taiwan, China, and other countries. Many home furnishing fabrics, also printed primarily by rotary screen, are produced in the United States, with various amounts printed in other countries, such as Spain, Italy, and Israel, as well as in the Far East. Technological advancements such as the use of computers in printing continue to impact and change the industry. This chapter explains the aspects of printing that designers should know: the most commonly used printing processes and the various color printing methods that are used to produce textiles.

A colorful patchwork design for apparel printed with eight rotary screens using the application wet printing method. *Designed by Gerard Bozett for The Cloth Company, a division of Cranston Print Works Co.*

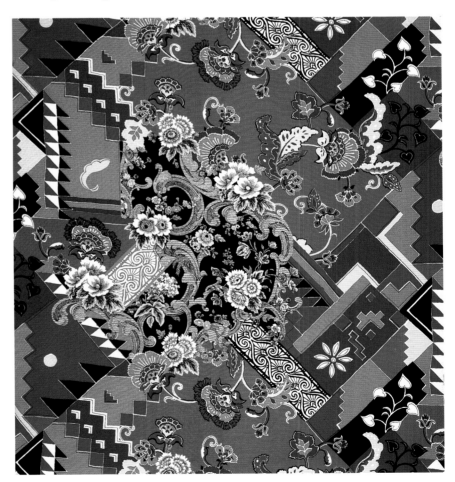

PRINTING METHODS

There are four primary textile printing machine processes: rotary screen, copper roller, flat-bed screen, and heat transfer. Hand screen printing, as its name implies, is done entirely by hand, and produces the most beautiful and expensive printed fabrics.

ROTARY SCREEN PRINTING

A rotary screen is a cylinder of thin flexible metal or plastic, usually with a circumference ranging from 25 1/4 to 36 inches. The circumference of the screen determines the size of the design repeat. A separate rotary screen is needed for each color in the design. The area of the design to be printed by the screen is an open fine mesh in the cylinder. Color is pumped from the press into each cylinder, and as the cylinders rotate the cloth passes beneath them. A magnetic rod within the cylinder forces color through the mesh onto the cloth. As in all methods of printing, each color in the design must be synchronized, so as to print the image on the fabric in perfect registration, or *in fit*. Today this method of printing fabric often incorporates laser engravers and computers to make the color separations.

Rotary screen printing is the fastest method of screen printing. At one time, the typical design printed by rotary screen had a maximum of 12 or 13 colors. During the late 1970s technological improvements accelerated, making it possible to print from 14 to 24 screens on a fully automatic machine. The use of finer mesh for the screens allows for greater flexibility in printing finer details and more vivid colors. These developments in rotary screen printing have enabled the American textile industry to remain competitive in both the high- and low-priced ends of the world market.

COPPER ROLLER PRINTING

In this printing process, the design is etched on copper rollers,

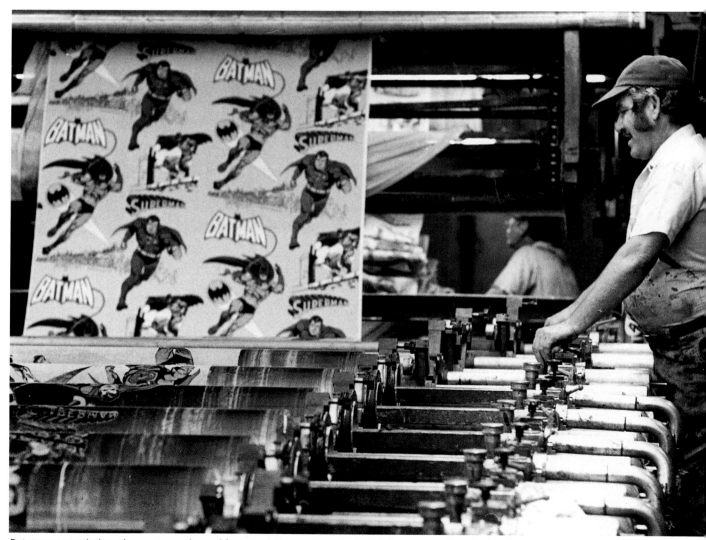

Rotary screen printing, the most popular and fastest printing process. As the fabric passes under cylindrical screens—one for each color—the pattern is printed. *American Textile Manufacturers Institute, Inc.*

which usually range from 15 to 18 inches in circumference. As with the rotary screen cylinder, the circumference of the copper roller determines the size of the design repeat. Each color in the design is etched on a separate roller; therefore, a five-color pattern would have five rollers. Color is picked up on each roller from a color trough, and the excess is scraped off by a blade known as the *doctor blade,* which leaves color only in the etched area of the roller. As the cloth passes through the printing machine, the rollers rotate, and each successive color in the design is printed on the fabric.

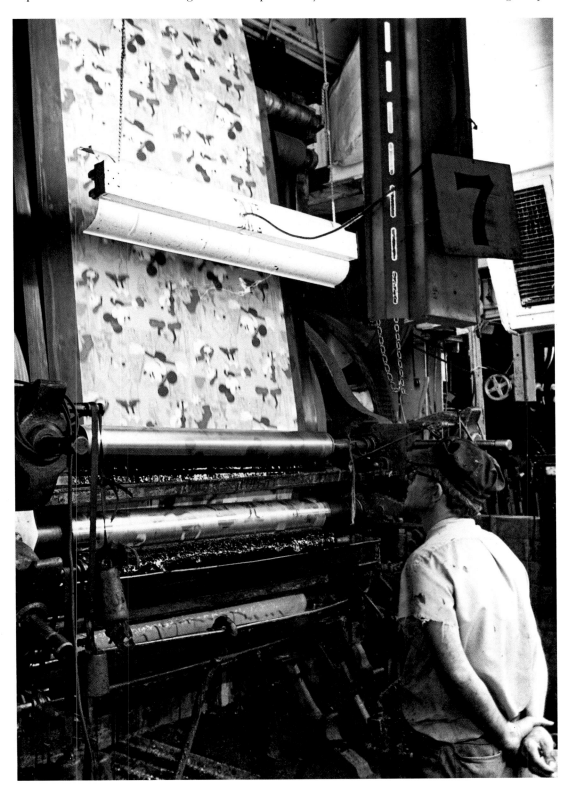

Roller printing. Each color in the design is engraved on a roller. As the cloth passes through the machine, each roller imparts its respective color and pattern to the fabric. *American Textile Manufacturers Institute, Inc.*

FLAT-BED SCREEN PRINTING

In flat-bed screen printing, the screens, which are usually made of strong nylon, are stationary. As the cloth passes beneath the screen, one repeat at a time, color is forced through the screen by a squeegee. The areas of the screen that are not used for printing are coated with a resist substance, and the color penetrates the screen only in areas where the nylon has been left porous. As in the other printing methods, a separate screen is used for each color.

HEAT TRANSFER PRINTING

Heat transfer printing (also known as *sublimation printing* and *dry printing*) was developed in France in 1966 and imported to the United States in 1968. Instead of printing the design directly on the fabric, as is done in other printing methods, the design is printed first on specially coated paper. The printed paper is then applied to the fabric, and through heat and pressure the design is transferred to the fabric. Often, the heat transfer process is more economical than rotary screen printing, and can reproduce precise detail and exact photographic images on fabric.

Originally, heat transfer printing was used only on nylon, polyester, and other manmade fabrics, as the dyes used were not suitable for natural fibers. However, improvements now permit the use of any blend of synthetic and natural fibers, such as rayon and cotton.

HAND SCREEN PRINTING

Hand screen printing is a slower method of flat-bed screen printing, which is done commercially on long tables up to 100 yards in length. Printers move the screens by hand with great care, one frame at a time, until the entire length of cloth is printed.

COLOR PRINTING TECHNIQUES

The most commonly used methods of color printing are direct or application, blotch prints, discharge or extract, resist, pigment or dry, and wet printing.

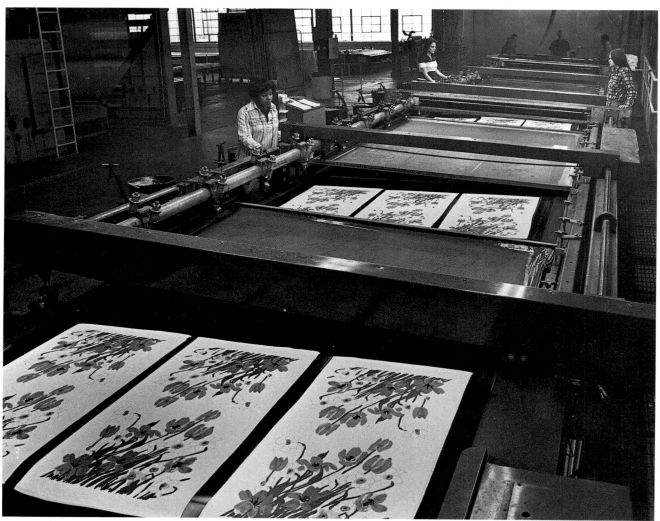

In flat-bed screen printing, color is poured onto the screen and applied to the fabric by means of a squeegee that passes back and forth over the screen. The designs are laid out on a porous cloth screen, which is usually made of nylon. *American Textile Manufacturers Institute, Inc.*

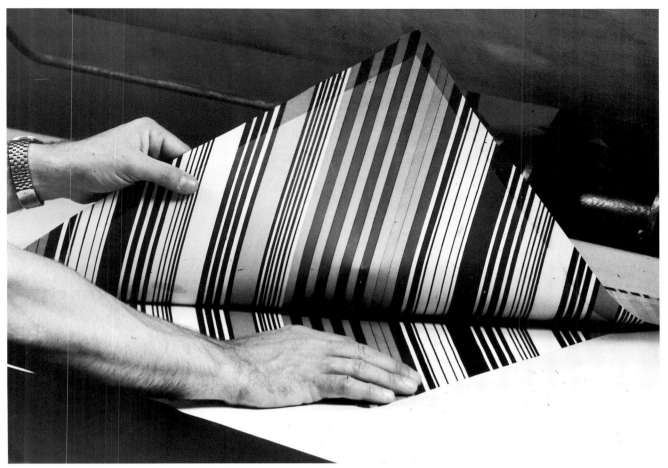

In heat transfer printing, the design is printed in special ink on paper and then transferred from the paper to the cloth through a combination of heat and pressure. Shown directional is the transfer-printed fabric being separated from exhausted paper. *Mayu International Ltd.*

DIRECT OR APPLICATION PRINTING

In direct or application printing, the design motif is printed directly on white or light-colored ground fabrics with a variety of pigment and dye colors. Although pigment colors have also been developed to cover medium- to dark-ground fabrics with white, light, or bright colors (an alternate method to discharge printing, described below), the ground shade will affect the application colors. Direct or application printing is the most popular color printing method.

BLOTCH PRINTS

Blotch prints are those in which the ground color and the colors in the design motifs are printed on white cloth in one step. It is a less expensive alternative to discharge and resist printing.

DISCHARGE OR EXTRACT PRINTING

In discharge or extract printing, medium to dark ground shades are dyed on the fabric first with specially prepared dyestuffs. The top colors, which are then printed on the dyed ground, contain a chemical that interacts with the dye. This interaction simultaneously bleaches color from the dyed ground and prints the desired color in its place. Areas can also be discharged out and left white.

The primary advantage of discharge printing is that bright and light colors or white can be printed on top of medium or dark grounds without the problem of fitting the background blotch around the motifs. Discharge prints can be produced by either rotary screen or roller printing.

RESIST PRINTING

In resist printing, the pattern is printed first on white fabric with a chemical substance that prevents the penetration of dyes. The fabric is then dyed, leaving the treated background with a white pattern. The resist printing method is the opposite of discharge printing, in which the fabric is dyed prior to printing.

PIGMENT OR DRY PRINTING

In this color printing method, pigment colors are mixed into a paste with a thickener and used to print the design by either rotary screen or copper roller. The colors tend to sit on top of the fabric rather than penetrate it. Pigment white can be used to highlight motifs.

WET PRINTING

In wet printing, dyes rather than pigment colors are used. Wet printing can be used in either the rotary screen or copper roller processes.

RESPONSIBILITIES OF MILL WORK

The stylist (or someone designated by the stylist, such as his or her assistant) is responsible for making sure that the designs are printed satisfactorily on the fabric, which requires going to the printing plant to supervise the printing and coloring. After learning mill work, a designer can command a higher salary. The purpose of supervising the printing is to ensure that the pattern printed on the fabric is clear and aesthetically acceptable, that the colors are correct, and that technical problems, such as bowing and warping of the fabric, are avoided.

The first run of printed fabric is called a *strike-off,* which the stylist examines and either approves or corrects. For example, the color may need to be *brought up* (made heavier or darker) or *brought down* (made lighter or duller). The printed colors are compared with the painted colorways, color chips, or a sample of previously printed fabric that are brought to the mill from the studio.

A newcomer is always accompanied by an experienced person on trips to the mill. I am always surprised at how quickly many of my students become proficient in mill work after only a short, on-the-job training period.

SUPERVISING PRINTING AT THE MILL

Unfortunately, there is nothing glamorous about going to the mill. Be prepared for long waits until your turn to print comes up, and don't be surprised if you are assaulted by a stench when you arrive at the plant.

You will work with the mill's head colorist, called the *color shader* or *color mixer,* who brings out the patches or samples for your inspection. Some mills have hand strike-off facilities that enable them to try different color choices before a final choice is made; in others, all the initial color experimentation must be done on the production print machine.

Know in advance what the stylist or design director wants or much time and cloth may be wasted. For instance, do you need to match a previous run of fabric, or should the colors coordinate with a wallpaper or with a companion or twin print? The more facts you have the better off you'll be.

It is best not to ask the color shaders for their opinions, as their primary interest is in running production. Do work *with* the color shaders, but don't tell them how to mix a color or what to do to arrive at a particular shade. It is their job to obtain the desired results as quickly as possible.

The color shader will then bring you the patches, which should always be seen against a white background. Step back and assess the overall look and quality of the strike-off. After you've spent sufficient time working with the color chips and seeing enough samples, begin to rely on your eye and make a clear decision. Don't continue to make minute color changes when it is obvious that a pattern balances as a whole. Sometimes compromise is necessary for some elements in the pattern.

If you like what you see, give the printer the go ahead. If not, request a second patch, but remember that most mills have a three-patch maximum. Make all your changes within the first three patches or they may *pull the pattern,* or take it off the machine.

Try to avoid such a situation. A pattern should only be pulled if it is improperly engraved or if something is wrong with one of the screens that cannot be fixed.

Always request to see a patch that goes from selvage to selvage, showing the full width of the goods, so you can check for side-to-side variations of shading or other problems.

Always stay on top of the printer; remember, you are the one who must report back to the studio. Be clear and direct, and establish yourself as a decisive person with the staff at the mill.

After you have approved the sample patch for fit and color, insist on a one-yard piece of each color combination to take back to the office. This is important, as the stylist will use them to compare against the sample fabrics that are sent to the studio after the mill completes the production run. It is also a good idea to take notes, recording all of the changes you request on each patch, as instructions may be forgotten or misinterpreted as they are sent from the shading room to the printing machine. It is advisable to note on each patch the time it was delivered, the number of the patch, and any comments that might prove helpful later. If you are coloring three or four patterns at once it will help answer the stylist's questions about changes, timing, and other details.

SUMMARY: WHAT TO CHECK AT THE MILL

1. Make sure that the ground shades and top colors are correct.

2. Check the strike-offs or sample patches for correct fit or registration of the motifs.

3. Check the sample patches for sharpness or clarity of printing.

4. Double-check that all of the colors are in their correct positions in the motifs.

RESOURCES

MAGAZINES

Architectural Digest
Condé Nast
699 Madison Avenue
New York, New York 10021
A business publication covering luxurious and unusual interior design and home furnishings.

Designers West
Designers World Corp.
Box 69660
Los Angeles, California 90069-0660
A business publication covering residential and contract design in the western United States.

Elle
Hachette Magazine Network
1633 Broadway – 42nd floor
New York, New York 10019-6741
A consumer magazine covering innovative developments in style and fashion.

Harper's Bazaar
Hearst Magazines
1700 Broadway – 28th floor
New York, New York 10019-5905
A consumer magazine reporting on a wide range of subjects concerning women, beauty, and fashion.

House Beautiful
Hearst Magazines
1700 Broadway – 28th floor
New York, New York 10019-5905
Publishes articles on a variety of interior design subjects, from advanced design concepts to practical home planning and maintenance.

House and Garden
Condé Nast
350 Madison Avenue
New York, New York 10017-3136
Covers ideas in home decorating, home furnishing, and other home design subject areas.

Vogue
Condé Nast
350 Madison Avenue
New York, New York 10017-3136
Reports on fashion, beauty, and a wide range of other subjects concerning women.

A wide range of internationally published magazines (available at many newsstands), including *Abitare, Bazaar Italia, Casa Vogue, Elegance, Gran Bazaar, Paris Bazaar, Paris Vogue, View Textiles,* and *World of Interiors,* are also excellent resources for reference material.

NEWSPAPERS

HFD—Retailing Home Furnishings
Fairchild Publications
7 West 34th Street
New York, New York 10001
Available through subscription only.

Women's Wear Daily
Fairchild Publications
7 West 34th Street
New York, New York 10001
Tuesday edition features textiles.

Furniture/Today
P.O. Box 1424
Riverton, New Jersey 08077
Available through subscription only.

TEXTILE COLLECTIONS

The Art Institute of Chicago
Michigan Avenue at Adams Street
Chicago, Illinois 60603

The Brooklyn Museum
Eastern Parkway
Brooklyn, New York 11238

Cooper-Hewitt Museum of Design
5th Avenue at 91st Street
New York, New York 10028

Costume and Textile Study Center
University of Washington
Seattle, Washington 98195

Fashion Institute of Technology
Design Laboratory
27th Street and 7th Avenue
New York, New York 10001

Los Angeles County Museum of Art
5905 Wilshire Boulevard
Los Angeles, California 90038

The Metropolitan Museum of Art
5th Avenue and 82nd Street
New York, New York 10028

Museum of Fine Arts
465 Huntington Avenue
Boston, Massachusetts 02115

Museum of the American Indian
One Bowling Green
New York, New York 10004

Philadelphia Museum of Art
Parkway at 26th Street
Philadelphia, Pennsylvania 19101

The Textile Museum
2320 S Street, N.W.
Washington, D.C. 20008

PROFESSIONAL ORGANIZATIONS

American Printed Fabrics Council
45 West 36th Street
New York, New York 10018
(212) 695-2254

Graphic Artists Guild
11 West 20th Street
New York, New York 10011
(212) 463-7730
Provides many services for textile designers, including health plans, legal referrals, and networking opportunities. Publishes the Graphic Artists Guild Handbook: Pricing & Ethical Guidelines, *an indispensable reference.*

COMPUTER RESOURCES

Two good places to investigate textiles on the web are:

www.fabriclink.com
Information about fabrics for apparel and home furnishings.

www.textileweb.com
Locates sources covering the textile industry.

Many textile printing houses also have web sites.

INDEX